Guide to BUDDHIST PHILOSOPHY

The
Asian
Philosophies
and
Religions
Resource
Guides

Guide to BUDDHIST PHILOSOPHY

KENNETH K. INADA

with contributions by
Richard Chi, Shotaro Iida,
and David Kalupahana

G.K.HALL &CO.

70 LINCOLN STREET, BOSTON, MASS.

Library of Congress Cataloging in Publication Data

Inada, Kenneth K.
Guide to Buddhist philosophy.

(The Asian philosophies and religions resources guide)
Includes indexes.
1. Philosophy, Buddhist—Bibliography. 2. Buddhism—Doctrines—Bibliography. I. Title. II. Series.
Z7128.B93I53 1985 [B162] 016.181'043 85-8530
ISBN 0-8161-7899-2

This publication is printed on permanent/durable acid-free paper
MANUFACTURED IN THE UNITED STATES OF AMERICA

Project on Asian Philosophies and Religions

Sponsoring Organizations
Center for International Programs and Comparative Studies of the New York State Education Department/University of the State of New York
Council for Intercultural Studies and Programs, Inc.

Steering Committee

Kenneth Morgan	Emeritus, Colgate University *Chairman*
Wing-tsit Chan	Chatham College Emeritus, Dartmouth College
David J. Dell	Foreign Area Materials Center Columbia University *Project Manager, 1975-77*
Edith Ehrman	Foreign Area Materials Center *Project Manager, 1971-74*
Robert McDermott	Baruch College, City University of New York
Bardwell Smith	Carleton College
H. Daniel Smith	Syracuse University
Frederick J. Streng	Southern Methodist University

Editorial Coordinators
David J. Dell
Edward S. Haynes

Preparation of this series of guides to resources for the study of Asian philosophies and religions was made possible by a grant from the National Endowment for the Humanities, supplemented through the Endowment's matching funds scheme, with additional financial support from the Ada Howe Kent Foundation, C. T. Shen, and the Council on International and Public Affairs, Inc. None of the above bodies is responsible for the content of these guides, which is the responsibility of those listed on the title page.

This project has been undertaken by the Foreign Area Materials Center, State Education Department, University of the State of New York, under the auspices of the Council for Intercultural Studies and Program, 60 East 42nd Street, New York, NY 10017.

IN MEMORY OF
EDITH EHRMAN
1932-1974

Straightway I was 'ware
So weeping, how a mystic shape did move
Behind me, and drew me backward by the hair
And a voice said in mastery while I strove, . . .
'Guess now who holds thee?—'Death', I said, but there
The silver answer rang . . . 'Not Death, but Love.'

Elizabeth Barrett Browning

Contents

Contents

Series Preface

Asian Philosophies and Religions and the Humanities in America

This guide is one of a series of books on resources for the study of Asian philosophies and religions. The series includes volumes on Chinese, Indian, Islamic, and Buddhist philosophies and religions. Since the preparation of the series has been undertaken as a contribution to advancing humanistic learning in America, it is important to place the study of these traditions in that larger context.

Humanistic scholarship and teaching in America has understandably concentrated on Western civilization of which we are a part. Yet Western civilization has historically drawn significantly upon the humanistic accomplishments of other traditions and has interacted with these traditions. Given the increasing mobility of scholars and students in the second half of the twentieth century and the rapidly advancing technological capacity of communicating ideas in the modern world, this interaction is accelerating as we approach the twenty-first century.

Liberal education for American students in the 1970s and 1980s must reflect not only our human heritage in all of its diversity as it has accumulated through past centuries, but also the nature of the future in its intellectual and cultural as well as economic, social and political dimensions. By the year 2000, a logical future reference point for today's college students who will spend most of their adult lives in the next century, four out of five human beings will live in the "Third World" of Asia, Africa, and Latin America about which we study least in our colleges and universities today.

Numerical distribution of humanity is certainly not the only criterion which should determine the content of humanistic learning in our institutions of higher education. But when orders of magnitude achieve the proportions which, according to most demographic projections, will exist in the year 2000, geographical location of humanity is certainly one criterion which will be applied by today's students in assessing the "relevance" of their undergraduate education to the real world of the future.

The argument becomes all the more compelling when the qualitative aspects of civilizations other than our own are considered. Western man can claim no corner on creative accomplishment, as Herbert Muller has rightly recognized in this passage from The Uses of the Past.

> Stick to Asia, and we get another elementary lesson in humility. Objectively its history looks more important than the history of Europe. . .It has produced more civilizations, involving a much greater proportion of mankind, over a longer period of time, on a higher level of continuity. As for cultural achievement, we have no universal yardstick; but by one standard on which Western Christendom has prided itself, Asia has been far more creative. It has bred all the higher religions, including Christianity.*

There is little doubt that the rapid growth of student interest in the study of these traditions is the result in part of their search for new value systems in contemporary society. But this interest is also a recognition of other civilizations as being intrinsically worthy of our attention.

Origins of the Project on Asian Philosophies and Religions

The project was initiated in response to this growth of student interest, which began in the 1960s and has persisted in the 1970s, notwithstanding a current general decline in the growth rates in American colleges and universities. Faculty members with specialized training in Asian philosophical and religious traditions, however, are still limited in number and most courses in these subjects are being taught by non-specialists. While the proportion of those with specialized training has certainly increased in recent years, the situation is unlikely to improve greatly due to the ceilings on faculty size which many institutions have imposed because of financial stringency.

The need for a series of authoritative guides to literature in these fields for use in both undergraduate and beginning graduate study of Asian philosophies and religions, which first prompted us to seek support from the National Endowment for the Humanities for the project in 1971, remains just as compelling as the project draws to a close.

Organization of the Project

The project on Asian philosophies and religions was conceived from the beginning as a cooperative venture involving scholars and teachers of these subjects. The key element in the organization of

*The Uses of the Past, New York: New American Library, 1954, p. 314.

of the project has been the project team or working group, a deliberately informal structure with its own leader, working autonomously but within a general conceptual framework developed early in the project by all of those who were involved in the project at that time.

The individual working groups have been linked together by a project steering committee, which has been concerned with the overall organization and implementation of the project. The members of the project steering committee, working group leaders, and other key project personnel are as follows:

Kenneth Morgan, Emeritus, Colgate University (Chairman of the Project Steering Committee)

Wing-tsit Chan, Chatham College and Emeritus, Dartmouth College (Member, Project Steering Committee; Leader of Working Group on Chinese Philosophy and Religion)

Bardwell Smith, Carleton College (Member, Project Steering Committee and Working Group on Buddhist Religion)

H. Daniel Smith, Syracuse University (Member, Project Steering Committee and Working Group on Hinduism)

Robert McDermott, Baruch College, City University of New York (Member, Project Steering Committee and the Working Group on Hinduism)

Thomas Hopkins, Franklin and Marshall College (Leader of the Working Group on Hinduism)

David Ede, Western Michigan University and McGill University (Leader of the Working Group on Islamic Religion)

Karl Potter, University of Washington (Leader of the Working Group on Indian Philosophy)

Frank Reynolds, University of Chicago (Leader of the Working Group on Buddhist Religion)

Kenneth Inada, State University of New York at Buffalo (Leader of the Working Group on Buddhist Philosophy)

Frederick J. Streng, Southern Methodist University (Member, Project Steering Committee and Working Groups on Buddhist Religion and Philosophy)

David Dell (Project Manager, 1957-77 and a Member of the Working Group on Hinduism)

Two characteristics of the project's organization merit mention. One has been the widespread use of other scholars and teachers, in addition to the members of the project steering committee and working groups, in the critical review of preliminary versions of the guides. Reviewers were asked to comment on both commissions and omissions, and their comments were used by the compilers in making revisions. A far more extensive exercise than the customary scholarly review of manuscripts, this process involved well over 200 individuals who contributed immeasurably to improving the quality of the end product.

A similar effort to enlarge participation in the project has been made through discussions at professional meetings about the project among interested scholars and teachers while it was in progress. Over the past four years a dozen such sessions, involving over 300 participants, have been held at both national and regional meetings of the American Academy of Religion and the Association for Asian Studies.

The Classification Scheme and Criteria of Selection for the Guide

Early in the project a conference of most of the key project personnel mentioned above, as well as other members of the project working groups, was held in New York City in June 1972 to develop a common classification scheme and criteria for inclusion of materials in the resource guides.

This task generated lively and intense debate because underlying any classification scheme are the most fundamental issues of conceptualization and periodization in the study of religious and philosophical traditions. The classification schemes for guides in religion and in philosophy have generally been followed by each working group, although there have been inevitable variations. Each of the traditions included in the project has distinctive qualities and characteristics which make it difficult to fit all aspects of all traditions into the same set of categories.

The objective of developing a common set of categories was to facilitate examination of parallel phenomena across traditions. We believe this objective has been at least partially achieved through this series, although we recognize the need for continued refinement before a common set of categories compatible with all the traditions being covered can be evolved.

If developing categories to span diverse religious and philosophical traditions has been difficult, definition and reasonably uniform application of criteria for inclusion of material in the guides has been no easier. The project's basic objective, as originally elaborated at the June 1972 working conference, has been to provide an authoritative guide to the literature, both texts in translation and commentary and analysis, for teachers and advanced undergraduate and beginning graduate students who are not specialized scholars with access to primary texts in their original languages. Because of the limited number of teachers in American colleges and universities who have the necessary language skills, particularly outside their own primary field of scholarly interest, it was expected that the guides would be useful to those teaching in the field who, even though they might have a high level of scholarly specialization on one tradition, would often find it necessary to deal with other traditions in their teaching.

We also sought to achieve some consistency in annotations of entries in the guides. The objective has been to provide short, crisp, critical annotations which would help the user of the guide in identifying material pertinent to his or her interest or most authoritative in its coverage of a particular topic. We recognize, of course, that we have not achieved this objective throughout the entire series of guides encompassing more than 12,000 individual entries.

Because of the difficulties in applying a common set of categories and subcategories to the diverse traditions being covered by the guides, not all categories have been covered in each guide, and in some cases, they have been grouped together as seemed appropriate to the characteristics of a particular tradition. Extensive cross-referencing has been provided to guide the user to related entries in other categories.

The Problem of Availability of Resources in the Guide and the Microform Resource Bank

We realized from the beginning that a series of guides of this character would have little value if the users could not acquire materials listed in the guides. We therefore sought the cooperation of the Institute for the Advanced Studies of World Religions, which is engaged in a major effort to develop a collection of resources for the study of world religions in microform, and through the Institute, have established a microform resource bank of material in the guides not readily available from other sources.

Subject to the availability of the material for microfilming and depending upon its copyright status, the Institute is prepared to provide in microform any item included in any of the guides out-of-print or otherwise not readily available, in accordance with its usual schedule of charges. Where an item is already included in the Institute's microform collection, those charges are quite modest, and an effort is being made by the Institute to increase its holding of materials in the guides. Material can also be provided in hard xerographic copy suitable for reproduction for multiple classroom use at an additional charge.

Under the terms of a project arrangement with the Institute, the Institute is undertaking the microfilming of some 30,000 pages of material included in these guides. In addition, the Institute already has in its microform collection a substantial number of titles in the fields of Buddhist and Chinese philosophy and religion.

The Institute will from time to time issue lists of material in microform from the guides available in its collections, but as its microform collections are continually being expanded, users are urged to contact the Institute directly to see if a particular title in which they are interested is available:

Institute for Advanced Studies of World Religions
Melville Memorial Library
State University of New York
Stony Brook, New York 11794

Acknowledgments

An undertaking of this scope and magnitude, involving such widespread participation, is bound to accumulate a long list of those who have contributed in one way or another to the project. It would be impossible to identify by name all of those who have contributed, and it is hoped that those who are not so identified will nonetheless recognize themselves in the categories which follow and understand that their help, interest, and support are also appreciated.

To begin with, primary thanks must be extended to the members of the project steering committee, the leaders of the various project working groups, and the members of each of the groups. Those responsible for each guide in the series are separately listed on the title page of that volume.

Thanks should also be expressed to the large number of scholars and teachers who served as critical reviewers of preliminary versions of the guides and the many who participated in sessions at regional and national meetings where the guides were subject to further scrutiny and where many constructive suggestions for their improvement were made.

We wish to acknowledge with grateful thanks the generous financial support of the National Endowment for the Humanities, and through its matching fund scheme, additional support from the Ada Howe Kent Foundation, C.T. Shen, and Council for International and Public Affairs, Inc. The patience and understanding of the Endowment's Education Division during the long and protracted period of completion of this project has been particularly noteworthy.

Many institutions have provided support to the project indirectly by making possible participation of their faculty in the various project working groups. In addition, both the South Asia Center at Columbia University and the Institute for Advanced Studies or World Religions have provided special assistance.

Series Preface

The project has been undertaken under the auspices of the Council for Intercultural Studies and Programs by the Foreign Area Materials Center, a project office of the Center for International Programs and Comparative Studies, State Education Department, University of the State of New York. The last-named institution, acting as the agent of the Council for Intercultural Studies and Programs, has been responsible for administering the National Endowment for Humanities grant and other financial support received for the project and has contributed extensively out of its own resources throughout the project, particularly in the concluding months, to assure its proper completion. Without the interest and support of key officials in the Center for International Programs and the New York State Education Department, the project could not have been completed.

A particular word of appreciation is in order for Norman Abramowitz of the Center, who succeeded me as Project Director after my resignation from the directorship of the Center in October, 1976 and to whom fell the unenviable task of overcoming administrative and financial obstacles in the final three years of the project. Appreciation should also be expressed to G.K. Hall and Company, the publishers of this series, and to its editorial staff. Their forebearance, as the manuscripts have been completed over a far longer time than we anticipated, has been exemplary.

Last but certainly not least are the project managers who have carried responsibility from day to day for implementing the project. Perhaps the most difficult and demanding role has been played by David J. Dell who came into the project at mid-stream and who struggled to assure its orderly completion. He and Edward Haynes have shared responsibility for final preparation of manuscripts for publication as editorial coordinators for the series, with the former handling two (Chinese Philosophy and Hindu Religion) and the latter, the remaining five titles in the series.

Different, but in many ways no less difficult, was the task confronting the interim project director, Josephine Case, whose services were kindly made available to the project by the New York Public Library in 1974 and 1975. She responded with dignity and sensitivity to the demands of this task.

But in many ways the most important figure in the project is one who is no longer with us. Edith Ehrman was the Manager of the Foreign Area Materials Center from its inception in 1963, a key figure in the conceptualization of this project, and its manager from the beginning until her untimely death in November, 1974. She was the moving spirit behind the project during its first three years. It is to her memory that this series of guides is dedicated by all those involved in the project who witnessed the extraordinary display of courage borne of her love of life during her last difficult illness.

Ward Morehouse, Chairman
Editorial and Publications Committee

Preface

This Guide to Buddhist Philosophy is a volume under the overall project of The Series of Guides to Resources for the Study of Asian Philosophies and Religions. It is also a sister volume to Guide to Buddhist Religion. Both volumes should be used in tandem to insure the greatest coverage of works in Buddhist studies. They mutually support each other in this respect.

Two other volumes worth mentioning here are the Guide to Indian Philosophy and the Guide to Chinese Philosophy. Both are notably philosophical in orientation as they are based on similar guidelines on philosophical categories. Both also have substantial works on Buddhism listed in the respective categories. Thus the reader of this guide will benefit greatly by correlating and supplementing resource materials from the above volumes. Overlapping and even duplication of materials are unavoidable and even expected where a central overall editor was wanting. Yet, taking all the volumes together, including the Guide to Buddhist Religion, the reader should derive a good measure of knowledge pertaining to Buddhist researches.

To be sure, there is no clearcut methodology or systematization applicable to the principles or doctrines of Buddhism; indeed, the principles or doctrines themselves defy, in a profound sense, any methodological assumptions. Fortunately, contemporary scholarship is moving significantly towards an objective view of Buddhism as a whole. Unfortunately, though, at the moment, scholars are sorely handicapped by the scarcity of purely philosophical treatises on Buddhism, be they classical or modern texts, and including works done by contemporary thinkers. The greater part of the problem lies in that, paradoxically enough, Buddhism was never seriously considered to be treated within the framework of a Western philosophical scheme, although it has all the ingredients for one. We are actually in a bind. We want to understand Buddhism philosophically, but at the same time we do not want to detract from or destroy its natural flavor and spirit in the process. We certainly tread on a thin line. The team members stand convinced, however, that the philosophical approach is legitimate and a necessary one. Indeed, there are already signs pointing in that direction.

Preface

The division of labor was generally carried out as follows: Richard Chi on Buddhist logical works; Shotaro Iida on Mahāyāna works; David Kalupahana on Theravāda works; Kenneth Inada on overall works as well as comparative works. In the process, however, each member contributed entries that covered other areas than his own and thereby helped to enrich the whole volume. Besides contributing my share of entries, I acted as chairman of the team, which included the editing of the manuscripts up to the final stages of publication.

In addition to the team members, Frederick Streng of SMU and Hajime Nakamura of the Eastern Institute (Tokyo), who was visiting professor of philosophy at SUNY/Buffalo in 1974-75, unstintingly gave valuable guidance and timely advice.

Finally, I wish to extend deep gratitude to Ward Morehouse, David Dell, and Edward Haynes, for their understanding, patience, and care with which they steered this guide to the press.

Kenneth K. Inada
SUNY at Buffalo

1 History of Buddhist Philosophy

1.1 Pan-Asian Surveys

(1) BAPAT, P.V. 2500 Years of Buddhism. New Delhi: Government of India Press, 1956, 503 pp.
A commemorative volume (Buddha Jayanti) contributed by outstanding scholars in the various fields on Buddhism. Good introduction.

(2) BAREAU, ANDRÉ. "Le Bouddhisme indien: Le Mahāyāna 1185-1203; Le Bouddhisme Indien Tadrdif ou Tantrique 1205-1212." In Histoire des Religions 1 (1970):1185-1203; 1205-12.
This excellent book is meant as an introduction to Mahāyāna Buddhism for a wider public. Authoritative and lucid presentation by Bareau, a leading European scholar on Buddhism.

(3) BERRY, THOMAS. Buddhism. New York: Hawthorne Books, 1967, 192 pp.
This succinct, clear and informative book on the history of Buddhism is a product of the "middle way" approach. Berry avoids the extremes of overspecialization and oversimplification. Primarily concerned with Indian Buddhism.

(4) BERVAL, RENÉ de, ed. Présence du Bouddhisme. Saigon: France-Asie, 1959, 1024 pp.
In this remarkably comprehensive volume on Buddhism, to which a number of eminent scholars contributed, the following articles are on Mahāyāna Buddhism: Tucci's interpretation of the spirit of Buddhism, Nalinaksha Dutt's analysis of the fundamental principles of Mahāyāna, S. Paranavitana's account of "Mahāyānism in Ceylon," and D.T. Suzuki's essays on Zen. For Tibetan Buddhism, Alexander David-Neel, D. Delannoy, and Marco Pallis deal with the monastic institutions.

1 History of Buddhist Philosophy

1.1 Pan-Asian Surveys

(5) BU-STON. History of Buddhism. Translated by E. Obermiller. Heidelberg, 1931. Reprint. Reprint Series 5. Tokyo: Suzuki Research Foundation, 1964.
Obermiller has done us a great service by translating two Tibetan works by Bu-ston (1290-1364). The first is The Jewelry of Scripture (185 pp.), which outlines the principal Mahāyāna works and their teachings; the second is The History of Buddhism in India and Tibet (231 pp.). Both constitute a wealth of information on doctrinal understanding and on the great Buddhist teachers in India and Tibet. Required reading for all.

(6) CH'EN, KENNETH K.S. Buddhism: The Light of Asia. Barron's Educational Series. Woodbury, N.Y., 1968, 297 pp.
Ch'en's approach in this work is primarily historical rather than philosophical. Doctrinal developments are sketched in the background of their historical setting. Ch'en does not shy away from the contemporary issues when he discusses the relevance of Buddhism in a modern world, swept by communism, racial tensions, and war.

(7) CHI, RICHARD S.Y. Buddhist Formal Logic. London: Royal Asiatic Society, 1969, 222 pp.
A work of substantial value, though highly technical in nature, covering logical development spanning India and China. Contains a lengthy bibliography.

(8) CONZE, EDWARD. Buddhism: Its Essence and Development. Oxford: Cassirer, 1951, 212 pp. Reprint. New York: Harper, 1959; London: Faber, 1963.
A highly readable introductory work covering the entire span of Buddhism, touching on the early beginnings, monastic life, popular Buddhism, old and new wisdom schools, Mahāyāna, devotional Buddhism, Yogācāra, magical Buddhism, and concluding with the non-Indian developments.

(9) CONZE, EDWARD, I.B. HORNER, D. SNELLGROVE, and A. Waley. eds. Buddhist Texts Through the Ages. New York: Philosophical Library, 1954, 322 pp.
Selected translations from the works of Theravāda, Mahāyāna, Tantrayāna, and the Chinese and Japanese schools. All are reliable renditions.

(10) CONZE, EDWARD. Thirty Years of Buddhist Studies: Selected Essays. Oxford: Cassirer, 1968, 274 pp.
In these fourteen essays, all of them previously published, Conze gathers a wealth of information: his historical sketch of the Prajñāpāramitā thought (pp. 123-147) is second to none. Two essays of comparative nature are "Buddhist Philosophy and its

European Parallels" (pp. 210 ff.) and "Spurious Parallels to Buddhist Philosophy."

(11) De BARY, WILLIAM THEODORE, ed. The Buddhist Tradition in India, China and Japan. New York: Modern Library, 1969.
An anthology of translations preceded by interpretative essays covering the entire range of Buddhism. The work is done by first-rate scholars and generally accurate. The section on Chinese Buddhism (pp. 125-255) covers the early years and includes two chapters on Chinese Buddhist sects. Good sections on T'ien-t'ai, Hua-yen, Pure Land, and Ch'an. A satisfactory text for beginning students.

(12) FRAUWALLNER, ERICH. Texte der indischen Philosophie. Vol. 2. Die Philosophie des Buddhismus. Berlin: Akademie-Verlag, 1958, 423 pp.
For those with knowledge of German, this is an indispensable anthology that has many translations of key works by the Buddhist masters, such as Nāgārjuna, Bhāvaviveka, Candrakīrti, Asaṅga, Vasubandhu, Dignāga, Sthiramati, and Dharmapāla.

(13) GODDARD, DWIGHT, ed. A Buddhist Bible. London: George G. Harrap & Co., [1932] 1956, 316 pp. Paperback reprint. Boston: Beacon Press, 1958.
Despite its title, this anthology contains some of the valuable translations from the Pali, Sanskrit, Chinese, Tibetan, and modern sources; however, it must be used selectively.

(14) HANAYAMA, SHŌYŪ, ed. A Guide to Buddhism. Yokohama: International Buddhist Exchange Center Press, 1970, 236 pp.
This guide to Buddhism, aimed at a wide public audience, includes such essays as "What is Buddhism?" and "Buddhism in Japan and the World." It has a useful chronological table, and an extensive bibliography.

(15) INTERNATIONAL BUDDHIST SOCIETY, ed. Studies on Buddhism in Japan. Vol. 3. Tokyo: Association for the Promotion of International Buddhism, 1936.
The volume contains the following important articles by eminent scholars: "Samgha" by Hakuji Ui, "Characteristics of Japanese Buddhism" by Bruno Petzold, "One Aspect of the Saddharmapuṇḍarīka Sūtra" by Mitsutaka Kimura, "Linee Generali Della Dottrina Shingon" by Giuliana Stramigioli, "The Seating Positions of Buddhas and Bodhisattvas in the Vajradhātumaṇḍala" by Ryujun Tajima, "The Protocanonical Languages of Buddhists in the Older Prakrit" by Horyu Kuno, and "Samāntamukha-Parivarta aus dem Sanskrit ubersetzt" by Ernst Leumann and Watanabe Syoko.

(16) de JONG, J.W. "A Brief History of Buddhist Studies in Europe and America." Eastern Buddhist 7 (May 1974):55-106; (Oct. 1974):49-82.
To date, the best accounting of Buddhist studies by Westerners in a compact form, conveniently divided into three periods: "Early" (300 B.C.-1877), "Middle" (1877-1942), and "Recent" (1943-1973). The work is largely philological, but it presents an excellent perspective on the scholars involved in the study and promotion of Buddhism. Here one will be introduced to such scholars as S. Levi, L. Poussin, H. Oldenberg, Th. Stcherbatsky, the Rhys-Davidses, E. Lamotte, S. Schayer, G. Tucci, Demieville, and their respective singular contributions. De Jong ends with a chapter on future perspectives in Buddhistic studies. Well worth perusing.

(17) KALUPAHANA, DAVID J. Buddhist Philosophy: A Historical Analysis. Honolulu: University Press of Hawaii, 1976, 189 pp.
An excellent philosophical treatment of early and later Buddhism. It treats such doctrines as causality, the three characteristics of existence, karma and rebirth, morality and ethics, and nirvāṇa, as well as the Mahāyāna schools of Mādhyamika and Yogācāra. Highly recommended for the beginner.

(18) KOLLER, JOHN M. Oriental Philosophies. New York: Scribner, 1970.
Part 2 (pp. 105-93) on Buddhist philosophies, while somewhat theologically oriented, gives an excellent synoptic view of the basic teachings and the nature of Buddhist reality. A useful general introduction.

(19) MOOKERJEE, S. The Buddhist Philosophy of Universal Flux: An Exposition of the Philosophy of Critial Realism as Expounded by the School of Dignāga. Calcutta: University of Calcutta, 1935. Reprint. Motilal Banarsidass, 1975.
This large work is actually a detailed survey of the entire realm of Buddhist philosophy. Much material is taken from the Tattvasamgraha, and there are good treatments of the controversies between Buddhist and other Indian schools. A good index and table of contents make this a most useful book. For the advanced student.

(20) McGOVERN, W.M. Introduction to Mahāyāna Buddhism. London: Kegan Paul, Trench, Trübner & Co., 1922. Reprint. Varanasi: Sahitya Ratan Mala Karyalaya, 1968.
The book begins with the "Doctrinal Evolution of Buddhism," followed by discussions of epistomology, logic, Buddhology, and psychology, which paves the way to "The Road to Nirvāṇa." A

short history of Buddhism and its principal sects forms the conclusion. The appendix is a survey of the sacred literature of the Buddhists. In short, a quick introduction to Mahāyāna Buddhism.

(21) MALALASEKERA, G.P., ed. Encyclopedia of Buddhism. Ceylon: Government Press, 1961-68. 1: (4 fasc.), 786 pp.; 2: (4 fasc.), 700 pp. Other vols. pending.
Granted that it is far from completion and its rate of publication is decreasing after the death of Dr. Malalasekera, one can still find valuable information in the several issues of the Encyclopedia. Destined to become the great resource work on all phases of Buddhism.

(22) MIZUNO, KŌGEN. Primitive Buddhism. Translated by Kōshō Yamamoto. Ube: Karinbunko, 1969, 293 pp.
A faithful translation of a pioneering work by an outstanding Japanese scholar of early Buddhism. It covers the early schools and includes a lengthy discussion of the characteristics of primitive Buddhism. Good for beginning students.

(23) MORGAN, KENNETH W., ed. The Path of the Buddha: Buddhism Interpreted by the Buddhists. New York: Ronald Press, 1956, 432 pp.
A highly readable introductory work containing a wide spectrum of essays contributed by Buddhist scholars of India, Tibet, Ceylon, Burma, and Japan. Of particular interest are U. Thittila's "The Fundamental Principles of Theravāda Buddhism," S. Yamaguchi's "Development of Mahāyāna Buddhist Beliefs," and H. Nakamura's "Unity and Diversity in Buddhism."

(24) NAKAMURA, HAJIME. "Buddhist Philosophy." In Encyclopedia Britannica. 15th ed., pp. 425-31.
A compact overview of Buddhist epistemology, metaphysics, ethics, psychology and logic.

(25) PARDUE, PETER A. Buddhism: A Historical Introduction to Buddhist Values and the Social and Political Forms They Have Assumed in Asia. New York: Macmillan, 1968, 203 pp.
A panoramic view of Buddhist advances in India, China, southeast Asia, Tibet, and Japan, and of the contemporary situation. A good beginning.

(26) PRATT, JAMES B. The Pilgrimage of Buddhism and a Buddhist Pilgrimage. New York: Macmillan Co., 1928, 758 pp.
A critical realist tries his hand at interpreting Buddhism in a sympathetic and unifying sense. Chapters worth perusing are

"Philosophy of the Mahāyāna," "Buddhist Thought in China," "Buddhist Thought in Japan," and "Zen."

(27) PREBISH, CHARLES S., ed. Buddhism: A Modern Perspective. University Park and London: Pennsylvania State University Press, 1975, 330 pp.
Eight contributors present a series of lectures on the general field of Buddhism from the pre-Buddhist background through the developments in Indian Buddhism and finally beyond India proper to Buddhism in China, Japan, Tibet, southeast Asia, and the West. The essays are of uneven quality, but they give a synoptic view of the whole range of Buddhism. A good introduction, especially handy for instructors.

(28) RAJU, P.T. Idealistic Thought of India. London: George Allen & Unwin, 1953, 454 pp.
Within the context of idealism, Buddhism is extensively treated (pp. 184-291) from the early teachings to the doctrinal developments in the various schools in India proper. A good beginning.

(29) RENOU, LOUIS, and FILLIOZAT, JEAN. L'Inde classique. Vol. 2. Hanoi: École française d'Extrême Orient, 1953, 564 pp.
Section C under the title of "Les doctrines du Grand Moyen de Progression (Mahāyāna)" covers "Origines du Mahāyāna," "Caractères principaux du Mahāyāna," "Bouddhologie," "La doctrine des corpus du Buddha," "Doctrines des sūtra mahāyāniques," "Théories des Mādhyamika," "Théories des Vijñānavādin Yogācāra," and "Les choses et la réalité." A solid work, profitable for those who read French.

(30) ROBINSON, RICHARD. The Buddhist Religion. Belmont, Calif.: Dickenson, 1970, 136 pp.
In this concise and excellent introductory work, Robinson sketches the origin and development of Buddhism in India, Tibet, China, and Japan.

(31) RUEGG, D. SEYFORT. The Study of Indian and Tibetan Thought. Leiden: E.J. Brill, 1967, 48 pp.
Ruegg undertakes a survey of the study of Indian and Tibetan thought and suggests areas fruitful for future research.

(32) SARKAR, ANIL KUMAR. Changing Phases of Buddhist Thought: A Study in the Background of East-West Philosophy. Patna: Bharatibhavan, 1968, 137 pp.
This is an interesting topical survey of Buddhist thought in India, covering such teachers as Aśvaghoṣa, Nāgārjuna, and Dignāga. Comparisons are drawn between the thought of Nāgārjuna

and Whitehead and that of the Western existentialists (Kierkegaard, Nietzsche, Jaspers, Marcel, Heidegger, and Sartre). Includes a short chapter on the four Buddhist schools (Vaibhāṣika, Sautrāntika, Mādhyamika, and Yogācāra).

(33) SCHUON, FRITHJOF. In the Tracks of Buddhism. Translated by Marco Pallis. London: Allen & Unwin, 1968.
Essentials of Buddhism described with clarity, making use of comparisons with Western religious thought. Emphasis on Japanese Buddhism.

(34) STRYK, LUCIEN, ed. World of the Buddha: A Reader--From the Three Baskets to Modern Zen. New York: Doubleday, 1968, 423 pp.
This is an ambitious anthology of selected translations of varying lengths that span the whole of Buddhist history, from the earliest literature to modern Zen. It gives the beginner a good overview.

(35) SUZUKI, BEATRICE L. Mahāyāna Buddhism: A Brief Outline. London: Allen & Unwin, [1939] 1948, 158 pp. Paperback reprint. New York: Macmillan, 1969.
This book furnishes a relatively simple introduction to the major tenets and terminology of Mahāyāna Buddhism. Outlines of some of the important Mahāyāna sūtras and analysis of their essential doctrines and practices are unpretentious and helpful. A selected list of books and a short glossary are included.

(36) SUZUKI, DAISETZ T. On Indian Mahāyāna Buddhism. Edited by E. Conze. New York: Harper & Row, 1968, 284 pp.
Suzuki develops the idea of the bodhisattva by introducing the concepts of śūnyatā and prajñā. Chapter 7 is of particular value since it analyzes the Gaṇḍavyūha or Avatamsaka sūtra, an analysis not readily found elsewhere. A solid work.

(37) SUZUKI, DAISETZ T. Outlines of Mahāyāna Buddhism. London: Luzac & Co., 1907, 383 pp. Reprint. New York: Schocken Books, 1963.
An early work by Suzuki but still valuable as an introduction to Mahāyāna. Good background study of early Buddhism and the beginnings of Mahāyāna. Covers such basic doctrines as bhūtatathatā, anātman, dharmakāya, trikāya, karma, bodhisattva, and the ten stages to bodhisattvahood.

(38) TAKAKUSU, JUNJIRŌ. Essentials of Buddhist Philosophy. Edited by C.A. Moore and W.T. Chan. Honolulu: University of Hawaii Press, 1945, 221 pp. 3d ed., 1956.
A highly technical but good introduction to Chinese and Japanese Buddhism. It contains a clear exposé of basic Mahāyāna ideas, followed by descriptions of the main schools and their texts. Solidly based on the Chinese source materials. Recommended for the advanced student.

(39) THOMAS, EDWARD J. The History of Buddhist Thought. London: Kegan Paul, Trench, Trübner, 1933, 316 pp. 2d ed., 1951.
Written by a historian, this is an excellent and reliable source on the development of Buddhist thought, covering such subjects as causation, karma, Buddha, emptiness, and consciousness. A solid beginning.

(40) WARD, C.H.S. Buddhism. Vol. 1, Hīnayāna. Vol. 2, Mahāyāna. Great Religions of the East Series, edited by Eric S. Waterhouse. London: Epworth Press, 1947, 1952. 1:143 pp. 2:222 pp.
In order to encompass the wide masses of material ranging from Tibet, Mongolia, China, Korea, and Japan, Ward masterfully divides the subject matter into: the origin and development of the doctrine of Buddhology, Theravāda and Mahāyāna philosophical ideas, and comparison and contrast. Ward's effective use of the writings of such specialists as Farquhar, de la Vallée Poussin, Stcherbatsky, Keith, Nariman, Thomas, Grousser, and others in the Encyclopedia of Religion and Ethics is commendable.

(41) WAYMAN, ALEX. "Buddhism." In Historia Religionum. Edited by C.J. Bleeker. Leiden: E.J. Brill, 1969, pp. 372-464.
A systematic survey of Buddhist development, covering such matters as the conception of deity, man, and worship, with a short history of Buddhist studies. A very good beginning.

(42) WELBON, RICHARD GUY. The Buddhist Nirvāṇa and Its Western Interpreters. Chicago and London: University of Chicago Press, 1968, 320 pp.
A lucid and informative account of the essential nature of nirvāṇa, which had been the subject of a great controversy in the West. In this work, therefore, the works of the most eminent scholars on the subject are presented and assessed. This, in turn, makes this book an excellent introduction to the history of Western approaches to Buddhism over the past century.

(43) YAMAKAMI, SŌGEN. Systems of Buddhist Thought. Calcutta: Calcutta University Press, 1912, 315 pp.
A dated but quite informative work dealing with the important doctrines of the various schools in India, China, and Japan. Highly technical and metaphysical in treatment.

(44) ZAEHNER, R.C., ed. The Concise Encyclopedia of Living Faiths. Boston: Beacon Press, [1959] 1967, 431 pp.
The following contributed chapters are highly recommended: "Buddhism: The Theravāda" (I.B. Horner), pp. 267-95; "Buddhism: The Mahāyāna" (E. Conze), pp. 296-320; "Buddhism: In China and Japan" (R.M. Robinson), pp. 321-47.

1.2 Indian Surveys

(1) BAHM, ARCHIE J. Philosophy of the Buddha. London: Rider & Co., 1958, 175 pp.
A Westerner's interpretive analysis of the principal teachings of the Buddha, covering such concepts as the four truths, craving, middle way, nirvāṇa, dhyāna, soul or no-soul, and the saṅgha. The critique is provocative and challenging but may mislead the unwary beginner.

(2) BURTT, E.A., ed. The Teachings of the Compassionate Buddha. New York: New American Library, 1955.
A good introduction to the ideas manifested in early Buddhism, Theravāda and Mahāyāna. Helpful introductory remarks to chapters and sections.

(3) CHATTERJEE, S., and D. DATTA. An Introduction to Indian Philosophy. Calcutta: University of Calcutta, 1954, 443 pp.
The chapter on Buddhism is a standard presentation focusing on the principal doctrines of the four noble truths, dependent origination, karma, impermanence, and non-soul. The four Indian Buddhist schools (Mādhyamika, Yogācāra, Sautrāntika, Vaibhāṣika) are also treated, and the chapter ends with the distinction between Theravāda and Mahāyāna. A good beginning.

(4) CONZE, EDWARD. Buddhist Thought in India: Three Phases of Buddhist Philosophy. London: George Allen & Unwin, 1962, 302 pp.
The three phases are Archaic Buddhism, the Sthāviras and the Mahāyāna. This is a comprehensive work that exhibits much maturity and originality. Recommended to all.

(5) DASGUPTA, SURENDRANATH. Indian Idealism. Cambridge: Cambridge University Press, 1962, 206 pp.
Chapters 4 and 5 (pp. 76-148) treat the Buddhist idealistic strains from Nāgārjuna, Aśvaghoṣa, Maitreya, Asaṅga, Vasubandhu, Śāntarakṣita, and Kamalaśīla. Very provocative and informative; however, some of the interpretations that suggest idealistic strains similar to those of the West are questionable.

(6) DASGUPTA, SURENDRANATH. A History of Indian Philosophy. Vol. 1. Cambridge: Cambridge University Press, [1922] 1951, 528 pp.
Chapter 5 (pp. 78-168) is a standard and reliable account of Buddhism by one of the leading Indian scholars.

(7) ELIOT, CHARLES. Hinduism and Buddhism: An Historical Sketch. 3 vols. London: Routledge & Kegan, 1921. Reprint. 1957.
An historical survey of Pali Buddhism and the Mahāyāna schools. Weak on doctrine and often erroneous.

(8) KEITH, ARTHUR B. Buddhist Philosophy in India and Ceylon. Oxford: Clarendon Press, 1923, 339 pp.
A somewhat outdated book, but it does contain important analysis of some of the essential doctrines in the different schools.

(9) PULIGANDLA, R. Fundamentals of Indian Philosophy. Nashville and New York: Abingdon Press, 1975, 363 pp.
The chapter on Buddhism (pp. 50-113) deals with the key philosophical concepts of suffering, four noble truths, nirvāṇa, dependent origination, impermanence, karma, and non-self. It also treats the four Indian Buddhist schools (Vaibhāṣika, Sautrāntika, Yogācāra, Mādhyamika), the Mādhyamika in detail, and ends with observations on Buddhist psychology and ethics. A solid beginning.

(10) RADHAKRISHNAN, S. Indian Philosophy. Vol. 1. London: George Allen & Unwin, 1923, 738 pp.
This volume contains three highly readable introductory chapters on Buddhism by the outstanding Indian philosopher.

(11) RADHAKRISHNAN, SARVAPALLI, and CHARLES A. MOORE, eds. A Source Book in Indian Philosophy. Princeton: Princeton University Press, 1957, 684 pp.
The Buddhist section (pp. 272-345) is relatively short, but it contains selections from previously translated works that give an overview of the doctrinal aspects of Buddhism from the early beginnings to the later Indian developments in the Vijñānavāda and Mādhyamika systems. A good introduction.

(12) RAHULA, WALPOLA. What the Buddha Taught. New York: Grove Press, 1959, 103 pp.
One of the best introductions to the study of basic Buddhist doctrines. It contains exhaustive analysis of the four noble truths, the doctrine of no-soul, and meditation or mental culture.

(13) RHYS-DAVIDS, T.W. Buddhist India. 3d Indian ed. Calcutta: Susil Gupta, 1957, 158 pp. (Orig. pub. London: Ernest Benn, 1903.)
One of the earliest and finest historical sketches of Buddhist India covering such matters as kings, clans, social and economic conditions, language and literature, and prevailing religions.

(14) ROBINSON, RICHARD H. "Classical Indian Philosophy." In Chapters in Indian Civilization. Edited by Joseph W. Elder. 2 vols. Dubuque: Kendall/Hunt, 1970. 1:127-227.
This chapter treats Indian philosophy as a whole but includes brief and lucid accounts of the foundations of such schools as the Abhidharma, Mādhyamika and Vijñānavāda. A good beginning for the serious student.

(15) SHARMA, CHANDRADHAR. A Critical Survey of Indian Philosophy. Delhi: Motilal Banarsidass, 1960, 415 pp.
Includes a critical assessment of Indian Buddhist developments from early Buddhism to Śūnyavāda, Vijñānavāda, and Svatantra-vijñānavāda. It also has some illuminating comparative analysis on Buddhist and Vedāntic doctrines. A good beginning.

(16) SMART, NINIAN. Doctrine and Argument in Indian Philosophy. London: George Allen & Unwin, 1964, 256 pp.
This is a highly interpretive account of Indian philosophical systems, in which Buddhist epistemology and metaphysics are generously treated. Recommended for the serious student.

(17) WARD, C.H.S. Buddhism (see 1.1[40]).
A general accounting of Theravāda and Mahāyāna Buddhism. More historical than doctrinal.

(18) WARDER, A.K. Indian Buddhism. Delhi: Motilal Banarsidass, 1970, 622 pp.
A panoramic view of the Indian Buddhist tradition from early beginnings to the Mādhyamika. Good for the beginner.

(19) WARDER, A.K. Outline of Indian Philosophy. Delhi: Motilal Banarsidass, 1971, 270 pp.
Contains an historical treatment of the principal schools of Buddhism in India. Very introductory.

(20) WINTERNITZ, MAURICE. A History of Indian Literature and Jaina Literature. Delhi: Motilal Banarsidass, 1983. (Orig. pub. Calcutta, 1933.)
An invaluable aid in understanding the different texts of Buddhism in general and Buddhist schools in particular.

(21) ZIMMER, HEINRICH. Philosophies of India. Edited by Joseph Campbell. Princeton: Bollingen paperback, [1951] 1969, 687 pp.
An excellent topical introduction to Indian philosophies. The Buddhist section (pp. 464-559) includes discussions on Buddhahood, Theravāda and Mahāyāna, and the way of the bodhisattva.

1.2.1 Early Indian

(1) BAGCHI, P.C. "Fundamental Problems of the Origins of Buddhism." France-Asie, n.s. 17 (July-Aug. 1961):2227-41.
An historian examines early Buddhism.

(2) BANERJEE, ANUKUL CHANDRA. Sarvāstivāda Literature. Calcutta: Calcutta Oriental Press, 1957, 271 pp.
A literary study of the Sarvāstivāda and the Vinaya texts.

(3) BAREAU, A. Les sectes Bouddhiques du petit véhicule. Saigon: École française d'Extrême Orient, 1955.
A very valuable treatment, in French, of the main doctrines of the various Hīnayāna schools of Buddhism. Discusses the rise of the eighteen schools with a minute and authoritative comparative study of the doctrines.

(4) BHATTACHARYA, VIDUSHEKHARA. The Basic Conception of Buddhism. Calcutta: University of Calcutta, 1934, 103 pp.
Comprises two lectures touching upon the early beginnings and the proper understanding of the basic doctrines. Good for the beginner.

(5) CHANDRA, PRATAP. "Was Early Buddhism Influenced by the Upanishads?" Philosophy East and West 21 (1971):317-24.
The author goes to the early texts to deny any Upanishadic influence.

(6) DUTT, NALINAKSHA. Buddhist Sects in India. Calcutta: Firma K.L. Mukhopadhyay, 1970.
Contains a classification of the different Indian Buddhist schools and an analysis of their respective doctrines.

(7) DUTT, SUKUMAR. The Buddha and Five After-Centuries. London: Luzac & Co., 1957, 259 pp.
The work covers the development of Buddhism from its origin through the Aśokan Age to the emergence of Mahāyāna. Reliable.

(8) FRAUWALLNER, ERICH. The Earliest Vinaya and the Beginnings of Buddhist Literature. Rome: Istituto italiano per il medio ed Estremo Oriente, 1956, 219 pp.
A comparative study of the early vinaya (discipline) in the various schools.

(9) LAMOTTE, ÉTIENNE. Histoire du Bouddhisme indien: Des Origines a l'ère Saka. Bibliothèque du Museon, vol. 43. Publications universitaires, 1958, 862 pp.
One of the finest historical works on Indian Buddhism done in recent years. Relatively weak on doctrines but a very reliable text in general for those who know French. A very conprehensive historical treatment of early Indian Buddhism.

(10) MEHTA, RATILAL N. Pre-Buddhist India. Bombay: Examiner Press, 1939, 461 pp.
A political, administrative, economic, social, and geographical survey of ancient India based mainly on the Jātaka stories. A good beginning for everyone.

(11) MURTI, T.R.V. The Central Philosophy of Buddhism: A Study of the Mādhyamika System. London: Allen & Unwin, 1955, 372 pp.
Contains introductory chapters on the Indian philosophical scene. Treats Mādhyamika philosophy and the Vijñānavāda system. Recommended for both the beginner and the advanced student.

(12) PANDE, GOVIND C. Studies in the Origins of Buddhism. Allahabad: University of Allahabad, 1957, 600 pp.
A scholarly account of the origin and development of the major concepts of Buddhism.

(13) PANDEYA, RAMCHANDRA, ed. Buddhist Studies in India. Delhi: Motilal Banarsidass, 1975, 208 pp.
A collection of essays of mixed philosophical value. The worthy ones are: "Early Buddhism and the Impact on the Gīta," "Buddhism and Change," "On Svabhāvavāda," "On Satyasiddhi," and "Buddhist Mysticism."

(14) RAHULA, WALPOLA. History of Buddhism in Ceylon: The Anuradhapura Period, 3rd B.C.-10th A.D. Gunasena & Co., 1966, 351 pp.
The most comprehensive and commendable work done in the area by a leading Buddhist thinker. Recommended for undergraduates.

(15) RHYS-DAVIDS, C.A.F. Śākya or Buddhist Origins. London: Kegan Paul, Trench, Trübner, 1931, 444 pp.
This is a mature and highly interpretive account of the beginnings of what we call Buddhism, capping her long career in Buddhist studies. Though controversial to some extent, her analysis of the founder, his message, and his mandate show rare insights into the philosophical dimensions of Buddhist thought. Recommended for the explorer.

(16) WAGLE, NARENDRA. Society at the Time of the Buddha. Bombay: Popular Prakashan, 1963, 314 pp.
An exhaustive analysis of such matters as patterns of settlement, social groups and ranking, kinship and marriage, and occupational divisions.

1.2.2 Later Indian: Prajñāpāramitā and the Rise of Mahāyāna

(1) CONZE, EDWARD. "The Development of Prajñāpāramitā Thought." In Buddhism and Culture (D.T. Suzuki Commemorative Volume). Edited by Susumu Yamaguchi. Kyoto: Nakano Press, 1960, pp. 24-45.
A definitive article on the subject by Conze, who has published a great number of books and articles dealing with Prajñāpāramitā literature.

(2) CONZE, EDWARD. The Prajñāpāramitā Literature. The Hague: Mouton & Co., 1960, 123 pp.
A basic text for the study of the literature on prajñā (wisdom) philosophy. The first chapter presents the basic ideas that run through the various sutras.

(3) DAYAL, HAR. The Bodhisattva Doctrine in Buddhist Sanskrit Literature. London: Kegan Paul, Trench, Trübner & Co., 1932, 392 pp.
An historian's approach to the bodhisattva concept. Excellent introduction.

(4) DUTT, NALINAKSHA. Aspects of Mahāyāna Buddhism and Its Relation to Hīnayāna. London: Luzac & Co., 1930, 356 pp. Rev. ed., 1973.
Excellent coverage of the early contact between the two traditions and analysis of basic doctrines. Recommended for all.

(5) DUTT, NALINAKSHA. "The Fundamental Principles of Mahāyānism." In Présence du Bouddhisme (see 1.1[4]), pp. 319-35.
A short overview of Mahāyāna principles.

(6) HANAYAMA, SHŌYŪ. "A Summary of Various Research on the Prajñāpāramitā Literature by Japanese Scholars." Acta Asiatica (Tokyo: Tōhō Gakkai) 10 (Feb. 1966):16-93.
A very detailed, comprehensive progress report on the various research on the Prajñāpāramitā literature in Japanese, which was not included in Conze's Prajñāpāramitā Literature (2), due to the obvious language barrier. Translations from some research articles are also included in this summary. A neglected but important study.

(7) HIKATA, RYŪSHŌ. Suvikrāntavikrāmi-paripṛcchā Prajñāpāramitāsūtra. Fukuoka: Kyushu University, 1958, 142 pp.
Although the bulk of the book is taken up by the edited Sanskrit text, there is a very helpful introductory essay on the prajñāpāramitā literature. Compare with E. Conze's Prajñāpāramitā Literature (2). Recommended for all.

(8) HOSAKA. G. "Development of the 'Pāramitā' Thought and the Establishment of Mahāyāna Sutras." Komazawa Daigaku Kenkyū Kiyō, 13 (1955):1-12.
The concept of pāramitā (perfection) is important not only in the Prajñāpāramitā-sūtras but also in other Mahāyāna sutras. This study traces the historical development of this thought.

(9) KAJIYAMA, YUICHI. "An Introduction to Buddhist Philosophy: An Annotated Translation of the Tarkabhāṣā of Mokṣākaragupta." Memoirs of the Faculty of Letters (Kyoto University) 10 (1966):1-173.
Contains a valuable discussion of the later Buddhist schools of Sautrāntika, Vaibhāṣika, Mādhyamika, and Yogācāra-Vijñānavāda.

(10) KANAKURA, YENSHŌ. "A Bibliographical Study of Aśvaghoṣa's Works." In Religious Studies in Japan. Tokyo: Maruzen, 1959, pp. 300-307.
A study of Aśvaghoṣa (first-second century A.D.), who linked Theravāda Buddhism with Mahāyāna. Kanakura has, among his numerous writings, a volume on Aśvaghoṣa entitled A Study of Aśvaghoṣa (in Japanese).

(11) KIMURA, R. A Historical Study of the Terms Hīnayāna and Mahāyāna and the Origin of Mahāyāna Buddhism. Calcutta: Calcutta University, 1927.
A comprehensive and scholarly work, but often neglected. Recommended to all.

(12) LAW, BIMALA CHURN. Buddhaghoṣa. Bombay: Bombay Branch, Royal Asiatic Society, 1946, 147 pp.
A good introduction to the great Theravāda master of the fifth century A.D., his works, and his philosophy.

(13) McGOVERN, WILLIAM M. An Introduction to Mahāyāna Buddhism (see 1.1[20]).
Contains a discussion of important Mahāyāna doctrines such as the trikāya concept and the Absolute, as developed by the different schools.

(14) NISHI, GIYU. "The Truth of the Original Purity of Mind." Religious Studies in Japan (see [10]), pp. 308-15.
This is a short article on "the motive force of the development of Mahāyāna Buddhism." The short articles by these prominent Japanese scholars in the volumes of Religious Studies in Japan are, needless to say, "a few drops" from their original Japanese works.

(15) YAMADA, RYŪJŌ. "A Study on the Formation of Mahāyāna Sūtras." Religious Studies in Japan (see [10]), pp. 316-28.
This is a synopsis of his voluminous work in Japanese entitled An Introduction to the Formation of Mahāyāna Buddhism (Daijō-bukkyō seiritsushi josetsu).

1.2.2.1 Mādhyamika

(1) DAYE, DOUGLAS D. "Major Schools of the Mahāyāna: Mādhyamika." In Buddhism: A Modern Perspective (see 1.1[27]), pp. 76-96.
An excellent introduction to the problematics of the Mādhyamika system of Nāgārjuna. It covers the epistemological and metaphysical nature of the system, treating such topics as causation, language, metalanguage, dharmic analysis, emptiness, prajñāpti, and the doctrine of two truths.

(2) La VALLÉE POUSSIN, L. de. "Réflexions sur le Mādhyamika." Mélanges chinois et bouddhique 2 (1933):1-59.
A noted Buddhologist reflects on past studies of the Mādhyamika system and then engages in an analysis of it, covering such topics as dependent origination, eight negations, conventional reality, middle way, prajñā, tathatā, and the controversy between Mādhyamika and Yogācāra. Well worth reading.

(3) MURTI, T.R.V. The Central Philosophy of Buddhism (see 1.2.1[11]).
Though controversial in parts (e.g., Murti's Kantian bias and his absolutistic treatment), this is still the definitive study of the Mādhyamika system. It can be recommended for serious students and scholars.

(4) MURTY, K.S. Nāgārjuna. New Delhi: National Book Trust, 1971.
A short, clear survey of the life, teachings, and influence of the founder of the Mādhyamika philosophy.

(5) PANDEYA, R.C. "The Mādhyamika Philosophy: A New Approach." Philosophy East and West 14 (1964):3-24.
Pandeya, an outstanding Indian philosopher, suggests a new approach for the understanding of Mādhyamika philosophy in a careful analysis of the Vaibhāṣika and Sautrāntika schools of Buddhism, regarding the nature of reality.

(6) PANIKKAR, RAIMUNDO. "The 'Crisis' of Mādhyamika and Indian Philosophy Today." Philosophy East and West 16 (1966): 117-31.
This stimulating article contains two parts: 1) criticism of the Mādhyamika, with an interesting summary and 2) the crisis of philosophy, with a solution.

(7) ROBINSON, RICHARD. Early Mādhyamika in India and China. Madison: University of Wisconsin Press, 1967, 347 pp.
An extremely learned and scholarly study of the Mādhyamika school in India and the introduction of its thinking into China in the fourth and fifth centuries. This study is solidly based on Sanskrit and Chinese texts, and the annotation is extensive. A must for advanced students.

(8) SHARMA, CHANDRAHAR. Dialectic in Buddhism and Vedānta. Banares: Nand Kishore & Bros.; New York: Hafner, 1952, 272 pp.
The first half of the book is devoted to an exposition of the Mahāyāna philosophy, and the second half deals with the attitude toward Buddhism by a Vedānta philosopher, Gaudapāda, a so-called crypto-Buddhist. Sharma attempts to show the totality of the Mahāyāna-Vedānta system which, he maintains, is a different stage of Upanishadic thought.

(9) SINGH, JAIDEVA. An Introduction to Mādhyamaka Philosophy. Delhi: Motilal Banarsidass, 1968, 59 pp.
A compact presentation of the Mādhyamaka system of Nāgārjuna with a good historical background study. In elucidating the system, it compares the Theravāda and Mahāyāna views on important doctrines, such as pratītya-samutpāda, nirvāṇa, arhatship and bodhisattvahood, dharma and śūnyatā. It presents the main arguments of the system with special emphasis on the use and significance of the dialectic. Recommended to all.

(10) VIDYĀBHŪṢAṆA, S. CH. "History of the Mādhyamika Philosophy of Nāgārjuna." Journal of the Buddhist Text Society 4 (1897):7-20.
A careful and critical analysis of the texts of the Mādhyamika.

(11) YAMAGUCHI, SUSUMU. "Criticism of the Mādhyamika School on Theism." Religious Studies in Japan (see 1.2.2[10]), pp. 329-35.
Criticisms of theism by the Buddha, Nāgārjuna, Candrakīrti, and Śāntideva.

(12) YAMAGUCHI, SUSUMU. Dynamic Buddha and Static Buddha (A System of Buddhist Practice). Translated by S. Watanabe. Tokyo: Risosha, 1958, 93 pp.
The work is a popularization of Yamaguchi's versatile knowledge, based on his painstaking textual studies.

1.2.2.2 Yogācāra-Vijñānavāda

(1) BHATTACHARYA, V. "Evolution of Vijñānavāda." Indian Historical Quarterly 10 (1934):1-11.
An interesting article that traces the origins of the "consciousness-only" doctrine back to the Upanishads and shows that the concept is similar to the Vedāntic point of view. For all students.

(2) CONZE, EDWARD. "The Yogācārin Treatment of Prajñāpāramitā Texts." In Proceedings of the Twenty-third International Congress of Orientalists, Cambridge, 1954, pp. 21-28.
An important article by the foremost authority on the Prajñāpāramitā literature.

(3) DASGUPTA, SURENDRANATH. "Philosophy of Vasubandhu in Viṃśatikā and Triṃśikā." Indian Historical Quarterly 4 (1928): 36-43.
A concise treatment of the principal ideas of Vasubandhu as seen in his twenty- and thirty-verse treatises. A good beginning.

(4) HAMILTON, CLARENCE H. "Buddhist Idealism in Wei Shih Er Shih Lun." In Essays in Philosophy of Seventeen Doctors of Philosophy of the University of Chicago. Chicago: University of Chicago Press, 1929, pp. 99-115.
An illuminating analysis of idealistic tendencies seen in the Chinese work of Hsuan-tsang. Recommended to all.

(5) JAINI, PADMANABH S. "On the Theory of the Two Vasubandhus." Bulletin of the School of Oriental and African Studies 21 (1958):48-53.
Originated by Frauwallner, the theory of the two Vasubandhus is still being debated (cf. Wayman's counterview as expressed in his Analysis of the Śrāvakabhūmi Manuscript [(12)]). Jaini's article appears in this context.

(6) JHA, GANGANATHA, trans. The Tattvasaṅgraha of Śāntarakṣita, with Commentary of Kamalaśīla. 2 vols. Gaekwad's Oriental Series, nos. 80, 83. Baroda: Oriental Institute, 1937, 1939.
An eighth-century work carrying on the Mādhyamika-Yogācāra tradition and which subsequently has had great influence on Tibetan Buddhism. For the advanced student who is familiar with the controversies surrounding Indian systems of the period.

(7) LÉVI, S. Un système de philosophie bouddhique: Matériaux pour l'étude du système Vijñaptimātra, histoire du système Vijñaptimātra, d'après D. Shimaji, par M.P. Demiéville. L'ālayavijñāna, d'après le Fan yi ming yi tai, traduit en collaboration avec E. Chavannes. Paris: Bulletin de l'école d'haute étude, 1932, 260 pp.
An invaluable book and a fine introduction to the Yogācāra school. The book contains an historical introduction to the school, annotated French translations of the Viṃśatikā and the Triṃśikā, and two important Yogācāra texts of Vasubandhu. There is also a short résumé of the Vijñaptimātra doctrines and long notes on the term ālayavijñāna. Essential for all advanced students who read French.

(8) MAY, JACQUES. "La philosophie bouddhique idéaliste." Asiatische Studien/Études asiatiques 25 (1971):265-323.
This is a concise and lucid introduction to the philosophy of Buddhist idealism centered around the notions of vijñāna and ālaya-vijñāna. For the educated public.

(9) UEDA, YOSHIFUMI. "Two Main Streams of Thought in Yogācāra Philosophy." Philosophy East and West 17 (1967):155-65.
The author takes up the two divergent streams of thought on consciousness-only (vijñāptimātra) doctrine as they occurred in China, one by virtue of Hsuan-tsang's translations of Indian texts and the other by those translations predating him.

(10) UI, HAKUJU. "Maitreya as an Historical Personage." In Indian Studies in Honor of Charles Rockwell Lanman. Cambridge: Harvard University Press, 1929, pp. 95-102.
In this article the author shows that Maitreya, whom tradition gives as the teacher of Asaṅga, is not a bodhisattva but an historical person. It is to him that the origins of the consciousness-only school (Vijñānavāda) must be traced.

(11) VERDU, ALFONSO. Dialectical Aspects in Buddhist Thought (Studies in Sino-Japanese Mahāyāna Idealism). East Asian Series, no. 8. Lawrence: University of Kansas Press, 1974.
Verdu traces in four essays the genesis, evolution, and Sino-Japanese development of the Ālayavijñāna. This is a product of his astonishment "at the breath-taking heights and depths of Buddhist philosophical insights." For the advanced student.

(12) WAYMAN, ALEX. Analysis of the Śrāvakabhūmi Manuscript. University of California Publications in Classical Philology, no. 17. Berkeley and Los Angeles: University of California Press, 1961, 185 pp.
A scholarly work on one of the chapters of the Yogācārabhūmi of Asaṅga. Contains much historical matter.

1.2.2.3 Buddhist Logic

See also Logic, 10

(1) CHATTERJI, D. "Buddhist Logic: An Introductory Survey." Annals of the Bhandarkar Oriental Research Institute 13 (1933):77-85.
A general introduction to early Buddhist logic, with special emphasis on the interdependence of Brahmanic, Jaina, and Buddhist logic.

(2) FRAUWALLNER, E. "Landmarks in the History of Indian Logic." Wiener Zeitschrift für die Kunde südasiens 5 (1961):125-48.
One of the few works of the Viennese master available in English, this article presents an historical overview of the main dates and events in Indian logic. As such, it is invaluable for beginning students.

(3) FRAUWALLNER, E. "Die Reihenfolge und Entstehung der Werke Dharmakīrtis." Asiatica, Festschrift Friedrich Weller. (Leipzig), 1954, pp. 142-54.
A basic and solid attempt to establish the chronology of the works of Dharmakīrti. The author also provides summaries of the contents of Dharmakīrti's two works, the Pramāṇavārttika and the Pramāṇaviniścaya. Invaluable for students interested in Dharmakīrti.

(4) KEITH, ARTHUR B. Indian Logic and Atomism: An Exposition of the Nyāya and Vaiśeṣkika Systems. Oxford: Oxford University Press, 1921, 291 pp.
A good introduction to Indian logic in general, including the contributions by Buddhist logicians Dignāga and Dharmakīrti.

(5) RANDLE, H.N. Indian Logic in the Early Schools. Oxford: Oxford University Press, 1930.
The work gives a coherent and systematic picture of the historical development of Indian logic. Unfortunately, the fact that it contains some controversial opinions which have since been revised by later scholars and the fact that the book itself is difficult, make it unsuitable for beginning students. The reader must be cautioned not to identify Buddhist logic with Western formal logic.

(6) SUGIURA, S. Hindu Logic as Preserved in China and Japan. Philadelphia: Ginn, 1900, 114 pp.
A pioneering and basic work which gathers and studies those texts on Buddhist logic that are preserved in Chinese translations. The book is now outdated but may still be useful if used in conjunction with the corrections and refinements of Tucci, Randle, Frauwallner, etc.

(7) TUCCI, GUISEPPE. "Buddhist Logic Before Diṅnāga (Asaṅga, Vasubhandhu, Tarkaśāstras)." Journal of the Royal Asiatic Society, Oct. 1929, pp. 870-71.
A reevaluation of the texts brought together by Sugiura. The author explains the various classification systems of pre-Dignāga thinkers, based on Chinese and Tibetan texts. The article contains useful correspondences between Chinese, Tibetan, and Sanskrit technical terms. Not for beginners.

(8) VIDYĀBHŪṢAṆA, S.C. History of the Medieval School of Indian Logic. Calcutta: Calcutta University, 1909.
This work, devoted to both Jaina and Buddhist logicians, presents a series of biographical sketches and resumés of important texts. The section on Dignāga (pp. 78-101) still contains much useful

information. Although criticized on certain points by later scholars, the work still remains perhaps the best short introduction to the subject. Recommended for all students.

1.2.2.4 Tantra

(1) BHARATI, AGEHANANDA. The Tantric Tradition. London: Rider, 1965.
A highly detailed exposition of both Hindu and Buddhist Tantra. Tantra is taken as a religious expression ultimately independent of any spiritual system. The practices and philosophical contents of Hindu and Buddhist Tantra are examined together so that they are seen both in their similarities and differences. The result is a thorough overview of the whole Tantric tradition. This is definitely meant for advanced studies, so those unfamiliar with Tantra would be advised to read a more general book first.

(2) BLOFELD, JOHN. The Tantric Mysticism of Tibet. New York: Dutton, 1970, 257 pp.
Blofeld, as a practitioner of the Vajrayāna, writes a good overview of Tantric background, theory and practices. It contains an easy-to-read discussion on the psychic symbols, the preliminaries, the sādhanas, the advanced practice, etc. Also contains a glossary, bibliography and an index. A good introductory book.

(3) DASGUPTA, SHASHIBHUSHAN. Introduction to Tantric Buddhism, 2d ed. Calcutta: University of Calcutta Press, 1958, 211 pp.
The book begins with a background discussion of earlier Buddhist systems, then looks at how they are present in the Tantras; also the Tantric schools, the esoteric symbology, and the yoga are discussed, ending with an interesting chapter on the arguments the Tantrics have presented in defense of their practices. Although the book is dry in its presentation, there are good explanations given of the significance behind the Tantric rites (particularly sexual ones), mantras, mudrās, deities, etc. Originally presented as a graduate thesis in 1931, this is a well-documented, scholarly study for advanced students but with some outdated bibliographic references.

(4) GUENTHER, HERBERT V., and CHOGYAM TRUNGPA. The Dawn of Tantra. Berkeley and London: Shambala, 1975, 78 pp.
This booklet is a seminar report covering the basics of Tantra, i.e., its origin, laying the foundation, Yogācāra, the maṇḍala principle, compassion, śūnyatā, the guru-disciple relationship,

and visualization. Questions and answers are also included. Good introduction to the subject.

(5) HADANO, HAKUTO. "A Historical Study in the Problems Concerning the Diffusion of Tantric Buddhism in India." Religious Studies in Japan (see 1.2.2[10], pp. 287-99.
A highly technical article on the problem of attributing authorship when a person has used various pseudonyms, or different persons have the same name. Hadano examines the case with the name or names of Advayavajra.

(6) MATSUNAGA, YŪKEI. "Indian Esoteric Buddhism as Studied in Japan." Mikkyōgaku Mikkyōshi Ronbunshū (Studies of Esoteric Buddhism and Tantrism) (Koyasan University, Koyasan), 1965, pp. 229-42.
This tightly packed, annotated bibliographical study is a key to the study of esoteric Buddhism.

(7) NAKAMURA, HAJIME. "A Critical Survey of Mahāyāna and Esoteric Buddhism Chiefly Based Upon Japanese Studies." Acta Asiatica (Tokyo: Tōhō Gakkai) 6 (1964):57-88.
A sister article to his survey on the philosophical schools of Mahāyāna.

(8) WAYMAN, ALEX. The Buddhist Tantras: Light on Indo-Tibetan Esotericism. New York: Samuel Weiser, 1973.
Wayman's Light, generated from his thirty years of Buddhist studies, certainly illuminates the dark and controversial corners, i.e., methodology, history, foundations and interpretation of symbolism, in the field of Indo-Tibetan esotericism. The value of the work perhaps lies in his presentation of many previously untranslated texts and a precise and yet imaginative interpretation of them.

(9) WAYMAN, ALEX. "Early Literary History of the Buddhist Tantras, Especially the Guhyasamāja Tantra." Annals of the Bhandarkar Research Institute, n.d., pp. 48-49, 99-110.
This is a discussion of the literary history of the Buddhist Tantras in general, based on some evidence from the Guhyasamāja cycle. It contains an interesting section entitled "Possible Greco-Roman Concepts in the Buddhist Tantras."

1.3 Buddhist Thought in China

(1) CHAN, WING-TSIT. A Source Book in Chinese Philosophy. Princeton: Princeton University, 1963, 856 pp.
There are seven chapters devoted to Buddhism (pp. 336-450), which cover the history and doctrinal development of Buddhism in China from the second to the tenth century. The book has a good bibliography, glossary, and index. A good text for an introductory course.

(2) CHAN, WING-TSIT. "Transformation of Buddhism in China." Philosophy East and West 7 (1957-58):107-16.
A brief account touching upon the Pure Land school, the doctrine of universal salvation, and Ch'an.

(3) CHANG, CHUNG-YUAN. Original Teachings of Ch'an Buddhism, Selected from the Transmission of the Lamp. New York: Pantheon Books, 1969, 333 pp.
A series of translations from the Ching-te ch'uan-teng-lu, the best-known of the Ch'an histories. The various Ch'an masters are grouped together according to chronology and philosophical affinity, and each section is prefaced by a short essay defining the doctrinal developments involved. The translations are reliable. There is a good bibliography of Chinese source materials and an index. One of the best books on Ch'an in China. Can be used by undergraduates.

(4) CH'EN, KENNETH K.S. The Chinese Transformation of Buddhism. Princeton: Princeton University Press, 1973.
This book is a study of the ways in which Buddhism was adapted to fit traditional Chinese attitudes. It is divided into five areas: 1) ethical life, 2) political life, 3) economic life, 4) literary life, and 5) education and social life. The main value of the book is its attempt to incorporate the Tun-huang materials into the general history of Buddhist studies in China. A useful and important book that is unfortunately marred by the author's lack of critical insight.

(5) DEMIÉVILLE, PAUL. "La pénétration du bouddhisme dans la tradition philosophique chinoise." Cahiers d'histoire mondiale 1 (1956):19-38.
A scholarly study of the transformation of the neo-Taoist concept of li (principle) into a Buddhist absolute. Also a discussion of sudden and gradual enlightenment. Fundamental for advanced students.

(6) DUMOULIN, H. The Development of Chinese Zen After the Sixth Patriarch in the Light of Mumonkan. Translated by Ruth F. Sasaki. New York: First Zen Institute of America, 1953.

An English translation of the author's original German article in Monumenta Serica 6 (1941):40-72. The article treats in detail the history of Zen in late T'ang and Sung times and deals with the evolution of the various schools. There are numerous appendices, glossaries, etc. A very useful work.

(7) FUNG, YU-LAN. A History of Chinese Philosophy. Translated by Derk Bodde. 2 vols. Princeton: Princeton University Press, 1953, 783 pp.
An important work that touches upon the principal schools and doctrines. Contains valuable translations from the original Chinese Buddhist sources, many of which are in running commentary form.

(7a) HAKEDA, YOSHITO S. The Awakening of Faith Attributed to Aśvaghosha. New York: Columbia University Press, 1967, 128 pp.
One of the most influential works produced in China, covering all the important phases of Mahāyāna Buddhism.

(8) HAMILTON, C.H. "Hsuan Chuang and the Wei Shih Philosophy." Journal of the American Oriental Society 51:291-308.
An interesting study of Hsuan-tsang and his interest in the consciousness-only doctrine. The author treats Hsuan-tsang's education in China, his trip to India, and his translation activities after his return to China. Good for beginners as an introduction to Hsuan-tsang.

(9) HAMILTON, C.H. "K'uei-chi's Commentary on Wei Shih Er Shih Lun." Journal of the American Oriental Society 53:144-51.
Good, short introduction to the conditions in which K'uei-chi wrote his commentary to the Viṃśatikā of Vasubhandhu. The author shows that K'uei-chi did not know Sanskrit.

(10) HURVITZ, LEON. "Chih-i (538-597): An Introduction to the Life and Ideas of a Chinese Buddhist Monk." Mélanges chinois et bouddhiques 12 (1962):372 pp.
An exhaustive and many-faceted study of the founder of the T'ien-t'ai sect of Chinese Buddhism. The work is divided into three parts: Chih-i's prehistory, his life, and his ideas. The first section contains a good historical and doctrinal survey of early Chinese Buddhism. The book is fundamental for studies in Chinese Buddhism. It suffers, however, from lack of an index or bibliography.

(11) HU SHIH. "Ch'an (Zen) Buddhism in China: Its History and Method." Philosophy East and West 3 (Apr. 1953):3-24.
A fundamental article for Ch'an studies, and the most famous of all the anti-Suzuki articles. Hu Shih attempts to show that there is nothing incomprehensible about Zen if it is viewed

within the historical and cultural framework in which it arose. Polemics aside, the article is a good, short, succinct introduction to Ch'an in China.

(12) LIEBENTHAL, WALTER. "Chinese Buddhism During the 4th and 5th Centuries." Monumenta Nipponica 11 (1955):44-83.
A valuable and scholarly study of the attitude of Taoists and of the government towards the Buddhists. Also contains a section on the controversy over immortality during this period. For advanced students.

(13) LIEBENTHAL, WALTER. "The World Conception of Chu Tao-sheng." Monumenta Nipponica 1-2 (1956):65-103; 3-4 (1956): 73-100.
An important collection and translation of the scattered remarks of this fifth-century Buddhist on a variety of topics. For advanced students.

(14) PETZOLD, BRUNO. "The Chinese Tendai Teaching." Eastern Buddhist 4 (1927-28):299-347.
The best short introduction to the teachings of the T'ien-t'ai sect available in English. Good for beginning students.

(15) SUZUKI, DAISETZ T. "The Laṅkāvatāra Sūtra, as a Mahāyāna Text in Special Relation to the Teaching of Zen Buddhism." Eastern Buddhist 4 (Oct. 1927-Mar. 1928):199-298.
A lengthy study of the position of the Laṅkāvatāra in Zen. The author's thesis is that the text's insistence on the experience of inner realization later becomes the cornerstone of Zen discipline. Covers somewhat the same ground as Suzuki's book on the Laṅkāvatārasūtra.

(16) TUCCI, GIUSEPPE. "Notes on Laṅkāvatāra." Indian Historical Quarterly 4 (1928).
A rambling series of observations on this important text of Chinese Buddhism. One of his remarks is that this work should not be treated as a textbook for the Yogācāra-Vijñānavāda school. Useful for students of the text.

(17) YAMPOLSKY, PHILIP B. The Platform Sutra of the Sixth Patriarch. New York: Columbia University Press, 1967.
This book supersedes all previous work done on this text. The author presents the text of the Tun-huang manuscript, a careful translation with good annotation, an almost complete bibliography, and 123-page introduction that is the best writing yet on the history of Ch'an in China. This book is fundamental for all students of Chinese Buddhism.

(18) ZURCHER, E. The Buddhist Conquest of China: The Spread and Adaptation of Buddhism in Early Medieval China. Leiden: E.J. Brill, 1959, 468 pp. Vol. 1, Text; Vol. 2, Notes, Bibliography, Indexes.
Perhaps the most ambitious and extensive work on the subject. Weak on doctrines but gives an excellent view of the whole Buddhist movement during the early formative period of Chinese Buddhism. Recommended for both undergraduate and graduate students.

1.4 Buddhist Thought in Japan

(1) ANESAKI, MASAHARU. The Buddhist Prophet, Nichiren. Cambridge: Harvard University Press, 1916.
This excellent, scholarly, and readable book depicts the life and mission of Prophet Nichiren, one of the most colorful Japanese monks.

(2) ANESAKI, MASAHARU. Religious Life of the Japanese People. Tokyo: Kokusai Bunka Shinkokai (Society for the Promotion of International Cultural Relations), 1970, 122 pp.
Dealing with Shintō, Confucianism, Taoism, Buddhism, and Christianity, Anesaki animates the usual materials in a manner which captures the interest of the reader. For example, in the chapter on Buddhism, he makes masterly comparisons among the various forms of Japanese Buddhism.

(3) BLYTH, REGINALD. Zen and Zen Classics. Vols. 1-4. Tokyo: Hokuseido Press, 1960-1970.
These volumes contain a wide-ranging collection of essays mainly centered around the history of Zen and its literature. The work is based on Japanese sources. Volume 4 is a collection of translations from the Mumonkan, the well-known Zen case book. The quality is uneven, but the work contains much useful information.

(4) COATS, H.H., and R. ISHIZUKA. Hōnen, the Buddhist Saint, His Life and Teaching. Kyoto: Sekai Seiten Kankōkai, 1949, 955 pp.
This is a translation of the authoritative biography of Hōnen, the founder of the Jōdo denomination.

(5) DUMOULIN, HEINRICH. A History of Zen Buddhism. Translated by Paul Peachey. New York: Pantheon Books, 1963.
An English translation of the 1959 German original. Dumoulin's book is the largest and best general history of Zen. The work is almost equally divided between the history of Ch'an in China

and that of Zen in Japan. Good bibliography and index. A pioneering effort in a difficult field. Useful for all levels of instruction.

(6) ELIOT, CHARLES. Japanese Buddhism. London: Routledge & Kegan Paul, 1959, 449 pp.
Historical survey of the schools and doctrines. Very introductory.

(7) HANAYAMA, SHINSHŌ. "Japanese Development of Ekayāna Thought." Religious Studies in Japan (see 1.2.2[10]), pp. 371-82.
This is a historical and ideological analysis of the doctrine of the one great vehicle.

(8) INABA, SHUKEN, and ISSAI FUNABASHI. Jōdo Shinshū. Kyoto: Ohtani University Press, 1961, 109 pp.
An introductory book on Shin Buddhism (Pure Land) for the general public.

(9) KISHIMOTO, HIDEO. "Mahāyāna Buddhism and Japanese Thought." Philosophy East and West 3 (1954):215-23.
An introductory survey of Buddhist principles as they relate to Japanese thought and culture.

(10) MASUNAGA, REIHŌ. "The Place of Dōgen in Zen Buddhism." Religious Studies in Japan (see 1.2.2[10]), pp. 339-49.
The contemporary value of Dōgen, who first brought Sōtō Zen to Japan, is mainly discussed in the context of the history of Buddhist meditation in India, China and Japan.

(11) MATSUNAGA, YŪKEI. "Tantric Buddhism and Shingon Buddhism." Eastern Buddhist, n.s. 2 (1969):1-14.
Modern scholarly approach; provides a short but reliable account based on the tradition kept in Kōyasan. It covers the differences between Jummitsu (pure esotericism) and Zōmitsu (miscellaneous esotericism).

(12) MIURA, ISSHŪ, and RUTH FULLER SASAKI. Zen Dust: The History of the Kōan and Kōan Study in Rinzai (Lin-chi) Zen. New York: Harcourt, Brace & World, 1966.
This is a valuable and useful work, much more extensive than the title indicates. The first part of the book is divided into three sections: 1) a history of the kōan in the Chinese and Japanese branches of the Lin-chi sect, 2) an essay on the use of the kōan in the modern Rinzai sect, and 3) selections from the Zen phrase anthology, Zenrin kushū, which dates from the end of the fifteenth century. For these three sections there are

extensive notes. However, the most useful part of the book is the extensive annotated bibliography (pp. 333-447), which gives detailed information on texts of Chinese and Japanese Buddhism. The book, although sometimes lacking in scholarly objectivity, is a gold mine of ready information.

(13) NAKAMURA, HAJIME. "A Brief Survey of Japanese Studies on the Philosophical Schools of the Mahāyāna." Acta Asiatica (Tokyo: Tōhō Gakkai) 1 (1960):56-88.
This work supplies not only a progress report on Japanese studies of the subject but also a general overview of the philosophical schools of Mahāyāna. Highly recommended.

(14) NAKAMURA, HAJIME. A History of the Development of Japanese Thought from 592 to 1868. 2 vols. Tokyo: Kokusai Bunka Shinkōkai (Society for the Promotion of International Cultural Relations), 1967, 326 pp.
This well-organized book contains the ideas of different Japanese thinkers from the time of Prince Shōtoku to the beginning of the Meiji Restoration. Nakamura succeeds in digging from the past for some new ideas of the present. The philosophical thought of Japanese Buddhist schools is dealt with in this context.

(15) OHTANI UNIVERSITY, ed. Jōdo Shinshū: An Introduction to the Authentic Pure Land Teaching (see [8]).
The work was originally written by Shūken Inaba and Issai Funabashi and translated into English by Ichirai Fukuhara and William Flygare. It includes: the life and teachings of Śākyamuni, the life of Saint Shinran and his teachings, the true vow, pure and true Action, true and genuine Mind, and faith and the true awakening.

(16) STEINILBER-OBERLIN, E. The Buddhist Sects of Japan: Their History, Philosophical Doctrines and Sanctuaries. London: Allen & Unwin, 1938, 303 pp.
A light, religiously oriented but informative discourse on the eleven Buddhist schools of Japan. Somewhat dated.

(17) SUZUKI, BEATRICE LANE. "The Shingon School of Mahāyāna Buddhism." Eastern Buddhist 5 (1931):291-311; 7 (1936): 1-38, 177-212.
Provides an interesting introduction to the Shingon School and Kōyasan, the school's head temple in Japan.

(18) SUZUKI, DAISETZ TEITARŌ. Essays in Zen Buddhism. First series. London: Rider, 1949, 383 pp.
Essay 4 gives the standard history of Zen Buddhism from Bodhidharma to Hui-neng (pp. 161-226).

(19) SUZUKI, DAISETZ TEITARŌ. Zen Buddhism and Its Influence on Japanese Culture. Kyoto: Eastern Buddhist Society, 1938. Paperback reprint. Princeton: Princeton University Press, 1970.
This is a collection of essays on different phases and aspects of Japanese cultural and intellectual life as influenced by Zen. The topics include: the Japanese people's "Love of Nature," "Zen and Samurai," "Zen and Swordsmanship," and tea ceremony. Recommended to all, for it gives a wealth of information on almost every aspect of Japanese culture and spiritual life.

(20) TAKEZONO, KENRYO. "The Syncretism of Buddhism and Shinto." Religious Studies in Japan (see 1.2.2[10]), pp. 383-88.
This is a short note on a unique characteristic of Japanese religious history. Takezono discusses the adaptations of the Buddha's statue and Buddhist ceremonies by the Jinguji temple.

(21) TAMAKI, KŌSHIRŌ. "On the Fundamental Idea Underlying Japanese Buddhism." Philosophical Studies of Japan, (1975), pp. 17-39.
A succinct analysis of the idea of the eternal Buddha realm and its manifestations in man as expounded by Prince Shōtoku, Kūkai, Ennin, Enchin, Shinran, Dōgen and Nichiren. A good beginning.

(22) VISSER, M.W. de. Ancient Buddhism in Japan. 2 vols. Leiden: E.J. Brill, 1935.
A scholarly work on the early history of Japanese Buddhism.

(23) WATANABE, SHŌKŌ. Japanese Buddhism: A Critical Appraisal. Tokyo: Kokusai Bunka Shinkōkai (Society for the Promotion of International Cultural Relations), 1970, 174 pp.
While laying bare the strong and weak points of Japanese Buddhism (p. xii), Watanabe reports on five trends of Japanese Buddhism: nationalism, magic, ceremonies for the dead, tendency to compromise, and formalism. Since he develops his thesis with a wealth of substantive information, this book deserves special attention.

1.5 Buddhist Thought in Tibet

(1) ANURUDDHA, R.P. An Introduction to Lamaism, the Mystical Buddhism of Tibet. Hospiarpur: Vishveshvaranand Research Institute, 1959, 212 pp.
This is a survey of basic features of Lamaism, its history, Tantricism, and iconography. A list of books for further study is included. Tontains a useful index.

(2) BAILEY, H.W., and E.H. JOHNSTON. "A Fragment of the Uttaratantra in Sanskrit." Bulletin of the School of Oriental and African Studies 8 (1935):77-89.
An important article on the authorship and doctrinal affiliation of the Uttaratantra. As a base for this discussion, the authors present a Sanskrit manuscript fragment from the Stein collection. Useful for advanced students of the Uttaratantra.

(3) BLOFELD, JOHN E.C. The Tantric Mysticism of Tibet: A Practical Guide (see 1.2.2.4[2]).
Discussion of the background, theory, and practice of the Tantric tradition. Good for the beginner.

(4) CHATTOPADHYAYA, A. Atīśa and Tibet: Life and Works of Dīpamkāra Śrījñāna in Relation to the History and Religion of Tibet. Translated by Lama Chimpa. Calcutta: Indian Studies, 1967, 600 pp.
Atīśa, also known as Dīpamkāra Śrījñāna, was the founder of the Great Kadam-pa, which was the original source for the Geluk-pa, the Yellow Order of the Dalai Lamas and Panchen Lamas. As the son of a king of Zahor, he studied every branch of Buddhism, but above all the Tantras. Chattopadhyaya's work, therefore, is an important contribution to the history and religion of Tibet.

(5) CH'EN, KENNETH. "Transformations in Buddhism in Tibet." Philosophy East and West 7 (1957-1958):117-25.
Treats the establishment of the Yellow Sect headed by the Dalai Lama and the beginnings of Tantrism, together with Mantrayāna and Vajrayāna.

(6) DALAI LAMA. The Opening of the Wisdom Eye. Bangkok: Social Science Association, 1968, 131 pp. Reprint. Theosophical Publishing House, 1972, 178 pp.
Written by Tenzin Byatsho, the present Dalai Lama, this is a brief outline of some of the basic tenets of Buddhism. A short history of Buddhism in Tibet is given, followed by chapters on Dharma, rebirth, the two levels of Truth, skandhas, Tripiṭaka, threefold training, levels of the path, and the bodies of virtue of a Buddha. The book is intended as an introductory text for those unfamiliar with Buddhist concepts and thus the topics are discussed in a very basic way. It is a good reference book for it has numerous lists and divisions (e.g., the precepts, states of mind, etc.) found in Buddhist doctrine. Photographs of Dharma practice in India are also included.

(7) DEMIÉVILLE, PAUL. La concile de Lhasa. Paris: Imprimerie nationale de France, 1952, 397 pp.
A heavily annotated translation of a Chinese account discovered at Tun-huang of the debate between the adherents of sudden and gradual enlightenment which took place at Lhasa in 792 A.D. The book also contains much information on Sino-Tibetan relations during the T'ang Period. For very advanced students and Tibetologists only. Later scholarship by the Japanese has proved that the debate was more alleged than real.

(8) GUENTHER, HERBERT V. Buddhist Philosophy in Theory and Practice. Baltimore: Penguin, 1972, 240 pp.
Contains a very helpful introduction to Tibetan Buddhism.

(9) GUENTHER, HERBERT V. Tibetan Buddhism Without Mystification: The Buddhist Way from the Original Tibetan Sources. Leiden: E.J. Brill, 1966, 156 pp.
This is one of the more important works by Guenther, who tries to present not only Tibetan Buddhism, but also Buddhist philosophy and psychology, without mystification. He always presents a lucid introduction before his translation of Tibetan original texts. One should, however, be accustomed to his unique terminology.

(10) GUENTHER, HERBERT V. Treasures on the Tibetan Middle Way. Berkeley: Shambala, 1971, 156 pp.
Originally entitled Tibetan Buddhism Without Mystification (see [9]), the book consists of five short essays on the reasons for and results of Buddhist practice, followed by translations of four texts by Ye-shes rgyal-mtshan, the tutor of the Eighth Dalai Lama. The four Tibetan texts complement the essays well, showing the traditional Tibetan way of introducing the Tantras. This is not a book for the person completely unacquainted with Buddhism, but with some background it will serve as an excellent primer on the Tibetan Dharma.

(11) HOFFMAN, HELMUT. The Religions of Tibet. Translated by E. Fitzgerald. London: Allen & Unwin, [1956] 1961.
A thorough historical survey which demands a careful reading. A detailed index makes this work an excellent reference guide.

(12) JONG, J.W. de, ed. Mi la ras pa'i rnam t'ar, texte tibétain de la vie de Milarepa. Gravenhage: Mouton, 1959, 218 pp.
A carefully edited Tibetan text of Milarepa's biography.

(13) NAKAMURA, HAJIME. A Critical Survey of Tibetology and Esoteric Buddhism Chiefly Based on Japanese Studies. Tokyo: Tokyo University Publications, 1965.
Unsurpassed.

(14) SANGHARAKSHITA, BHIKSHU. The Three Jewels: An Introduction to Buddhism. London: Rider, 1967.
Sangharakshita, an Englishman who has been a Buddhist monk for twenty years, mostly in India, introduces the wider public to Buddhism centered around its Three Jewels, Buddha, Dharma and Saṅgha, with readable and reliable accounts and an air of refreshing, detached involvement.

(15) SCHLAGINWEIT, EMIL. Buddhism in Tibet, Illustrated by Literary Documents and Objects of Religious Worship, with an Account of the Buddhist Systems Preceding It in India. New York: Augustus Kelley, [1863] 1969, 403 pp.
Although it is somewhat outdated, the short survey of Indian Buddhism and Tibetan Buddhism in part 1 is still useful. The value of the book, however, from a historical point of view, is found in part 2, "Present Lamaic Institutions."

(16) SNELLGROVE, DAVID. Buddhist Himālaya: Travels and Studies in Quest of the Origins and Nature of Tibetan Religion. Oxford: Oxford University Press, 1957, 324 pp.
In this scholarly travelogue, the basic texts and tenets of Tibetan Buddhism are also discussed. The work is, therefore, a travelogue in depth, or an on-the-spot introduction to Tibetan Buddhism.

(17) SNELLGROVE, DAVID, and HUGH RICHARDSON. A Cultural History of Tibet. London: Weidenfeld & Nicolson, 1968, 291 pp.
As for the Tibetan development of Mahāyāna-Vajrayāna Buddhist philosophy, the following chapters are recommended: "Introduction of Buddhism," "A Later Literary View," "The Middle Ages," "Religious Preoccupations," and "The Twentieth Century." The book is enjoyable and informative for a wider public as well as for specialists.

(18) STEIN, ROLF A. Tibetan Civilization. Translated by J.E.S. Driver. Stanford: Stanford University Press; London: Faber & Faber, [1962] 1970, 333 pp.
This is an excellent introduction to Tibetan civilization, i.e., the habitat, inhabitants, historical events from ancient times to modern, the structure of Tibetan society, religious life and customs. A selected bibliography contains the modern critical studies as well as the Tibetan sources.

1.5 Buddhist Thought in Tibet

(19) TUCCI, GIUSEPPE. Tibetan Painted Scrolls. 3 vols. Rome, 1949.
The introduction presents an excellent survey of Tibetan Buddhism.

2 Theory of Human Nature

(1) BAHM, ARCHIE J. Philosophy of the Buddha (see 1.2[1]).
A critical assessment of the Buddha's humanistic philosophy. It touches upon the basic doctrines, but some of the Western interpretations are questionable.

(2) CHOU, S.C., G.P. MALALASEKARA, and W.G. WEERARATNE. "Arahant." In Encyclopaedia of Buddhism (see 1.1[21]): 41-54.
Three scholars present an exhaustive analysis of the enlightened man, the arhat, from the time of the Buddha to the later developments in China. Some overlapping in the contributions but packed with helpful information.

(3) GUENTHER, HERBERT V. The Tantric View of Life. Berkeley: Shambala, 1972, 175 pp.
Despite similarities in the title, this is not the same book as his earlier work, Yuganaddha: The Tantric View of Life. Guenther here interprets Buddhist Tantra as an integrated world-view, without delving into either its historical aspects or the techniques of practice. The goal of Tantra is simply to be. Guenther feels that "Tantrism in its Buddhist form is of the utmost importance for the inner life of man and so for the future of mankind."

(4) HISAMATSU, SHIN'ICHI. "Zen: Its Meaning for Modern Civilization." Eastern Buddhist, n.s. 1 (1965):22-47.
An interesting article that analyzes the following: Zen and Buddhist sutras, the meaning of "killing the buddha," the method of Zen, Zen understanding of man, and the nature of formless beauty.

(5) HORNER, I.B. The Early Buddhist Theory of Man Perfected. London: Williams & Norgate, 1936, 328 pp.
This is a most comprehensive analysis of the concept of arahant, the goal of a perfected man in early Buddhism, gleaned from the canons.

(6) MALALASEKARA, G.P. "The Status of the Individual in Theravāda Buddhism." Philosophy East and West 14 (1964):145-56.
A clear analysis of the concept of man, bringing together the basic doctrines.

(7) MIYAMOTO, SHŌSON. "Freedom, Independence, and Peace in Buddhism." Philosophy East and West 1, no. 4 (Jan. 1952): 30-40; 2, no. 3 (Oct. 1952):208-25.
A Buddhist treatment of the several concepts from a modern perspective.

(8) PARSONS, HOWARD L. "Buddha and Buddhism: A New Appraisal." Philosophy East and West 1 (1951):8-37.
An heroic attempt to reappraise the Buddha's basic teachings. There are a few keen insights into the problem of human nature, but the analysis is still tainted with Western misunderstandings of the Buddhist nature of the mind or intellect, the middle way, and the void or emptiness.

(9) PULIGANDLA, R., and K. PUHAKKA. "Buddhism and Revolution." Philosophy East and West 20 (1970):345-54.
The authors examine, from a Buddhist perspective, how man should take up the challenge of capitalism, communism, and the one-dimensional nature imposed by modern society.

(10) RAHULA, WALPOLA. What the Buddha Taught (see 1.2[12]).
A lucid account of the basic teachings of early Buddhism, especially the four noble truths (ārya satya), attempting to remove a number of current misconceptions about Buddhism.

(11) RHYS-DAVIDS, C.A.F. Śākya or Buddhist Origins (see 1.2.1[15]).
Rhys-Davids's most mature work on the nature of Buddhism and the Buddhist ideal of person.

(12) STCHERBATSKY, TH. "The Soul Theory of the Buddhists." In Bulletin de l'Académie des sciences de Russie. Leningrad: Academy of Sciences of the USSR, 1919, pp. 823-958.
A translation and discussion of the concept of a person (pudgala) in Vasubandhu's work, Abhidharmakośa.

(13) UEDA, YOSHIFUMI. "The World and the Individual in Mahāyāna Buddhist Philosophy." Philosophy East and West 14 (1964): 157-66.
This study surveys the ontological status of the "self" and the bifurcation of "subject/object structure" in the world and the resolution of the bifurcation in the Yogācāra Buddhist philosophy. For the advanced student.

(14) WAYMAN, ALEX. "The Meaning of Unwisdom (avidyā)." Philosophy East and West 7 (1957):21-25.
A short but clear analysis of the concept of avidyā (usual translation: ignorance) in the Indian and Buddhist traditions.

3 Ethics

(1) ANESAKI, MASAHARU. "Ethics and Morality." In Encyclopedia of Religion and Ethics. Vol. 5, pp. 447-55.
The article attempts to show that the fundamental feature of Buddhist morality consists in its autonomic and personal principle, in contrast with the legal and social principle of Brahmanism. Ethics is analyzed in terms of aims of morality which, according to the author, is the attainment of nibbāna.

(2) BHAGVAT, DURGA N. Early Buddhist Jurisprudence: Theravāda Vinaya-Laws. Poona: Oriental Book Agency, 1939, 204 pp.
An examination of the monastic life and the disciplines (vinaya) as the foundation of Buddhist ethics.

(3) BLOOM, ALFRED. "Buddhism, Nature and the Environment (Views and Reviews)." Eastern Buddhist, n.s. 6, no. 1 (1973): 115-29.
Discusses the role of nature in Buddhist experience and thought, together with Buddhism and the quality of life. A timely essay.

(4) BREAR, A.D. "The Nature and Status of Moral Behavior in Zen Buddhist Tradition." Philosophy East and West 24 (1974): 429-41.
Argues for the ethical elements in the Zen tradition.

(5) FOX, DOUGLAS A. "Zen and Ethics: Dōgen's Synthesis." Philosophy East and West 21 (1971):33-41.
An analysis of Dōgen's Zen as a unity of concepts and deeds, an actualization or realization of an absolute in terms of the non-originated nature of things (anutpāda).

(6) HORNER, I.B. The Basic Position of Sīla. Colombo: Buddha Sahitya Sabha, 1950, 27 pp.
This short essay consists of an analysis and evaluation of the moral precepts (sīla) in early Buddhism, showing their importance in the Buddha's path to spiritual perfection.

(7) JACOBSON, NOLAN PLINY. "The Purification of Post-Modern
    Man." In Bonnō no Kenkyū (A Study of Kleśa). Edited by
    Genjun Sasaki. Tokyo: Shimizukobundo, 1975, pp. 134-49.
A proposal of a "New Life Style" through an examination of the
"New Meaning of Pollution."

(8) JAMES, E., trans. A Treasury of Aphoristic Jewels.
    Bloomington: Indiana University Press, 1969.
A collection of short, pithy verses by the Tibetan Sākya Paṇḍita.
Modeled after Nāgārjuna, Sākya Paṇḍita's maxims are in the tradi-
tion of collections of proverbial wisdom. This genre of moral-
istic stanzas was maintained and developed later by the Ninth
Panchen Lama, the Eleventh Dalai Lama, etc.

(9) JAYATILLEKE, K.N. "The Principles of International Law in
    Buddhist Doctrine." Recueil des cours 2 (1967):445-566.
Consists of five lectures dealing with the problem of ethics and
law from the Buddhist perspective, with special emphasis on early
Buddhism.

(10) KALUPAHANA, DAVID J. Buddhist Philosophy: A Historical
    Analysis (see 1.1[17]), pp. 56-68.
An examination of the basis of ethical judgments in early
Buddhism, especially in comparison with the positivist analysis
of ethics in Western philosophy.

(11) KHANTIPALO, PHRA. Tolerance: A Study from Buddhist
    Sources. London: Rider & Co., 1964, 191 pp.
A good introductory book on Buddhist praxis of tolerance,
patience, and compassion.

(12) La VALLÉE POUSSIN, L. de. "Bodhicaryāvatāra: Introduction
    à la pratique de la sainteté boudhique (bodhi) par
    Çāntideva. Chapitres 1, 2, 3, 4, 10." Le Muséon 11 (1892):
    68-82, 87-109. "Chapitre 5." 15 (1896):306-18. "Bodhi-
    caryāvatāra: Introduction à la pratique des futurs Bouddhas,
    poème de Çāntideva, traduit du sanscrit et annoté." Revue
    d'histoire et de litérature religieuses, 1907, pp. 10-12.
It is difficult to imagine that so much has been achieved single-
handedly by de La Vallée Poussin through his numerous editions,
translations, and expositions of Buddhist literature in many
areas and in several languages. This is another fine work, which
demands the attention of beginners as well as adepts. The best
translation available for those who read French.

(13) La VALLÉE POUSSIN, L. de. La morale bouddique. Paris: Nouvelle librairie nationale, 1927.
Although the book is meant for a wider public, it retains a high standard of scholarship. One of a few books written on the subject.

(14) MALALASEKARA, G.P., and JAYATILLEKE, K.N. Buddhism and the Race Question. Paris: UNESCO, 1958, 72 pp.
An authoritative account of the early Buddhist conception of man and his place in the universe. The Buddha's attitude towards questions of caste and race are discussed in the light of modern theories on the subject.

(15) MATICS, MARION L., trans. Entering the Path of Enlightenment: The Bodhicaryāvatāra of the Buddhist Poet Śāntideva. London: Macmillan, 1970.
This newest English translation is preceded by a lengthy and helpful introduction to Mahāyāna ideas.

(16) NAGAO, GADJIN M. "Buddhist Subjectivity." Religious Studies in Japan (see 1.2.2[10]), pp. 257-62.
Nagao, a leading authority on Buddhist studies in Japan, suggests that Buddhism has difficulty in establishing subjectivity due to its no-self doctrine, but that by taking recourse to the three self-natures doctrine of the Yogācāra school, subjectivity can be reestablished on a deeper level.

(17) NAKAMURA, HAJIME. "The Indian and Buddhist Concept of Law." Religious Pluralism and World Community: Interfaith and Intercultural Communication. Edited by Edward Junji. Leiden: E.J. Brill, 1969, pp. 131-74.
Nakamura's writings are well organized, well documented, and well written. Recommended to all.

(18) NAKAMURA, HAJIME. "Interrelational Existence." Philosophy East and West 17 (1967):107-12.
A short but interesting analysis of the theory of interrelational existence advocated by Eastern thinking, as seen in the Avataṃsaka-sūtra and elsewhere and by Western mystics, e.g., Plotinus, Enneads, and Eckhart. Discusses the nature of ethics in terms of the concept of dependent origination (pratītya-samutpāda).

(19) RUPP, GEORGE. "The Relationship between Nirvāṇa and Saṃṣāra: An Essay on the Evolution of Buddhist Ethics." Philosophy East and West 21 (1971):55-67.
Some good insights on Theravāda and Mahāyāna views on nirvāṇa and its ethical role in everyday experience (saṃsāra). Contemporary

viewpoints are expressed. The author tries a new and systematic approach to the question of the meaning of <u>nirvāṇa</u> in Buddhism. A thought-provoking article.

(20) SADDHATISSA, H. <u>Buddhist Ethics</u>. New York: G. Braziller, 1971, 202 pp.
A traditional analysis of the action of morality (<u>sīla</u>) in early Buddhism.

(21) SPIRO, MELFORD E. <u>Buddhism and Society</u>. New York: Harper & Row, 1970, 510 pp.
A lengthy analysis of some of the basic doctrines of Buddhism, such as karma, and their sociological ramifications, especially as seen in Theravāda countries like Burma.

(22) STCHERBATSKY, TH. "Philosophical Doctrine of Buddhism." In <u>Further Papers of Stcherbatsky</u>. Translated by H.C. Gupta. Calcutta: K.L. Mukhopadhyaya, 1971, pp. 11-33.
Translated from the Russian, this short article succinctly deals with the question, "What is the basis of the moral laws of Buddhism," Buddhism being a religion which does not subscribe to the existence of God and the immortality of the soul. Good introductory essay.

(23) TACHIBANA, SHUNDO. <u>Ethics of Buddhism</u>. London: Oxford University Press, 1926, 288 pp.
Represents one of the earliest attempts at the classification of ethical concepts of Buddhism, rather than a purely theoretical discussion of the major problems of ethics from the Buddhist standpoint. Having classified Buddhist morality, Tachibana discusses the following elements: self-restraint, abstinence, temperance, contentment, patience, celibacy, chastity, purity, humility, benevolence, liberality, reverence, gratitude, tolerance, veracity, and righteousness.

(24) VARMA, V.P. "The Origins and Sociology of the Early Buddhist Philosophy of Moral Determinism." <u>Philosophy East and West</u> 13 (1963):25-47.
An analysis of the Buddhist concept of karma, with introductory comparisons with Vedic and Upanisadic traditions.

(25) VARMA, VISHWANATH PRASAD. "The Sociology of Early Buddhist Ethics." <u>Journal of the Bihar Research Society</u> (Patna) 2 [Buddha Jayanti Special Issue] (1956):395-420.
A solid article dealing with the evolution of moral ideas in India, the sociology of early Buddhist ethics, and the social and political ethics of early Buddhism. Buddhist morality concerns

not only with the performance of external actions but with the intuition that must be purified by philosophic insight into Buddhist truth (dharma).

(26) WARDER, A.K. Indian Buddhism (see 1.2[18]), pp. 157-200.
A comprehensive account of the Buddha's conception of society and social values.

(27) WIJESEKARA, O.H. de A. Buddhism and Society. Colombo: Bauddha Sahitya Sabha, 1951, 23 pp.
A short but excellent analysis of the Buddha's social philosophy.

4 Paths of Liberation

(1) BARUA, B.M. "Some Aspects of Early Buddhism." In Cultural Heritage of India. Vol. 1. Calcutta: Radhakrishna Mission Institute of Culture, 1953-62, pp. 442-55.
The article attempts to explain the significance of the concept of right (samma) as a characteristic of the noble eightfold path (aṭṭhaṅgika magga) which represents the middle (majjhima) standpoint.

(2) BOLLE, KEES W. "Devotion and Tantra." Mikkyōgaku Mikkyōshi Ronbunshū (Studies of Esoteric Buddhism and Tantrism) (Koyasan University, Koyasan), 1965.
This is a discussion of the role of devotion (bhakti) in both esoteric practice (sādhanas) and popular religion.

(3) CHEN, C.M. "Comment on Śamatha, Samāpatti, and Dhyāna in Ch'an (Zen)." Philosophy East and West 16 (1966):84-87.
An article in refutation of Charles Luk's handling of these terms in his translation of the Sūtra of Complete Enlightenment in Ch'an and Zen Teachings Series 3: (London: Rider, 1962), pp. 147-278). Though it is somewhat technical, it is a good discussion of these difficult and often misunderstood terms.

(4) CHIH-K'AI [Chih-I]. "Mahāyāna Method of Cessation and Contemplation." In A History of Chinese Philosophy (see 1.3[7]), 2:310-86).
Fung concentrates on the work of Chih-k'ai (patriarch of the T'ien-t'ai school), Ta-sheng chih-kuan fa-men, to expound on the method of cessation and contemplation. Good translations of passages are included. Compare with Leon Hurwitz's "Chih-I" (see 1.3[10]).

(5) CONZE, EDWARD, trans. Aṣṭasāhasrikā Prajñāpāramitā (The Perfection of wisdom in eight thousand ślokas). Calcutta: Asiatic Society, 1958, 225 pp. The Perfection of Wisdom in Eight Thousand Lines and its Verse Summary. Bolinas: Four Seasons Foundation, 1973, 325 pp.

A translation of one of the most important works in the wisdom (prajñā) literature, describing the nature and development of bodhisattvahood.

(6) CONZE, EDWARD. Buddhist Meditation. London: George Allen & Unwin, 1956, 183 pp.
A standard exposition of the methods of meditation taken from the canons, including some selected translations. Provides a general view of meditation, its purpose, components, and textual sources. Most of the doctrines of early Buddhism, such as the three marks, dependent arising, and nirvāṇa are analyzed in the context of meditation.

(7) DAYAL, H. The Bodhisattva Doctrine in Buddhist Sanskrit Literature (see 1.2.2[3]).
A definitive and most influential work on the subject.

(8) EVANS-WENTZ, W.Y., ed. Tibet's Great Yogi Milarepa: A Biography from the Tibetan. 2d ed. New York: Oxford University Press, [1928] 1951, 315 pp.
This is the inspiring biography of the great poet-yogin, Milarepa. The story traces his life from his childhood to his experiences as a black sorcerer, his renunciation of his evil ways, his study under Marpa the Translator, and his subsequent years meditating in mountain caves. The translator's understanding of the Vajrayāna is cluttered with his own interpretations and his comparisons of Tantra to other spiritual systems, which are often misleading. Nonetheless, until someone retranslates it, this book remains an important text in Tibetan studies.

(9) FUNG, YU-LAN. "The Ch'an School." In History of Chinese Philosophy (see 1.3[7]) 2:386-406.
A short analysis of Ch'an and its famous masters with translated passages from their works.

(10) sGAM.PO.PA. The Jewel Ornament of Liberation. Translated by H.V. Guenther. Berkeley: Shambala, 1971, 333 pp.
This book clearly lays down the requirements for the practice of Mahāyāna Buddhism. Each chapter deals with a certain part of the path, for example, karma or one of the six pāramitās, breaking it down into its various aspects and discussing it in full. While the style of teaching is classical Tibetan--sGam.po.pa was the eleventh-century disciple of Milarepa--its straightforward presentation makes it easy to understand the analogies, terms, etc. explained by Guenther's footnotes. It is one of Guenther's most easily read books, having little of his usually complicated style of writing and translating. This is an important and

popular text with Tibetans, a classic that is recommended for everyone.

(11) GONDA, J. "'Ways' in Indian Religions." Mikkyōgaku Mikkyōshi Ronbunshū (Studies of Esoteric Buddhism and Tantrism) (Koyasan University, Koyasan), 1965, pp. 47-66.
This is a learned and detailed study of the synonyms which convey the meanings of "way," "path," "vehicle," etc.

(12) GRIMM, GEORGE. The Doctrine of the Buddha: The Religion of Reason and Meditation. 2d. ed. Edited by M. Keller-Grimm and Marc Hoppe. Translated by Bhikkhu Sīlacāra. Berlin: Akadamie-Verlag, 1958, 413 pp.
A lucid account of the path to freedom as enunciated in the early Buddhist discourses.

(13) GUENTHER, H.V. Philosophy and Psychology in the Abhidharma. Lucknow: Buddha Vihara, 1959, 405 pp.
A clear exposition of the process of meditation (dhyāna) presented on the basis of the source material found in both Pali and Sanskrit. The concluding chapter (pp. 290-377) deals with the various interpretations of the path to freedom presented by the different Abhidharma schools.

(14) HAYASHIMA, KYŌSHŌ. "Abhisamaya." In Encyclopaedia of Buddhism (see 1.1[21]), 1:105-14.
A lengthy study on the paths leading to the realization of enlightenment. It treats the concept rather technically in early Buddhism, Sarvāstivāda, and Vijñānavāda schools. For the advanced student.

(15) HORNER, I.B. "The Concept of Freedom in the Pali Canon." In Présence du Bouddhisme (see 1.1[4]), pp. 337-47.
A concise account of the concept of freedom culled from the early scriptures.

(16) HYERS, CONRAD M. "The Ancient Zen Master as a Clown-figure and Comic Midwife." Philosophy East and West 20 (1970): 3-18.
In Zen pedagogy, there is time for humor, which the Zen master utilizes whenever the occasion calls for it, either to lead one to enlightenment or to dissuade one from taking the wrong path.

(17) KANEKO, DAIEI. "The Meaning of Salvation in the Doctrine of Pure Land Buddhism." Eastern Buddhist, n.s. 1 (1965):48-63.
An authoritative article by Kaneko, who was a leading authority on Pure Land Buddhism.

(18) La VALLÉE POUSSIN, L. de. "Bodhicaryāvatāra: Introduction à la pratique de la sainteté boudhique (bodhi) par Çāntideva. Chapitres 1, 2, 3, 4, 10." Le Muséon 11 (1892): 68-82, 87-109. "Chapitre 5." Le Muséon 15 (1896):306-18. "Bodhicaryāvatara: Introduction à la pratique des futurs Bouddhas, poème de Çantideva, traduit du sanscrit et annoté." Revue d'histoire et de littérature religieuses (see 3[12], [15], 1907, pp. 10-12).

(19) La VALLÉE POUSSIN, L. de. The Way to Nirvāṇa. Cambridge: Cambridge University Press, 1917, 172 pp.
A good introduction to understanding the nature of Buddhist salvation.

(20) LOUNSBERY, G. CONSTANT. Buddhist Meditation in the Southern School. London: Luzac & Co., [1936] 1950, 177 pp.
A rather faithful and traditional Theravāda explication of the theory and practice of meditation. For the beginner.

(21) MASUNAGA, REIHŌ. A Primer of Sōtō Zen. Honolulu: East-West Center Press, 1971, 119 pp.
This is a translation of the Shōbōgenzō Zuimonki of Dōgen, the great thirteenth-century Japanese Zen master. It comprises talks, remarks, and practical instructions on sitting. Good introduction to Sōtō Zen.

(22) MATICS, MARION L., trans. Entering the Path of Enlightenment: The Bodhicaryāvatāra of the Buddhist Poet Śāntideva (see 3[15]).

(23) MERTON, THOMAS. Mystics and Zen Masters. New York: Farrar, Straus & Giroux, 1961, 303 pp.
A series of essays comparing Western mystics with the Zen masters. As usual with Merton, the approach is ecumenical and always highly stimulating. A good book for a course on mysticism.

(24) NYANAPONIKA, Thera. The Heart of Buddhist Meditation. London: Rider & Co., 1962.
This excellent work represents a handbook of mental training based on the Buddha's way of mindfulness (saṭipatthāna). It also contains an anthology of relevant texts translated from Pali and Sanskrit.

(25) OBERMILLER, E. "The Doctrine of Prajñāpāramitā as Expounded in the Abhisamayālaṃkāra of Maitreya." Acta Orientalia 11 (1932):1-181, 334-54.
A good analysis of the wisdom (prajñā) philosophy in the work by Maitreya. The aim of this treatise is to elucidate how one

realizes the truth of being or liberation through wisdom (prajñā). This is a thorough and excellent study, with an introductory section on pertinent literature in Sanskrit and Tibetan and a useful glossary of technical terms (pp. 101-31). Recommended for serious students.

(26) PIYADASSI, Thera. The Buddha's Ancient Path. London: Rider & Co., 1964, 239 pp.
A clear exposition of the four noble truths (ariya sacca) and the eightfold path (aṭṭhaṅgika magga) from a very traditional point of view.

(27) ROBINSON, RICHARD H. "Mysticism and Logic in Seng-chao's Thought." Philosophy East and West 8 (1958-59):99-120.
A solid examination of Seng-chao, who belongs to the Chinese Mādhyamika school. His thoughts are explicated by way of a logical analysis which, in turn, introduces translations from original sources.

(28) SCHAYER, STANISLAV. Mahāyāna Doctrines of Salvation. Translated from German by R.T. Knight. London: Probastain & Co., 1923, 53 pp.
Schayer discusses the Buddhology of Mahāyāna, the idea of bodhisattvahood, the doctrine of emptiness, and the doctrine of the dual truth.

(29) SHIBATA, MASUMI. Les maîtres du Zen au Japon. Paris: Maisonneuve et Larose, 1969, 246 pp.
The author attempts to show that Zen is not simply a religious practice but a vast synthesis of Japanese culture.

(30) SUZUKI, D.T. Essays in Zen Buddhism. First, Second, and Third Series. London: Rider & Co., 1950, 383 pp., 351 pp., 384 pp.
The fundamental writings of Suzuki are contained in these three volumes. They comprise essays on the history and doctrine of Zen, as well as extensive translations from Zen texts. Good indexes facilitate the use of the works. Indispensable for students of Zen. See also 1.4(18).

(31) SUZUKI, D.T. An Introduction to Zen Buddhism. 2d ed. London: Buddhist Society, 1959, 136 pp. Reprint. New York: Grove Press, 1964.
A collection of ten of Suzuki's most fundamental essays on various Zen topics, including satori and the kōan. There is a helpful foreword by Carl Jung.

(32) SUZUKI, D.T. Manual of Zen Buddhism. Kyoto: Eastern Buddhist Society, 1935, 232 pp. Reprint. London: Rider, 1957.
Contains authoritative descriptions of the theory and practice of Zen. Can be recommended without reserve to all students of Buddhism.

(33) SUZUKI, D.T. The Training of the Zen Buddhist Monk. Kyoto: Eastern Buddhist Society, 1934, 161 pp. Reprint. New York: University Books, 1965.
A most compact and informative accounting of the life of a Zen monk by the leading Zen scholar. Excellent introduction to the practice of Zen.

(34) SUZUKI, SHUNRYŪ. Zen Mind, Beginner's Mind. New York and Tokyo: Weatherhill, 1970, 138 pp.
A highly readable and worthy compact volume for the beginner. From the Sōtō Zen standpoint.

(35) SWEARER, DONALD K. "Control and Freedom: The Structure of Buddhist Meditation in the Pali Suttas." Philosophy East and West 23 (1973):435-55.
Analysis of the important stages in the traditional meditative exercise.

(36) TUCCI, GIUSEPPE. "The Contents of the First Bhāvanākrama." Minor Buddhist Texts Serie Orientale Roma pt. 2,9 (1958): 155-82.
The Bhāvanākrama of Kamalaśīla is an interesting text that reflects the famous debate (792-94) between the Chinese monk Mahāyāna and Kamalaśīla, a representative of Indian Buddhism. While the Chinese upheld "the sudden path," the Indian rejoined with the "gradual, step-by-step" journey to the final release.

(37) VAJIRANANA, PARAVAHERA. Buddhist Meditation in Theory and Practice. Colombo: M.D. Gunasena, 1962, 498 pp.
An exhaustive analysis of the various meditative practices discussed in the Pali canons.

(38) WAYMAN, ALEX. "The Lamp and the Wind in Tibetan Buddhism." Philosophy East and West 5 (1959):149-54.
An historical discussion of the doctrines of calm (śamatha) and insight (vipaśyanā) in Tibetan Buddhism.

(39) WAYMAN, ALEX. "Purification of Sin in Buddhism by Vision and Confession." In Bonnō no Kenkyū (A Study of Kleśa (see 3[7]), pp. 58-79.

4 *Paths of Liberation*

In this interesting volume, Wayman masterfully deals with the topic of defilement and purification from the point of view of the prevalent position of Buddhism, i.e., "the defilement in man is to be removed by man himself; no one else can do it for him" (p. 73). Wayman, as usual, introduces many Indian and Tibetan materials to illuminate this important aspect of Buddhism.

5 Philosophy of Religion

(1) BHARATI, AGEHANANDA. "Śakta and Vajrayāna, Their Place in Indian Thought." Mikkyōgaku Mikkyōshi Ronbunshū (Studies of Esoteric Buddhism and Tantrism) (Koyasan University, Koyasan), 1965.
Having carefully defined his usage of "philosophical analysis," Bharati analyzes the major contents of Indian Tantric systems. His constant references to Western philosophy make this study almost comparative and evaluative.

(2) CONZE, EDWARD. "The Mahāyāna Treatment of the Viparyāsas." Oriens Extremes 9 (1962):34-46.
Starting with the Hīnayanist concept of "perverted views" (viparyāsa), Conze elucidates six innovations by Mahāyāna Buddhists. An important article for the study of the "right view."

(3) EVANS-WENTZ, W.Y., ed. The Tibetan Book of the Great Liberation: Or the Method of Realizing Nirvāṇa Through Knowing the Mind. London, New York, and Toronto: Oxford University Press, 1954, 64 + 261 pp. Illus.
The first part of this work contains the descriptions of illustrations (9 plates in color), a psychological commentary by the celebrated psychologist Jung, a lengthy and helpful introduction (pp. 1-100) by the editor, and an epitome of the life and teachings of Tibet's great guru, Padma Sambhava (pp. 101-92). The second part contains the English translation of the various important Tibetan texts, including the last testamentary teachings of the guru Phadampa Sangay. In short, a very important work for everybody.

(4) HORNER, I.B. The Early Buddhist Theory of Man Perfected (see 2[5]).

(5) JACOBSON, NOLAN PLINY. Buddhism, the Religion of Analysis. London: George Allen & Unwin, 1966, 202 pp.
A Westerner's interpretation of the key doctrines of Buddhism, conveyed with great sympathy and understanding. Good philosophical introduction to the tenets, especially in the Theravāda tradition.

(6) KAPLEAU, PHILIP, ed. and comp. The Three Pillars of Zen: Teaching, Practice and Enlightenment. New York: Harper & Row, 1966, 363 pp. Paperback reprint. Boston: Beacon Press, 1971.
By presenting the detailed accounts of the process of satori and interviews with Yasutani Roshi, the book gives an intimate, inside picture of life in a Zendō and the working of the minds of disciples there.

(7) KIYOTA, MINORU. "Presuppositions to the Understanding of Japanese Buddhist Thought." Monumenta Nipponica 22:251-59.
This is a discussion on the transformation of Japanese Buddhism from Triyāna (Three Vehicles) to Ekayāna (One Vehicle) and from the mere observance of śīla to the downright transgression and rejection of it. This requires the practice of compassion directed toward humanity and finding therein the source of enlightenment.

(8) La VALLÉE POUSSIN, LOUIS de. The Way to Nirvāṇa (see 4[19]).
A good introduction to the nature of Buddhist salvation.

(9) LESSING, FERDINAND D., and ALEX WAYMAN, trans. Mkhas Grub rje's Fundamentals of the Buddhist Tantras. Indo-Iranian Monographs, no. 8. The Hague and Paris: Mouton, 1968, 382 pp.
A monumental work that opens up the subject of Buddhist Tantras to Western readers. This is because, as the translators assert, "it represents the fundamentals along with important bibliography of all four divisions of Tantras and indicates the non-Tantric Buddhist topics which the disciples were expected to master in preparation for the Tantras; and it presents these fundamentals with a minimum of quotations and other complications." The copious notes are a mine of information. The book is richly enhanced further by a thorough index.

(10) MASUTANI, FUMIO. "Two Types of Faith in Buddhism." Religious Studies in Japan (see 1.2.2[10]), pp. 169-84.
Having reduced types of faith into two, i.e., "faith through understanding" and "faith through person," Masutani describes the regional variants of these two in India, China, and Japan.

(11) NAKAMURA, HAJIME. "Pure Land Buddhism and Western Christianity Compared: A Quest for Common Roots of the Universality." International Journal for Philosophy of Religion 1 (1970):77-96.
A good comparative study on salient points of difference between the two great religions.

(12) NISHITANI, KEIJI. "On the I-Thou Relationship in Zen Buddhism." Eastern Buddhist, n.s. 2 (1969):71-87.
Another interesting and penetrating article by Nishitani which expands on Buber's ideas.

(13) SASAKI, GESSHŌ. "Philosophical Foundations of the Shinshū Doctrine." Eastern Buddhist 1 (1921):38-46.
An important article asserting the religion of salvation in contrast to traditional Buddhism, which is taken to be a religion of enlightenment.

(14) SEN, SUKUMAR. "On Dhāraṇī and Pratisāra." Mikkyōgaku Mikkyōshi Ronbunshū (Studies of Esoteric Buddhism and Tantrism), (Koyasan University, Koyasan), 1965, pp. 67-72.
This is a short but extremely informative article on the difference between the rites involving dhāraṇī (magic formula) and pratisāra (counter-magic).

(15) STRENG, FREDERICK J. Emptiness: A Study in Religious Meaning. Nashville and New York: Abingdon Press, 1967, 252 pp.
A novel attempt at understanding Nāgārjuna's philosophy of emptiness or ultimate reality. For the advanced student.

(16) SUZUKI, D.T. "Passivity in Buddhist Life." In Essays in Zen Buddhism. Second Series. (See 4[30]), pp. 253-333.
A masterful account of passivity in the Buddhist way of life, but Suzuki invariably focuses on Zen and its doctrines.

(17) SUZUKI, D.T. "Infinite Light." Eastern Buddhist, n.s. 4 (1971):1-29.
Sheds light on the doctrine of "Infinite Light" (amitābha) from the angles of: Shinran's Wasan [Songs in praise of Amitābha], Amida and his original vow, and the original vow and self.

(18) SUZUKI, D.T. The Training of the Zen Buddhist Monk (see 4[33]).
A most compact and informative accounting of the life of a Zen monk by the leading Zen scholar. Excellent introduction to Zen. An early classic in the field.

(19) TAKASAKI, JIKIDŌ. "The Tathāgatagarbha Theory in the Mahāparinirvāṇasūtra." Indogaku Bukkyōgaku Kenkyū (Journal of Indian and Buddhist Studies) 19 (1971):1-10.
An important article by one of the world's authorities on the Tathāgatagarbha (womb of Enlightenment) theory.

(20) WAYMAN, ALEX. "The Five-fold Ritual Symbolism of Passion." Mikkyōgaku Mikkyōshi Ronbunshū (Studies of Esoteric Buddhism and Tantrism)(Koyasan University, Koyasan), 1965, pp. 117-44.
Wayman, a prolific writer on the Buddhist Tantra, treats the sādhana (evocation of deity) formula and its symbolic elements. He makes comparisons not only with the Brahmanical tradition but also with the Greco-Roman tradition.

(21) YAMAGUCHI, SUSUMU. "The Concept of the Pure Land in Nāgārjuna's Doctrine." Eastern Buddhist, n.s. 1 (1966): 34-47.
Having pointed out the three aspects of śūnyata, i.e., the operation, the expression, and the emptying function of discursive thought, Yamaguchi attempts to explain the necessary connection with the Pure Land doctrine set forth in the Daśabhūmikaśāstra.

6 Philosophy of Psychology

(1) ANACKER, STEFAN. "Vasubandhu's Karmasiddhiprakaraṇa and the Problem of the Highest Meditation." Philosophy East and West 22 (1972):247-58.
The author explains the intricacy of acts (karma) as they relate to the meditative or concentrative aspect of consciousness. Rather technical but important discussion of the so-called Yogācāra idealism.

(2) ANDERSON, TYSON. "Anattā--A Reply to Richard Taylor." Philosophy East and West 25 (1975):187-93.
Examines Taylor's interpretation of the non-self (anattā) doctrine (85).

(3) ANESAKI, MASAHARU. "Transmigration." In Encyclopedia of Religion and Ethics. Vol. 12, pp. 429-30.
This brief article tries to explain the early Buddhist notion of rebirth as a continuing revolution or stream (saṃsāra) of existences, contrasting it with the animistic theory of soul and its transmigration.

(4) BAHM, ARCHIE J. Philosophy of the Buddha (see 1.2[1]).
A critical assessment of Buddha's philosophy. Touches upon the basic doctrines, but some of the Western interpretations are questionable.

(5) BENOIT, HUBERT. The Supreme Doctrine: Psychological Studies in Zen Thought. London: Routledge & Kegan Paul, 1955, 248 pp. (English translation of French 1951 edition.)
This book is a series of essays, not by a student of religion, but by a professional psychologist. He is not interested in presenting Zen in a scholarly or systematic way but uses Zen teachings as a criticism of Western psychiatry. A good book for those interested in psychiatry, but could be harmful if presented as an objective account of Zen.

(6) BEYER, STEPHAN. The Cult of Tārā: Magic and Ritual in Tibet. Berkeley: University of California Press, 1973, 542 pp.

The Cult of Tārā is a detailed examination of the rituals built around the worship of Tārā, the Mother of Compassion. Several complete rituals are transcribed in their entirety, with mantras, mudrās, and other ritual actions given and explained. As well as describing the rituals themselves, Beyer provides his own interpretations of their spiritual meaning and the reasons for and results of them. The subtitle, Magic and Ritual in Tibet, is actually more indicative of the subject matter. The whole of Tibetan ritual is covered, taking the popular Tārā rituals as the focal point from which to examine Tibetan Buddhism as the "performing art" Beyer feels it to be. This is an important book, for it gives the reader an insight into the complexity of everyday religious life among the Tibetans.

(7) BLOFELD, JOHN E.C. The Tantric Mysticism of Tibet: A Practical Guide (see 1.2.2[4]).

Divided into two parts--background and theory, and practice--the book briefly outlines the various aspects of Tibetan Buddhism. The value of visualization, the role of the guru, the various symbols and deities, prostrations, meditation, and several sādhanas are among the topics covered. An intelligent use of illustrations as well as a logical arrangement of subject matter aid in presenting in a concise manner what might otherwise be a confusing topic. Blofeld's book lacks the depth of Guenther's or Lama Govinda's but nonetheless stands on its own as a valuable book on Tibetan Buddhism.

(8) CAIRNS, GRACE E. "The Philosophy and Psychology of the Oriental Maṇḍala." Philosophy East and West 11 (1962): 219-29.

The philosophical basis of the maṇḍala is seen as (1) the teaching of the Yogācāra school that all things are manifestations of Absolute Mind, (2) the Mādhyamika concept that the Absolute Mind in its transcendental form is śūnyatā (void), and (3) the central idea of the Buddhāvataṃsaka Sūtra, the interpenetration of the transcendental Void with saṃsāra. It is this idea of the Buddhāvataṃsaka-sūtra that is taken to be central in maṇḍala symbolism.

(9) CHAN, W.T. "The Treatise on the Establishment of the Doctrine of Consciousness-only." In A Source Book in Chinese Philosophy (see 1.3[1]), pp. 374-95.

The selections are from Hsuan-tsang's Ch'eng wei-shih lun and also from the Chinese Trimśikā (Thirty verses) of Vasubandhu. The same verses can also be found in A Sourcebook in Indian

Philosophy (see 1.2[11]). A good introduction to the Vijñānavāda (onsciousness) school.

(10) CHANG CHEN-CHI. The Nature of Ch'an (Zen) Buddhism." Philosophy East and West 6 (Jan. 1957):333-55.
The author addresses himself to four topics: (1) Is Zen incomprehensible as Suzuki maintains? (2) What is Zen enlightenment? (3) the relationships among Zen and Yogācāra and Mādhyamika Mahāyāna, and (4) Can Zen be made more intelligible? A good, sound article, worth reading.

(11) CHANG, GARMA C.C., ed. Teachings of the Tibetan Yoga. Secaucus: Citadel Press, 1963, 128 pp.
Part one of the book contains the Zen-like "Song of Mahāmudrā" by Tilopa, "The Vow of Mahāmudrā" by Garmapa Rangjang Dorje and the "Essentials of Mahāmudrā Practice" by the Ven. Lama Kong Ka, which explains how the adept is to realize the Mahāmudrā. Part two consists of "The Epitome of an Introduction to the Profound Path of the Six Yogas" by Drashi Namjhal. These texts outline how the yogi gains control over the nāḍīs (psychic nerves) and breath in order to perfect gTum. Mo (the mystic fires of Heat Yoga), the illusory-body, dream, light, bardo, and transformation yogas are also covered.

(12) CHATTERJEE, HERAMBA. "A Critical Study of Buddhistic Conception of Nirvāṇa." Journal of the Bihar Research Society (Patna) 2 [Buddha Jayanti Special Issue] (1956):492-97.
A brief but penetrative analysis of the concept, starting with the etymological construction and ending with the various interpretations and uses seen in the Theravāda, Mādhyamika, and Yogācāra systems.

(13) CHIH-K'AI [Chih-I]. "Mahāyāna Method of Cessation and Contemplation" (see 4[4]).

(14) CHOGYAM TRUNGPA. Cutting Through Spiritual Materialism. Edited by John Baker and Marvin Casper. Berkeley: Shambala, 1973, 250 pp.
The work consists of two series of lectures given in 1970-71. Cutting Through progresses from the relatively simpler topics of beginning spiritual practice, opening to the guru, etc., through developing compassion and insight, and finally to the "crazy wisdom" of Tantra, thus tracing the Theravāda, Mahāyāna, and Vajrayāna disciplines. The chapters are followed by questions and answers, which help to clarify various points, although a certain amount of repetition and digression occurs.

(15) CHOGYAM TRUNGPA. Meditation in Action. Berkeley: Shambala, 1969, 74 pp.
Originally given as talks at the Samye-Ling Tibetan Centre in Scotland, the book covers several topics related to the meditative experience: the life and example of Buddha, the manure of experience and the field of Bodhi, transmission, generosity, patience, and wisdom. As meditation itself is nothing more than a practical technique for getting to know the world, the book remains faithful to its subject and gives the reader a good feeling for the simplicity of the topic. This is the Zen-mind of the Vajrayāna.

(16) CONZE, EDWARD. Buddhist Meditation (see 4[6]).
A standard exposition of the methods of meditation taken from the canons, including some selected translations. Provides a general view of meditation, its purpose, components, and textual sources. Most of the doctrines of early Buddhism, such as the three marks, dependent arising, and nirvāṇa, are analyzed in the context of meditation. A good place to begin.

(17) CONZE, EDWARD. "The Ontology of the Prajñāpāramitā." Philosophy East and West 3 (1953):117-29.
Introductory remarks on the nature of the several doctrines occurring in the wisdom sūtras.

(18) CROWE, C.L. "On the 'Irrationality' of Zen." Philosophy East and West 15 (1965):31-36.
This article is a general attack on Suzuki's labeling of Zen as "irrational." The author concentrates on the Zen concept of satori, or enlightenment, and concludes that there is nothing in Zen that differs from other mystical approaches to religion. A good, general "anti-Suzuki" article.

(19) DASGUPTA, SURENDRANATH. "Philosophy of Vasubandhu in Viṃśatikā and Triṃśikā" (see 1.2.2.2[3]).
A short and succinct summary of the doctrines of Vasubandhu contained in these two Yogācāra-vijñānavāda tracts. Good for beginning students.

(20) DHAMMARATANA, U. "The Methodology of Vibhaṅgaprakaraṇa." Nava-Nālandā Mahāvihāra Research Publication 2 (1960): 235-320.
A very helpful discussion of the various chapters of the work, which belongs to the Abhidhamma. For those interested in psychical factors of existence.

(21) DOWMAN, KEITH, trans. Lama Mi-pham: Calm and Clear. Berkeley: Dharma, 1973, 127 pp.
The work contains two short meditation texts: "The Wheel of Analytic Meditation" and "Instructions on Vision in the Middle Way," written by Lama Mi-pham, the famous nineteenth-century Nyingma scholar. The texts deal with the analysis of impermanence, selflessness, etc., as practiced in certain forms of calm (śamatha, Tibetan zhi-gnas) and clear (vipaśyanā, Tibetan lhagmthong) meditation.

(22) DUMOULIN, H. "Technique and Personal Devotion in the Zen Exercise." Studies in Japanese Culture, 1963, pp. 17-40.
Provides an interesting discussion on the relationship between "self-power" and "other-power" in Buddhism.

(23) EVANS-WENTZ, W.Y., ed. Tibetan Yoga and Secret Doctrines. New York: Oxford University Press, [1935] 1967, 389 pp.
This is Evans-Wentz's translation of the Seven Books of Wisdom of the Great Path, dealing with the practice of various yogic meditations. The translations are awkward and the commentary misleading.

(24) FUKAURA, SEIBUN. "Ālaya-vijñāna." In Encyclopaedia of Buddhism (see 1.1[21]) 1:382-88.
A rather technical presentation of the concept of storehouse consciousness as seen in the various developments, especially in the Vijñānavāda and the Chinese She-lun school.

(25) FUNG YU-LAN. "The Ch'an School" (see 4[9]).

(26) GOMEZ, LUIS O. "Some Aspects of the Free-will Question in the Nikāyas." Philosophy East and West 25 (1975):81-90.
Advances the free-will doctrine in early Buddhism.

(27) GOVINDA, ANAGARIKA B. Foundations of Tibetan Mysticism, According to the Esoteric Teachings of the Great Mantra: Oṁ Maṇi Padme Hūṁ. London: Rider & Co., [1959] 1967, 311 pp.
Taking the mantra "Oṁ Maṇi Padme Hūṁ Hrīḥ," Lama Govinda examines the spiritual teachings associated with each of the mantra's five parts. Special attention is also paid to the yogic exercises involving the psychic centers (cakras), nerves, breath, inner heat (gtum-mo), etc. The beauty of Foundations comes from the masterly way Lama Govinda ties diverse topics together to make the book a continuous whole. As both an Austrian scholar and a Vajrayāna lama, Lama Govinda succeeds in covering his subject matter skillfully.

(28) GOVINDA, LAMA ANAGARIKA. The Psychological Attitude of Early Buddhist Philosophy. London: Rider & Co., 1961, 191 pp.

An analysis of the four noble truths (ariya sacca) in terms of the psychological approach in the Abhidhamma. Contains a lengthy discussion of the factors of consciousness as represented in the Theravāda Abhidhamma.

(29) GRIMM, GEORGE. The Doctrine of the Buddha: The Religion of Reason and Meditation (see 4[12]).

One of the chapters presents a lengthy discussion of the third noble truth, namely cessation of suffering (dukkha), i.e., nirvāṇa. Nirvāṇa is here defined as the "unnameable" state of peace.

(30) GUENTHER, HERBERT V., and CHOGYAM TRUNGPA. The Dawn of Tantra (see 1.2.2.4[4]).

This is the edited transcript of a seminar given in Berkeley in 1972. Various aspects of tantra, such as the maṇḍala principle, initiations, and guru-student relationship, are discussed. The chapter on visualization speaks of the reason for that practice and the difficulties and dangers of unprepared Westerners involving themselves in it. The last two chapters are questions and answers with Guenther and Trungpa respectively. A good beginning in Tantrism.

(31) GUENTHER, H.V. Philosophy and Psychology in the Abhidharma (see 4[13]).

Contains a very critical and lucid account of the Abhidharma conception of mind (citta) and mental factors, or concommitants (cetasika or caitta). Also includes comparative study of the different schools of Abhidharma on the conception of the external world as represented by form (rūpa).

(32) HAMILTON, C.H. "Buddhist Idealism in Wei Shih Er Shih Lun" (see 1.2.2.2[4]).

A paraphrase of the text with some remarks on the milieu in which the Yogācāra arose and on the influence of the Yogācāra on modern-day Buddhism in East Asia. Very useful for beginning students who cannot tackle the Chinese text itself.

(33) HISAMATSU, SHIN'ICHI. Zen and the Fine Arts. Translated by Gishin Tokiwa. Tokyo and Palo Alto: Kodansha International, 1971, 400 pp., 313 plates.

Though the topic of the book is the influence of Zen on art and culture, it maintains a highly philosophical tone. Having defined Zen as "the self-awareness of the formless self," Hisamatsu goes on to discuss the essentials of Zen in order to show the concrete expressions of the "formless self."

(34) HOSAKA, GYOKUSEN. "Āsrava." In Encyclopaedia of Buddhism (see 1.1[21]) 2:201-14.
An exhaustive analysis of the nature and function of the important concept of āsrava, usually translated as outflows, and closely related to the nature of defilements or impediments relative to the enlightened realm of existence. For the advanced student.

(35) HSUAN-TSANG. "Completion of the Doctrine of Mere Ideation." In A History of Chinese Philosophy (see 1.3[7]) 2:299-338.
Hsuan-tsang presents a very fine analysis of the eight-consciousness theory as expounded in Ch'eng wei-shih lun. Many important translated passages are included.

(36) HUI-NENG, "Platform Scripture;" SHEN-HUI, "Recorded Conversations;" I-HSUAN, "Recorded Conversations." In A Source Book in Chinese Philosophy (see 1.3[1]), pp. 425-49.
Important translations of treatises by three Ch'an masters of the school of sudden enlightenment.

(37) INADA, KENNETH K. "The Ultimate Ground of Buddhist Purification." Philosophy East and West 18 (1968):41-53.
An analysis of the human situation and problem of possible means of resolution of the so-called impure nature.

(38) JAINI, PADMANABH S. Abhidharmadīpa with Vibhāshāprabha[v]ritti. Patna: Kashi Prasad Jayaswal Research Institute, 1959.
While the volume is a Sanskrit edition of the newly discovered work, Jaini has added a very long and informative introduction, which exposes the content of the work and its role in the Abhidharma philosophy. Recommended for advanced students.

(39) JAM-mGON KONG-sPRUL. A Direct Guide to Enlightenment. Translated by Ken McLeod. Vancouver: Kagyu Kunkhyab Chuling, 1975, 82 pp.
Jam-mGon Kong-sPrul was a famous nineteenth-century lama who was one of the key figures in the ecumenical movement that revitalized Tibetan Buddhism. This is his explanation of Atīśa's "The Seven Points of Mind Training," a meditation text that is used to this day by all four sects. The meditation deals with the generation of bodhicitta (enlightened attitude) through examination of suffering, impermanence, etc.

(40) JAYASURIYA, W.F. The Psychology and Philosophy of Buddhism. Colombo: Y.M.B.A. Press, 1963, 254 pp.
This is a well-researched study of Abhidhamma philosophy. Rather technical but challenging for those whose interests lie in the area of Buddhist psychology, especially in the nature of mind-function.

(41) JAYATILEKE, K.N. Survival and Karma in Buddhist Perspective. Kandy: Buddhist Publication Society, 1969.
This short work represents an attempt to explain the early Buddhist notions of karma and rebirth in the light of recent researches into paranormal phenomena.

(42) JOHANSSON, RUNE E.A. "Citta, Mano, Viññāṇa--A Psychosemantic Investigation." University of Ceylon Review 23 (1965):165-215.
A very interesting analysis of the three Pali terms expressing mind or psychic phenomena. The author attempts to demarcate the meanings of the three terms based on an analysis of the textual passages where they occur.

(43) JOHANSSON, RUNE E.A. The Psychology of Nirvāṇa. London: George Allen & Unwin, 1969, 142 pp.
One of the more recent attempts to expound on the early Buddhist notion of freedom (nirvāṇa) on the basis of the material found in the Pali Nikāyas and to relate it to modern Western psychology.

(44) JUNG, CARL G. Psychology and Religion: East and West. Edited by Herbert Read, Michael Fordham and Gerhard Adler. Translated by R.F.C. Hull. Bollingen Series, no. 20, The Collected Works of C.G. Jung, vol. 2. London: Routledge & Kegan Paul, 1969, 669 pp.
Contains Jung's lectures and articles on the subject. Good introduction to those interested in comparative psychology as he focuses on his renowned "collective unconscious" and makes excursions into Eastern concepts, notably Buddhism.

(45) KALUPAHANA, DAVID J. Buddhist Philosophy: A Historical Analysis (see 1.1[17]).
An examination of the Buddha's conception of existence, including an analysis of the doctrines of karma and rebirth. Also includes (in the second selection) an examination of the doctrine of freedom (nirvāṇa) in early Buddhism, including a critique of Johansson's views as expressed in his Psychology of Nirvāṇa (43).

(46) KARUNARATNA, UPALI. "Anusaya." In Encyclopaedia of Buddhism (see 1.1[21]) 1:775-77.
Discussion of an important concept, that of inherent tendencies that lead to evil inclinations.

(47) KITAYAMA, J. Metaphysik des Buddhismus: Versuch einer philosophischen Interpretation der Lehre Vasubandhus und seiner Schule.

The author attempts a philosophical interpretation of the consciousness-only doctrine of Vasubandhu. A German translation of the Viṃśatikā is appended (pp. 234-68). For advanced students only.

(48) La VALLÉE POUSSIN, LOUIS de. Nirvāṇa. Études sur l'histoire des religions, no. 5. Paris: G. Beauchesne, 1925.

One of the earliest attempts at expounding the notion of freedom (nirvāṇa) in Buddhism. An important work, though superseded by more modern works on the subject.

(49) La VALLÉE POUSSIN, LOUIS de. "Note sur l'Ālayavijñāna. Pour servir d'Introduction à la traduction du Mahāyāna-samgraha (Chap. de l'Ālaya) par E. Lamotte." Mélanges chinois et bouddhiques 3 (1934):145-68.

An interesting article on early Buddhist theories of the soul, the "mind-only" doctrine (cittamātra), and the relationship between the receptable (ālaya) and psychological processes. For advanced students.

(50) LEGETT, TREVOR, ed. and trans. A First Zen Reader. Rutland: C.E. Tuttle, 1960, 236 pp. Illus.

Contains the following translations: a sermon on "The Original Face" by Daito Kokushi (fourteenth century), a collection of discourses by Takashina Rōsen entitled "A Tongue-tip Taste of Zen," a commentary by Amakuki Sessan on Hakuin's "Song of Meditation," a sermon on "The Two Poems" by Oka Kyūgaku, and the kōan "Bodhidharma and the Emperor."

(51) LÉVI, SYLVAIN. Un système de philosophie bouddhique: Matériaux pour l'étude du système Vijñaptimātra (see 1.2.2.2[7]).

(52) LINDQUIST, SIGURD. Siddhi und Abhiññā. Uppsala: Uppsala University, 1935, 98 pp.

An authoritative account of psychokinesis (iddhi, siddhi) and higher knowledge (abhiññā) recognized in early Buddhism.

(53) LOKESH, CHANDRA. "Maṇḍalas of a Tantra Collection." Mikkyōgaku Mikkyōshi Ronbunshū (Studies of Esoteric Buddhism and Tantrism) (Koyasan University, Koyasan), 1965, pp. 253-68,

This is a classification of the maṇḍalas, which are "veritable psychocosmograms," into the classes of Kriyā, Carya, Yoga,

Anuttara-yoga, Advaya, the Amnata cycle, and into those which are auspicious at the end.

(54) MALALASEKERA, G.P. "Anattā." In Encyclopaedia of Buddhism (see 1.1[21]) 1:567-76.
A comprehensive analysis of the early Buddhist notion of non-substantiality (anattā) in the light of the pre-Buddhist background.

(55) MALALASEKERA, G.P. "The Status of the Individual in Theravāda Buddhism" (see 2[6]).
A clear analysis of the concept of man, bringing together the basic doctrines.

(56) MASUNAGA, REIHŌ. A Primer of Sōtō Zen (see 4[21]).

(57) MIYAMOTO, SHŌSON. "Freedom, Independence and Peace in Buddhism" (see 2[7]).

(58) NANANANDA, Bhikkhu. The Magic of the Mind in Buddhist Perspective. Kandy: Buddhist Publication Society, 1974.
Represents an exposition of a canonical discourse--the Kālakarma-sutta--where the main theme is the illusory nature of consciousness. The exposition centers on a discussion of the doctrine of dependent arising (paṭiccasamuppāda).

(59) NEBESKY-WOJKOWITZ, RENÉ de. Oracles and Demons of Tibet: The Cult and Iconography of the Tibetan Protective Deities. The Hague: Mouton, 1956, 666 pp.
This monumental work is a fascinating study of "black magic" practices.

(60) NYANAPONIKA, Thera. Abhidhamma Studies: Researches in Buddhist Psychology. Colombo: Island Hermitage Publications, 1949, 86 pp.
These studies are based on the Dhammasaṅgaṇi and its commentary, the Atthasālinī. These include philosophical and psychological investigations with emphasis on the practical application of the teachings.

(61) NYANAPONIKA, Thera. Anattā and Nibbāna. The Wheel Publications, no. 11. Kandy: Buddhist Publication Society, 1959, 28 pp.
This small essay deals with the traditional interpretation of the doctrine of nonsubstantiality (anattā) and its relation to the notion of freedom (nibbāna).

(62) NYANATILOKA, Mahathera. Karma and Rebirth. The Wheel Publications, no. 9. Kandy: Buddhist Publication Society, 1959, 22 pp.
An attempt to present the Theravāda doctrines of karma and rebirth to the Western world.

(63) OBERMILLER, E. "The Doctrine of Prajñāpāramitā as Expounded in the Abhisamayālaṁkāra of Maitreya" (see 4[25]).

(64) OLSCHAK, BLANCE CHRISTINE. Mystic Art of Ancient Tibet. New York: McGraw-Hill, 1973, 224 pp.
It is important that the student of the Vajrayāna philosophy become acquainted in some way with its artistic form, for, to put it another way, Tibetan painted scrolls are what philosophy represents. The work contains numerous maṇḍalas of deities and their manifestations.

(65) OLSON, ROBERT. "Candrakīrti's Critique of Vijñānavāda." Philosophy East and West 24 (1974):405-11.
The critique is by a Mādhyamika thinker and is centered on the storehouse consciousness (ālaya-vijñāna) and the mind-only (cittamātra) doctrines of the Vijñānavāda.

(66) PARSONS, HOWARD L. "Buddha and Buddhism" (see 2[8]).

(67) POTT, P.H. "Some Remarks on the 'Terrific Deities' in Tibetan 'Devil Dances.'" Mikkyōgaku Mikkyōshi Ronbunshū (Studies in Esoteric Buddhism and Tantrism) (Koyasan University, Koyasan), 1965, pp. 269-78.
Pott observes a very systematic application of the fundamental ideals of Mahāyāna in the movements of Tibetan "devil dances" and the glances of the terrific deities. An interesting article, not only for philosophers but also for dancers.

(68) RAHULA, WALPOLA. What the Buddha Taught (see 1.2[12]).
A lucid account of the basic teachings of early Buddhism, especially the four noble truths (ārya satya), which attempts to remove a number of current misconceptions about Buddhism.

(69) RHYS-DAVIDS, C.A.F. Buddhist Psychology. 2d ed. London: Luzac & Co., 1924, 302 pp.
One of the earlier and more reliable works of the author. Includes a clear exposition of the conception of mind in early Buddhism, followed by an analysis of the later developments in the Theravāda Abhidhamma.

(70) ROBINSON, RICHARD H. "Mysticism and Logic in Seng-chao's Thought" (see 4[27]).

(71) ROBINSON, RICHARD H. "Some Buddhist and Hindu Concepts of Intellect-will." Philosophy East and West 22 (1972): 299-307.
A comparative study of the concept of buddhi in both traditions.

(72) SAKURABE, HAJIME. "Abhidharmāvatāra by an Unidentified Author, Some Introductory Remarks." Nava-Nālandā Mahāvihāra Research Publication 2 (1960):359-69.
Relates an Abhidharma work to works from the Tibetan and Chinese sources. For the advanced student.

(73) SARATCHANDRA, E.R. Buddhist Psychology of Perception. Colombo: Ceylon University Press, 1958.
After an examination of the material found in the Pali Nikāyas, the author comes to the conclusion that early Buddhism considered the mind as an epiphenomenon. Developments in the Abhidharma as well as Yogācāra are discussed. For the advanced student.

(74) SASTRI, AIYASWAMI N. "Some Abhidharma Problems." Adyar Library Bulletin 18 (1954):81-98, 217-28.
Analysis of concepts, such as sensation (vedanā), perception (samjñā), dispositions (samskāra), and consciousness (vijñāna) in the Abhidharma.

(75) SAUNDERS, DALE. "Some Tantric Techniques." Mikkyōgaku Mikkyōshi Ronbunshū (Studies in Esoteric Buddhism and Tantrism) (Koyasan University, Koyasan), 1965, pp. 167-77.
An article on sādhana, which Saunders calls "in-corporation" of the three fundamental elements, i.e., the flesh, the living cosmos, and time.

(76) SCHOTT, M. Sein als Bewusstein: Ein Beitrag zur Mahāyāna-Philosophie. Materialeu zur Kunde des Buddhismus, no. 20. Heidelberg, 1935, 50 pp.
A short but very dense study of the consciousness-only doctrine, based on the Ālambanaparīkṣa and the Vijñāptimātratāsiddhi. Good for advanced and serious students.

(77) SIERKSMA, FOKKE. "Tibet's Terrifying Deities: Sex and Aggression in Religious Acculturation." In Art in Its Context: Studies in Ethno-Aesthetics. Edited by Adrian A. Gerbands. Museum Series 1. The Hague: Mouton & Co., 1966. 288 pp., 45 plates.
This is an interesting and important book on tankas, the Tibetan painted scrolls.

(78) SILVA, C.L.A. de. *The Four Essential Doctrines of Buddhism.* Colombo: Lake House, 1940, 1948, 203 pp.
One of the best orthodox interpretations of dependent origination, *nirvāṇa*, karma, and rebirth. Rather technical; excellent for the serious student.

(79) STCHERBATSKY, TH. "Dignāga's Theory of Perception." *Journal of the Taishō University* (April 1930). Reprinted in *Wogibara Commemorative Volume* (Tokyo: Taisho University, 1930), pt. 2, pp. 89-130.
A clear and concise account of Dignāga's theory of perception. For all students.

(80) STCHERBATSKY, TH. *The Soul Theory of the Buddhists* (see 2[12]).
This small treatise examines the Buddhist doctrine of nonsubstantiality (*anātman*) and includes a translation of the appendix to Vasubandhu's *Abhidharmakośa* on "Determination of Individuality" (*pudgalaviniścaya*), together with Yaśomitra's commentary (*vyakhyā*). This important chapter deals with the heretical view of the *Pudgalavāda* which posited a substantialist individuality (*pudgala*), as opposed to the traditional Buddhist view of nonsubstantiality.

(81) STRENG, FREDRICK. "Reflections on the Attention Given to Mental Construction in the Indian Buddhist Analysis of Causality." *Philosophy East and West* 25 (1975):71-80.
Examines mental constructions as they relate to the Buddhist concept of causality.

(82) SUZUKI, D.T. "Zen, a Reply to Hu Shih." *Philosophy East and West* 3 (1953):25-46.
Suzuki's reply to Hu Shih's study on the history and methods of Zen (see 1.3[11]). The two should be read together by every student of Chinese Buddhism; they represent diametrically opposite vantage points.

(83) SUZUKI, SHUNRYŪ. *Zen Mind, Beginner's Mind* (see 4[34]).
A highly readable and worthy compact volume for the beginner.

(84) SWEARER, DONALD K. "Two Types of Saving Knowledge in the Pali Suttas." *Philosophy East and West* 22 (1972):355-71.
Examines the difference between discriminating knowledge (*viññāṇa*) and intuitive knowledge (*paññā*) in the Pali tradition.

(85) TAYLOR, RICHARD. "The Anattā Doctrine and Personal Identity." *Philosophy East and West* 19 (1969):359-66.

The author takes a look at the anattā (non-self) doctrine in terms of the concept of a person rather than the ordinary nature of a self. An interesting approach.

(86) THOMAS, E.J. The History of Buddhist Thought (see 1.1[39]). Chapters 8 and 9 analyze the doctrines of non-self and karma, respectively, and chapter 10 treats the doctrine of nirvāṇa in early Buddhism.

(87) TUCCI, GUISEPPE. The Theory and Practice of the Maṇḍala, with Special Reference to the Modern Psychology of the Subconscious. London: Rider, 1961, 156 pp.
An informal and easily read treatise.

(88) UI, HAKUJU. "On Nibbāna." In Studies on Buddhism in Japan, I. Tokyo: International Buddhist Society, 1939, pp. 37-52.
A leading Japanese Buddhist scholar examines the nature of nirvāṇa from its early beginnings to the later developments in the Mahāyāna. A good beginning.

(89) WALEY, ARTHUR. "On Trust in the Heart." In Buddhist Texts through the Ages, by Edward Conze. New York: Harper & Row, 1964, pp. 295-98.
A poetic translation of the famous Hsin-hsin ming by the third patriarch, Seng-ts'an (d. 606). A good introduction to Buddhist devotional poetry. Another translation is in D.T. Suzuki's Manual of Zen Buddhism (see 4[32]), pp. 76-82 in 1957 reprint.

(90) WAYMAN, ALEX. "Female Energy and Symbolism in the Buddhist Tantras." History of Religions 2 (1962):73-111.
The importance of Wayman's articles lies in their originality, freshness of materials used, and thoroughness. This in turn requires the concentrated effort of the reader.

(91) WEINPAHL, PAUL. Zen Diary. New York: Harper & Row, 1970, 244 pp.
The author elaborates on the daily experience of the Zen life of meditation, zazen and sanzen, also recording his personal thoughts and reactions.

(92) WIJESEKERA, O.H. de A. "The Concept of Viññāṇa in Theravāda Buddhism." Journal of the American Oriental Society 84 (1964):254-59.
The article attempts to delineate four different meanings of the term viññāṇa (consciousness), as used in the Pali canons.

7 Epistemology

(1) BHATTACHARYA, VIDHUSHEKHARA. The Basic Conception of Buddhism (see 1.2.1[4]).
Consists of a discussion of the Buddha as a rationalist and a pragmatist relative to his own context and exemplified in a discussion of his silence. Buddha's silence is interpreted as a recognition that his experience was too subtle for words. Comparisons are drawn with Vedānta and Mahāyāna.

(2) CHANG, CHUNG-YUAN. "Ch'an Buddhism: Logical and Illogical." Philosophy East and West 17 (1967):37-49.
The author takes up two divergent approaches, logical and illogical, used by the Chinese Zen masters.

(3) CHATTERJI, D. "The Problem of Knowledge and the Four Schools of Later Buddhism." Annals of the Bhandarkar Oriental Research Institute 12 (Apr. 1931):205-15.
A short exposition of the views of the Sautrāntikas, Vaibhāṣikas, Yogācāras, and Mādhyamikas on sources of knowledge (pramāṇa). According to the author, the first two schools admit the reality of the external world, but the latter two do not. A good, succinct article.

(4) CHATTERJI, D. "Sources of Knowledge in Buddhist Logic." Indian Culture 1 (1934):263-73.
A general account of the different ways of knowing in Buddhist logic.

(5) DEMIÉVILLE, PAUL. "Sur la mémoire des existences antérieures." Bulletin de l'École française d'Extrême Orient 27 (1927):283-98.
A discussion of retrocognition as a higher form of knowledge recognized in early Buddhism, based on the material found in the Chinese Āgamas.

(6) FRAUWALLNER, ERICH. "Dharmottara's Kṣaṇabhaṅgasiddhi. Text und Uebersetzung." Wiener Zeitschrift für die Kunde des Morgenlandes 42 (1935):217-58.
Establishes that Dharmottara was active about 750. His work on universal flux is here edited in the Tibetan version and translated into German. Useful material on the concept of kṣaṇabhaṅga (momentariness).

(7) FRAUWALLNER, ERICH. "Dharmakīrti's Sambandhaparīkṣā. Text und Uebersetzung." Wiener Zeitschrift für die Kunde des Morgenlandes 41 (1934):261-300.
A small tract by Dharmakīrti refuting the existence of relationships (sambandha) between various dharmas is here presented in its Tibetan version with a German translation. A useful study on the concept of sambandha.

(8) FRAUWALLNER, ERICH. "Dignāga's Ālambanaparīkṣā: Text, Uebersetzung und Erläuterungen." Wiener Zeitschrift für die Kunde des Morganlandes 37 (1930):174-94.
A translation in German from the Tibetan and Chinese versions of a fundamental tract of Dignāga on perception. Frauwallner was the leading pioneer in German-speaking countries on Buddhist logic and epistemology. All his articles are essential for advanced students who can read German.

(9) GUENTHER, HERBERT V. "The Levels of Understanding in Buddhism." American Oriental Society 78, no. 1 (1958): 19-28.
A clear and forceful analysis of three levels of understanding in Buddhism, drawing heavily from Tibetan sources.

(10) HATANI, RYŌTAI. "Dialectics of the Mādhyamika Philosophy." In Studies on Buddhism in Japan, I. Tokyo: International Buddhist Society, 1939, pp. 53-71.
A leading Japanese authority on the Mādhyamika system unravels the dialectical movements of Nāgārjuna's thought, centering on the Mūlamadhyamakakārikā and introducing cognate ideas from the Prajñāpāramitā Sūtras, Milindapañha, and even Chinese sources of the Sanron (Three Treatises) school. For the advanced student.

(11) HATTORI, MASAAKI, trans. Dignāga on Perception. Harvard Oriental Series, no. 47. Cambridge: Harvard University Press, 1968, 265 pp.
This is a solid translation with copious annotations on the concept of perception (pratyakṣa) from Dignāga's Pramāṇasamuccaya. For the advanced student.

(12) INADA, KENNETH K. "Some Basic Misconceptions of Buddhism." International Philosophical Quarterly 9 (1969):101-19.
Clarification of some labels attached to Buddhist thought, such as pessimism, nihilism, agnosticism, relativism, and monism.

(13) JAYATILLEKE, K.N. "Avijjā." In Encyclopaedia of Buddhism (see 1.1[21]) 2:454-59.
A fine analysis of ignorance (avidyā) by an authority on Buddhist epistemology.

(14) JAYATILLEKE, K.N. Early Buddhist Theory of Knowledge. London: George Allen & Unwin, 1963, 519 pp.
The most comprehensive and authoritative account of early Buddhist theory of knowledge; problems of authority, reason, analysis and meaning, logic and truth, means and limits of knowledge, are analyzed in great detail. Recommended for all serious students.

(15) KALUPAHANA, DAVID J. "Aññā." In Encyclopaedia of Buddhism (see 1.1[21] 1:693-96.
The article examines the nature of the insight a saint develops with the attainment of freedom (nirvāṇa).

(16) KALUPAHANA, DAVID J. Buddhist Philosophy: A Historical Analysis (see 1.1[17]).
A brief statement on the early Buddhist theory of knowledge, indicating its empirical approach.

(17) KALUPAHANA, DAVID J. "A Buddhist Tract on Empiricism." Philosophy East and West 19 (1969):65-67.
A brief exposition of the significance of the discourse on everything (sabba-sutta) of the kindred sayings of the Buddha (Saṃyutta-nikāya), containing the early Buddhist statement of empiricism.

(18) La VALLÉE POUSSIN, LOUIS de. "Documents d'Abhidharma. Les deux, les quatre, les trois vérités." Mélanges chinois et bouddhiques 5 (1937):159-87.
A French translation of selections from the Abhidharma texts, such as the Vibhāṣā and Saṅghabhadra's commentary on Vasubandhu's Abhidharmakośa, dealing with the problems of two, four and three truths.

(19) LINQUIST, SIGURD. Siddhi and Abhiññā (see 6[52]).

(20) MIYAMOTO, SHŌSON. "Voidness and Middle Way." In Studies on Buddhism in Japan, I (see [10]), pp. 73-92.
An early exposition on the tenets of Mādhyamika philosophy by an authority. Quite technical at times but gives a comprehensive view of the ultimate identity of the middle-way doctrine and voidness (śūnyatā). For the advanced student.

(21) NARAIN, HARSH. "Śūnyavāda: A Reinterpretation." Philosophy East and West 13 (1964):311-38.
The reinterpretation consists of a return to earlier interpretations by Indians and Westerners alike that Śūnyavāda (i.e., Mādhyamika) is a form of absolute nihilism rather than absolutism or absolutistic monism. Some of the readings of Nāgārjuna's ideas are strained.

(22) PANDEYA, R.C. "The Mādhyamika Philosophy: A New Approach" (see 1.2.2.1[5]).
The author reduces the Mādhyamika (Śūnyavāda) to an analytical philosophy, engaged in concepts and language, which reduction has a definite modern Western influence. He concludes that it is an analytic system with a negative function.

(23) POTTER, KARL H. Presuppositions of India's Philosophies. Englewood Cliffs: Prentice-Hall, 1963, 276 pp.
A serious attempt to consider the basic conditions leading to the life of freedom (mokṣa). Contains analysis of Buddhist systems, such as Mādhyamika, Yogācāra, and that of the logicians. An indispensable guide.

(24) PRAKASH, BUDDHA. "Buddhist Methodology." Journal of the Bihar Research Society (Patna) [Buddha Jayanti Special Issue] (1956):35-46.
A succinct and helpful essay that points to the experimentalistic and practical nature of Buddhist approaches to truth and reality.

(25) PRASAD, JWALA. "Discussion of the Buddhist Doctrines of Momentariness and Subjective Idealism in the Nyāyasūtras." Journal of the Royal Asiatic Society, Jan. 1930, pp. 31-39.
A confused article, dealing not with the concept of momentariness, but trying to ascertain whether the Nyāyasūtras belong to either Mādhyamika or Yogācāra.

(26) RAMANAN, VENKATA KRISHNIAH. Nāgārjuna's Philosophy as Presented in the Mahā-Prajñāpāramitā-Śāstra. Rutland: Charles E. Tuttle, 1966, 409 pp.
Although the work used is dubiously attributed to Nāgārjuna, it still belongs to the Mahāyāna tradition, presenting essentials of

the Mādhyamika position. This is a formidable work, worthy of attention. A helpful introduction to Nāgārjuna's philosophy is included.

(27) RHYS-DAVIDS, C.A.F. "Reality." In Encyclopaedia of Religion and Ethics. Vol. 10, pp. 592-93.
A very brief article representing an attempt to explain the notion of reality or truth (satya) in early Buddhism and its development in Theravāda Abhidhamma. The early Buddhist emphasis on the unreality of the five aggegates (khandha) is contrasted with the later decadent Indian Buddhist and Vedantist sense of the ontological unreality of the objects and impressions of sense.

(28) ROBINSON, RICHARD H. "The Classical Indian Axiomatic." Philosophy East and West 18 (1967):139-54.
A brilliant presentation of certain axiomatic presuppositions in classical Indian philosophy, drawing mainly from Śaṅkara and Nāgārjuna.

(29) ROBINSON, RICHARD. "Did Nāgārjuna Really Refute All Philosophical Views?" Philosophy East and West 22 (1972):325-31.
The author examines the assumptions that underlie Nāgārjuna's critique of opposing views.

(30) ROBINSON, RICHARD H. "Some Methodological Approaches to the Unexplained Points." Philosophy East and West 22 (1972): 309-23.
Analysis of the ten or fourteen indeterminate questions (avyākṛta vastuni).

(31) RUEGG, D. SEYFORT. "On the Knowability and Expressibility of Absolute Reality in Buddhism." Indogaku Bukkyōgaku Kenkyū (Journal of Indian and Buddhist Studies) 20 (1971): 489-95.
Based on his monumental work on the Tathāgata-garbha, Ruegg discusses the epistemology and expressibility of absolute reality in Buddhism.

(32) SASAKI, GENJUN M. "The Three Aspects of Truth in Buddhist Epistemology." Journal of the Oriental Institute, Baroda, 1965, pp. 236-51.
The author analyzes the three forms of truth (satya), i.e., absolute (paramārtha), conventional (saṃvṛtti), and existence (bhāva), by examining the etymological roots as reflected in the Pali and Sanskrit sources. Somewhat technical but worth reading.

(33) SHASTRI, DHARMENDRA NATH. Critique of Indian Realism: A Study of the Conflict between the Nyāya-vaiśeṣika and the Buddhist Dignāga School. Agra: Agra University, 1964, 562 pp.
A solid comparative work on logic and epistemology in the Indian tradition. For the advanced student.

(34) SPRUNG, MERVYN, ed. The Problem of Two Truths in Buddhism and Vedānta. Dordrecht: Reidel Pub. Co., 1973, 125 pp.
Nine contributors, including the editor, have confronted the basic epistemological dichotomy in Buddhist and Vedantic truths. Most of the papers are concentrated on the Mādhyamika system. Much old ground is covered, but some new ground is broken. For the advanced student.

(35) SUZUKI, D.T. "Zen, A Reply to Hu Shih" (see 6[82]).

(36) SWEARER, DONALD K. "Two Types of Saving Knowledge in the Pāli Suttas" (see 6[84]).

(37) TAMURA, YOSHIRŌ. "Affirmation and Negation." In Encyclopaedia of Buddhism (see 1.1[21]) 1:237-39.
An overview of the concepts as seen in Buddhist literature. A good introduction.

(38) TATIA, NATHMAL. "The Avyākṛtas or Indeterminables." Nava-Nālandā Mahāvihāra Research Publication 2 (1960):139-60.
An attempt to clarify the problems involved in interpreting the nature of the indeterminate.

(39) UEDA, YOSHIFUMI. "Thinking in Buddhist Philosophy." Philosophical Studies of Japan 5 (1964):69-94.
A profound analysis of the nature of Buddhist wisdom (prajñā) by an outstanding Japanese Buddhist thinker. Thinking involves the cognizing self as well as the cognized self or the intuitive as well as the discriminative natures. Wisdom encompasses and penetrates both realms. For the advanced student.

(40) UEDA, YOSHIFUMI. "The World and the Individual in Mahāyāna Philosophy" (see 2[13]).
Discussion of the fundamental way of thinking in Buddhist philosophy, where the true nature of the self is ultimately known, resolving all dichotomies, and where the individual and the world, the one and many, are finally accommodated. This study surveys the ontological status of "self" and the epistemological picture of the bifurcation of "subject/object structure" in the world and the resolution of that bifurcation in the Yogācāra Buddhist philosophy.

(41) No entry

(42) WAYMAN, ALEX. "The Buddhist 'Not This, Not That.'" Philosophy East and West 11 (1961):99-114.
A good textual presentation of the various basic doctrines as related to the indeterminate nature of things.

(43) WOLFF, ERICH. Zur Lehre vom Bewusststein (Vijñānavāda) bei den spateren Buddhisten: Unter besonderer Berucksichtigung des Laṅkāvatārasūtra. Materialien zur Kunde des Buddhismus, no. 17. Heidelberg, n.p., 1930, 90 pp.
The work is divided into two parts: 1) a historical survey of the concept of consciousness from the earliest times to the Yogācāra school, and 2) a systematic presentation of the concept of consciousness based on the first seven chapters of the Laṅkāvatāra. A fundamental work for advanced students who read German.

(44) YAMAGUCHI, S. "Examen de l'objet de la connaissance (Ālambanaparīkṣā). Textes tibetain et chinois et traduction des stances et du commentaire. Éclaicissements et notes d'après le commentaire tibetain de Vinitadeva--en collaboration avec Henriette Meyer." Journal asiatique, Jan.-Mar. 1929, pp. 1-65.
Contains much more information and a better discussion of the Ālambanaparīkṣā than the translation and study of Frauwallner (8). Since this work of Dignāga is not on logic, but relates to the doctrines of the Vijñānavādins, it is extremely important for gaining insight into the larger philosophical thought of Dignāga. Fundamental for students of Dignāga.

(45) ZEYST, M.G.A. van. "Analogies." In Encyclopaedia of Buddhism (see 1.1[21]) 1:518-27.
An illuminating essay on the analogies found so abundantly in Buddhist literature. A helpful aid.

(46) ZEYST, M.G.A. van. "Avyākata." In Encyclopaedia of Buddhism (see 1.1[21]) 2:464-66.
A brief analysis of the concept of the indeterminate or the unexplained with respect to Buddhist reality.

8 Metaphysics and Ontology

(1) BAREAU, A., Y. TAMURA, and H.G.A. van ZEYST. "Absolute." In Encyclopaedia of Buddhism (see 1.1[21]) 1:140-51.
Three scholars contribute different aspects of the concept of absolute in Buddhism. Some overlapping, but they form a good introduction to the concept.

(2) BAREAU, A. "The Notion of Time in Early Buddhism." East-West 7 (1957):353-64.
A detailed analysis of the controversies concerning the notion of time in the ancient Buddhist schools.

(3) BARUA, B.M. "Pratītyasamutpāda as a Basic Concept of Buddhist Thought." B.C. Law Memorial Volume. 2 vols. Calcutta: Bhandarkar Oriental Institute, 1945. 1:574-89.
Discusses the centrality of the doctrine of causation in Buddhist philosophy and examines some epistemological questions regarding freedom from the chain of causation represented by the twelvefold formula of causation.

(4) BHATTACHARYA, VIDHUSHEKHARA. The Basic Conception of Buddhism (see 1.2.1[4]).
Analysis of the Buddha's position on nonsubstantiality (anātman) in the context of dependent origination (pratītyasamutapāda). The exposition is from the viewpoint of Mādhyamika and interprets early canonical works in that light.

(5) CHANG, GARMA C.C. The Buddhist Teaching of Totality: The Philosophy of Hwa Yen Buddhism. University Park: Penn State University Press, 1971, 270 pp.
A comprehensive book on Hua-yen Buddhism. The work is divided into two parts, a study of the philosophical foundations of Hua-yen Buddhism and a selection of translations from Hua-yen texts. The book is often lacking from the point of view of the professional scholar, but the subject is too important to deny the value of the book. Should be used with caution.

(6) CHATTERJEE, ASHOK KUMAR. The Yogācāra Idealism. Banaras Hindu University, 1962, 309 pp.
The author examines the principal doctrines of Buddhist idealism, i.e., the Yogācāra system. Although he does not use any Tibetan or Chinese texts or their French translations, this philosophical treatise is a contribution based on the Sanskrit texts. It should, however, be used with caution due to its Vedantic bias and Western interpretation.

(7) CHI, RICHARD S.Y. "Topics on Being and Logical Reasoning." Philosophy East and West 24 (1974):293-300.
Discussion on the Buddhist concept of being (bhāva) and the nature of logical reasoning in Buddhism, especially Zen.

(8) CHI-TSANG. "Theory of Double Truth." A History of Chinese Philosophy (see 1.3[7]) 2:293-99.
Translation and running commentary of Chi-tsang's short but important treatise on the twofold nature of Buddhist truth. Compare with W.T. Chan's translation in his Source Book in Chinese Philosophy (9).

(9) CHI-TSANG. "Treatise on the Two Levels of Truth and the Profound Meaning of the Three Treatises." In A Source Book in Chinese Philosophy (see 1.3[1]), pp. 357-69.
Basic ideas on the Mādhyamika system expressed by a Chinese Buddhist thinker.

(10) COLLINS, WILLIAM J.H. "The Middle Way in Clear Words." Eastern Buddhist, n.s. 5 (1972):130-38.
This is a refreshing short article on the Middle Way. Collins compares the notion of causation of the Abhidharmikas and the Mādhyamikas.

(11) CONZE, EDWARD, trans. Aṣṭasāhasrikā Prajñāpāramitā (see 4[5]).

(12) CONZE, EDWARD. "The Ontology of the Prajñāpāramitā" (see 6[17]).
The Prajñāpāramitā-sūtras do not merely discuss the concept of emptiness. Its basis is the solid ontology that is analyzed authoritatively in the article. The ontological status of dharmas is considered in six ways, including psychological attitudes and religious motives.

(13) CONZE, EDWARD, ed. and trans. Vajracchedikā Prajñāpāramitā. Serie Orientale Roma, no. 13. Rome: Istituto italiano per il medio ed Estremo Oriente. 1957, 113 pp.

The best translation of this short but significant treatise so far (popularly referred to as the "Diamond Sutra") on attaining the nature of wisdom (prajñā). A helpful introduction, together with the Sanskrit text, is included.

(14) COOK, FRANCIS H. "The Meaning of Vairocana in Hua-yen Buddhism." Philosophy East and West 22 (1972):403-15.
An analysis of the concept of absolute reality (Vairocana) in Hua-yen metaphysics. A good place to begin.

(15) EDGERTON, FRANKLIN. "Did the Buddha Have a System of Metaphysics?" American Oriental Society 79 (1959):81-85.
A short but critical analysis by one of the leading scholars in Indian and Buddhist thought and language. Worth reading.

(16) FALK, MARYLA. "Nairātmya and Karman." In Louis de La Vallée Poussin Memorial Volume. Edited by N.N. Law. Calcutta: Calcutta Oriental Press, 1940, pp. 429-64.
Falk takes up de La Vallée Poussin's lifelong problem of seeking a rationale in the coexistence of the Buddhist concepts of non-self (nairātmya) and deed (karma). La Vallée Poussin ends up rather weakly in a soteriological solution.

(17) FA-TSANG. "Essay on the Gold Lion." In A History of Chinese Philosophy (see 1.3[7]) 2:339-59.
Fung presents a reliable accounting of this highly metaphysical work on the nature of Buddhist reality. Good excerpted translations included.

(18) FA-TSANG. "Treatise on the Golden Lion, Hundred Gates to the Sea of Ideas of the Flowery Splendor Scripture." In Source Book in Chinese Philosophy (see 1.3[1]), pp. 406-24.
Important translation of this profound work by one of China's greatest Buddhist minds.

(19) GEIGER, MAGDALENE, and WILHELM GEIGER. Pali Dhamma. Munich: Bavarian Academy of Science, 1921, 129 pp.
The most exhaustive account of the various meanings of the term dhamma occurring in Pali literature. In German.

(20) GOKHALE, V.V. "Gotama's Vision of the Truth." Adyar Library Bulletin 30 (1966):105-21.
A short doctrinal analysis of the development of Gotama's vision when he saw "the Truth of the Total Universe in a flash of Enlightenment." Gokhale describes the transformation of that vision to philosophy in the Mādhyamika and Yogācāra schools.

(21) GRIMM, GEORGE. The Doctrine of the Buddha: The Religion of Reason and Meditation (see 4[12]), pp. 163-226.
An exhaustive analysis of the doctrine of dependent origination (paṭiccasamuppāda) consisting of the twelvefold formula.

(22) GUENTHER, HERBERT V. "Concept of Mind in Buddhist Tantrism." Journal of the Oriental Society 3 (1965):261-77.
Guenther deals with the two major elements of Buddhist Tantrism, i.e., the religiophilosophical and the psychomeditational backgrounds.

(23) GUENTHER, HERBERT V. "The Levels of Understanding in Buddhism" (see 7[9]).

(24) GUENTHER, HERBERT V. "Philosophical Background of Buddhist Tantrism." Journal of the Oriental Society 5 (1959-62): 45-64.
The psychomeditational nature of Tantrism.

(25) HAMILTON, CLARENCE. "Encounter with Reality in Buddhist Mādhyamika Philosophy." Journal of Bible and Religion 26 (1958):13-22.
Prompted by T.R.V. Murti's The Central Philosophy of Buddhism, Hamilton, an expert on Yogācāra Buddhism, discusses an "encounter with reality" in Mādhyamika. An interesting article.

(26) HAYASHIMA, KYŌSHŌ. "Dialogue Relating to Ātman and Anātman in Milindapañha." Toyo University Asian Studies 1 (1961): 7-13.
A short but illuminating analysis of both concepts as they appear in the Milindapañha.

(27) HIRAKAWA, AKIRA, et al. Index to the Abhidharmakośabhāṣya. Part One: Sanskrit-Tibetan-Chinese. Tokyo: Daizo Shuppan Kabushiki Kaisha, 1973, 437 pp.
This is a monumental indexing work done by Hirakawa in collaboration with four other scholars. Special attention is called to the introduction, rendered into readable English, which outlines the history of the Abhidharmakośa. Also includes a brief but helpful analysis of the contents of the eight chapters.

(28) IINO, NORIMOTO. "Dōgen's Zen View of Interdependence." Philosophy East and West 12 (1962):51-57.
An estimation of a Japanese Zen Master's view on the reality of things.

(29) INADA, KENNETH K. "Buddhist Naturalism and the Myth of Rebirth." International Journal for Philosophy of Religion 1 (1970):46-53.
A reappraisal of Buddhist philosophy construed from within a naturalistic framework and the reinterpretation of the concept of rebirth.

(30) INADA, KENNETH K. "Time and Temporality--A Buddhist Approach." Philosphy East and West 24 (1974):171-79.
An examination of the conventional (limited) nature of time leads the Buddhist to widen his perspective by way of the nonconventional (nonlimited) nature of experience, i.e., the unique way in which temporal events or experiences actually take place.

(31) JAINI, PADMANABH S. Abhidharmadīpa with Vibhāshaprabhā[v]ritti (see 6[38]).

(32) JONG, JAN W. de. Review of Douze Chapitres de la Prasannapadā, by J. May. Indo-Tranian Journal 5 (1961): 161-63.
An important review of an important work (55) by one of the best reviewers in the fields of Indian and Buddhist studies. In French.

(33) JONG, JAN W. de. "Le problème de l'Absolu dans l'école Mādhyamika." Revue philosophique 140 (1950):322-27.
In this learned article, de Jong demonstrates that it is impossible to consider the absolute of Mādhyamika, whether as the totality of being or as nothingness (néant). He also demonstrates the danger of a hasty analogy with Western philosophical systems.

(34) KAJIYAMA, YUICHI. "Bhāvaviveka and the Prāsaṅgika School." Nava-Nālandā-Mahāvihāra Research Publications 1 (1957): 291-331.
Within the Mādhyamika school, the Prāsaṅgika considers the absolute as entirely transcendent, while the Svātantrika takes the absolute as immanent. A fine account of this important aspect of the Mādhyamika philosophy and logic.

(35) KAJIYAMA, YUICHI. "Trikapañcakacinta: Development of the Buddhist Theory on the Determination of Causality." Miscellanea Indologica Kiotiensia 4-5 (1963):1-15.
An important, tightly-packed article by an outstanding Japanese scholar.

(36) KALUPAHANA, DAVID J. "The Buddhist Conception of Time and Temporality." Philosophy East and West 24 (1974):181-91.
Analysis of the different conceptions of time and temporality in early Buddhism, the Abhidharma, and Mādhyamika.

(37) KALUPAHANA, DAVID J. Buddhist Philosophy: A Historical Analysis (see 1.1[17]).
A summary of the essential elements of the doctrine of causation in early Buddhism as presented in the author's Causality: The Central Philosophy of Buddhism (38).

(38) KALUPAHANA, DAVID J. Causality: The Central Philosophy of Buddhism. Honolulu: University of Hawaii Press, 1975, 265 pp.
A comprehensive analysis of the doctrine of causality (pratītya-samutpāda) in early Buddhism as embodied in the Pali Nikāyas and the Chinese Āgamas, together with a description of the development of the doctrine in the later schools of scholasticism (abhidharma) and Mahāyāna.

(39) KALUPAHANA, DAVID J. "The Philosophy of Relations in Buddhism." University of Ceylon Review 19 (1961):167-94; 20 (1962):19-54, 188-208.
These two articles are devoted to an analysis of the Abhidamma doctrine of causal correlations (paccaya) as enunciated in the Paṭṭhāna.

(40) KARUNARATNE, W.E., K. MIZUNO, and H.G.A. van ZEYST. "Abhidhamma." In Encyclopaedia of Buddhism (see 1.1[21]) 1:37-49.
Three scholars contribute to an understanding of the Buddhist metaphysics of experience. They analyze the method, characteristics, and subject matter of the Abhidhamma. Some overlapping information but generally sound presentations. Cf. Mizuno's lengthy article on "Abhidharma Literature" in the same volume (pp. 64-80).

(41) KARUNADASA, Y. Buddhist Analysis of Matter. Colombo: Department of Cultural Affairs, 1970, 186 pp.
A detailed study of the conception of matter (rūpa), with emphasis on interpretations drawn from the Abhidharma literature.

(42) KING, WINSTON L. "Causality: Eternal or Momentary." Philosophy East and West 13 (1963):117-35.
This is a comparative study of Śaṅkara's concept of the eternal nature of Brahman and the later Buddhists' (Śāntarakṣita, Kamalaśīla) concept of the momentary nature of existence. The author first shows the difference but in the end attempts to conciliate the two realms of existence.

(43) KIYOTA, MINORU. "The Three Modes of Encompassing in the Vijñaptimātratā System, Their Correlated Meaning in the Structural Totality of the Human Consciousness." Journal of Indian and Buddhist Studies 10 (1962):386-81.
An analysis of the svabhāva-traya (three self-natures) doctrine of the Yogācāra.

(44) KONOW, STEN, ed. The Two First Chapters of the Daśasāhasrikā Prajñāpāramitā: Restoration of the Sanskrit Text, Analysis and Index. Oslo: Jacōb Dywad, 1941.
A good analysis of this restored text (from the Tibetan) expounding on the quest for wisdom (prajñā) by the bodhisattva.

(45) KOROS, ALEXANDER CROMA de. "Notes on Mādhyamika Philosophy." Journal of the Buddhist Text Society of India 6 (1898):22.
One of the earliest accounts on the subject to have been based on Tibetan sources.

(46) LANCASTER, LEWIS R. "Discussion of Time in Mahāyāna Texts." Philosophy East and West 24 (1974):209-14.
Succinct.

(47) La VALLÉE POUSSIN, LOUIS de. "Buddhica." Harvard Journal of Asian Studies 3 (1938):137-60.
An important article by de La Vallée Poussin, who selects several topics pertaining to Mahāyāna Buddhist sūtras and concepts. Definitely for advanced students.

(48) La VALLÉE POUSSIN, LOUIS de. "Documents d'Abhidharma la controverse des temps." Mélanges chinois et bouddhiques 1 (1931-32):65-112.
French translation of selections from the Abhidharma texts pertaining to the problem of time. Selections are 1) a fragment of the Vibhāṣā, and 2) a part of the commentary on Vasubandhu's Abhidharmakośa by Saṅghabhadra. A note on the controversy regarding the moment (kṣaṇa) between the Sarvāstivāda and Sautrāntika schools is also included.

(49) La VALLÉE POUSSIN, LOUIS de. Théorie des douze causes. Ghent: University of Ghent, 1913.
Examination, in French, of the twelvefold chain of causation on the basis of the discussion in the Āryaśālistambasūtra, reconstructed by the author from Chinese and Tibetan translations.

(50) La VALLÉE POUSSIN, LOUIS de. "The Mādhyamikas and the Tathatā." Indian Historical Quarterly 9 (1933):30-31.
Poussin's articles are very important, even when they are only a page or two long like this one, as they are the result of extensive research in original materials.

(51) LEDI, SAYADAW. "On the Philosophy of Relations." Translated into English and annotated by S.Z. Aung. Journal of the Pali Text Society, 1916, pp. 21-53.
A comprehensive analysis of the doctrine of causal correlations (paccaya) of the Theravāda school of Buddhism, based on the author's own work written in Pali, Paccayatthadipani.

(52) LIEBENTHAL, WALTER, trans. Chao Lun: The Treatises of Seng-chao. Hong Kong: Hong Kong University Press, 1968, 152 pp.
A rather faithful rendition of the four treatises of Seng-chao, a disciple of Kumārajīva and a follower of the Mādhyamika school. The treatises are: "On Time"; "On Śūnyatā"; "On Prajñā not Cognizant"; and "Nirvāṇa Is Unnameable." There is a lengthy and very helpful introduction to Seng-chao's thought. For the advanced student. Compare selections with W.T. Chan's Sourcebook (1.3[1]) and R.H. Robinson's Early Mādhyamika (1.2.2.1[7]).

(53) MALALASEKERA, G.P. "Anattā." In Encyclopaedia of Buddhism (see 6[54]).

(54) MASSON-OURSEL, P. "Essai d'interprétation des théories des douze conditions." Revue de l'histoire des religions 71 (1915):30-46.
The article deals with the twelvefold formula of causation in early Buddhism.

(55) MAY, JACQUES. Candrakīrti, Prasannapadā Mādhyamikavṛtti: chapitres traduits du sanscrit et du tibetain, accompagnés d'une introduction, de notes et d'une édition critique de la version tibetaine. Paris: Adrien-Maissonneuve, 1959.
Since the 1903-13 publication by de La Vallée Poussin of the Prasannapāda, it has been rendered into western languages by five men, i.e., Stcherbatsky (chapters 1 and 25, 1927), Schayer (chapters 5, 10, and 12-16, 1931), Lamotte (chapter 17, 1936), de Jong (chapters 18-22, 1949), and May (chapters 2-4, 6-9, 23-24, and 26-27, 1959). Of these, all but Lamotte and May have translated into a language not their mother tongue. May's excellent translation brought this half-century-old endeavor to fruition.

(56) MAY, JACQUES. "Kant et le Mādhyamika." Indo-Iranian Journal 3 (1959):102-11.
While reviewing Murti's Central Philosophy of Buddhism (see 1.2.1[11], 1.2.2.1[3]), May criticizes him on several points. For example, Mādhyamika's fusion of subject/object in absolute reality excludes any Kantian "Copernican revolution." A valuable resource for a comparative study.

(57) MAY, JACQUES. "La philosophie bouddhiste de la vacuité." Studia Philosophica 18 (1958):123-37.
An illuminative analysis of the Buddhist notion of emptiness by the translator of twelve chapters of the Prasannapadā, one of the most important texts on Buddhist emptiness.

(58) McDERMOTT, A. CHARLENE. "The Sautrāntika Arguments Against the Traikālyavāda in the Light of Contemporary Tense Revolution." Philosophy East and West 24 (1974):193-200.
Illuminating analysis of the notion of three temporal moments in the Sautrāntika-Sarvāstivādin debate and viewed in the light of modern tense logic.

(59) McDERMOTT, JAMES P. "The Kathāvatthu Kamma Debates." Journal of the American Oriental Society 95 (1975):424-33.
Exposition of the concept of kamma as developed in one of the Abhidhamma works. Recommended to all.

(60) MITCHELL, DONALD W. "Analysis in Theravāda Buddhism." Philosophy East and West 21 (1971):23-31.
The author starts with the Humean analysis of the self and then shows that the Buddhist concept of the self, due to its inherent non-self, is different. Where Humean analysis is epistemologically oriented, the Buddhist is religious in the end.

(61) MITCHELL, DONALD W. "An Early View of Man in Indian Buddhism." International Philosophical Quarterly 14 (1974):189-99.
An expository essay on the nature of man in the Sarvāstivāda tradition with a critique from the Sautrāntika school. A good start.

(62) MITCHELL, DONALD W. "The No-Self Doctrine in Theravāda Buddhism." International Philosophical Quarterly 9 (1969): 248-60.
A faithful analysis of the nature of man and the path of purification that he must take. Good beginning in the study of early Buddhist thought.

(63) MIYAMOTO, SHŌSON. "The Logic of Relativity as the Common Ground for the Development of Middle Way." In Buddhism and Culture (Suzuki Festschrift). Tokyo: Suzuki Foundation, 1960, pp. 67-88.
The article surveys the prevailing views of the nature of relativity at the time of the rise of the "Middle Way" concept.

(64) MIYAMOTO, SHŌSON. "The Middle Path Concept in History and Society." In Tōyō Bunka Ronshū (Fukui Festschrift). Tokyo: Waseda University Press, 1969, pp. 35-57.
Another essay on the "Middle Way" concept as it is related to social and historical forces.

(65) MIYAMOTO, SHŌSON. "The Middle Way from the Standpoint of the Dharma." Indogaku Bukkyōgaku Kenkyū (Journal of Indian and Buddhist Studies) 17 (March 1969):963-932.
An attempt to tie in the "Middle Way" concept with the nature of Buddhist reality.

(66) MIYAMOTO, SHŌSON. "A Re-appraisal of Pratītyasamutpāda." Studies in Indology and Buddhology (Susumu Yamaguchi Commemoration Volume), 1955, pp. 152-64.
A solid essay exploring the problems and facets of the concept of dependent origination.

(67) MIYAMOTO, SHŌSON. "'Ultimate Middle' as the Fundamental Principle of Buddhism." Religious Studies in Japan (see 1.2.2[10]), pp. 235-56.
Compared with Miyamoto's numerous writings on the subject of the ultimate middle and emptiness, his English articles are rather limited. This article, therefore, gives us the essentials of his ideas.

(68) MOOKERJEE, S. "A Buddhist Estimate of the Universals." Indian Culture 1 (1934):359-74.
A discussion of the Buddhist arguments against the Nyāya-vaiśeşika realistic schools based on the Tattvasamgraha. For advanced students only.

(69) MOOKERJEE, SATKARI. The Buddhist Philosophy of Universal Flux (see 1.1[19]).
Although basically a treatise on critical realism as expounded by Dignāga, the work contains a lengthy discussion on the conception of time of the Sautrāntika school of Buddhism.

(70) MOOKERJEE, SATKARI. "The Nature of Ultimate Reality." Nava-Nālandā Mahāvihāra Research Publication 2 (1960): 47-74.

This is a general essay on Indian concepts of reality as seen in the various schools but includes an interesting comparative analysis of Vedantic and Buddhist (mainly Sarvāstivāda and Mādhyamika) views.

(71) NAGAO, GADJIN M. "Buddhist Subjectivity" (see 3[16]).

(72) NAGAO, GADJIN M. "An Interpretation of the Term Saṃvṛti (Convention)." Sōritsu Nijugoshūnen Kinen Ronbunshū (Silver Jubilee Volume of the Institute of Humanistic Studies, Kyoto University) 1 (1957).
Having established the two possible roots of the word saṃvṛti, i.e., sam-vṛ, "to conceal," and sam-vṛt, "to become," Nagao further suggests that this difference may indicate the difference in attitude between the Mādhyamika and the Yogācāra schools.

(73) NAGAO, GADJIN M. "The Silence of the Buddha and its Mādhyamic Interpretation." Studies in Indology and Buddhology (S. Yamaguchi Commemorative Volume), 1955, pp. 137-51.
One of the best articles on "the Silence of the Buddha." Nagao examines the questions of language, logic and absolute reality from the point of view of the Mādhyamika school as expressed by Buddha's silence. Recommended to all.

(74) NAGAO, GADJIN. "On the Theory of Buddha-Body." Eastern Buddhist, n.s. 6 (1973):25-53.
This is a clear and authoritative analysis of the theories concerning the Buddha-body (buddha-kāya), which underwent various developments during the course of the spread of Buddhism in Asia.

(75) NAKAMURA, HAJIME. "Interrelational Existence" (see 3[18]).

(76) ÑĀṆAMOLI, Bhikkhu. "Anicca." In Encyclopaedia of Buddhism (see 1.1[21]) 1:657-63.
A solid essay on the concept of impermanence as seen in early Buddhist literature. A good beginning.

(77) NISHITANI, KEIJI. "Nihilism and Śūnyatā." Eastern Buddhist, n.s. 4, no. 1 (1971):30-49; 5, no. 1 (1972): 55-69; 5, no. 2 (1972):95-106.
Nishitani deals with the problem of personality and materiality, and also the problem of the modes of being of a thing and of a self. A highly original interpretation. For the serious student.

(78) NISHITANI, KEIJI. "The Standpoint of Śūnyatā." Eastern Buddhist, n.s. 6, no. 1 (1973):68-91; 6, no. 2 (1973): 58-86.
Provides a penetrating analysis of śūnyatā or emptiness by a leading Japanese philosopher. Originally written in Japanese.

(79) NYANAPONIKA, Thera, ed. The Basic Facts of Existence. 3 volumes. Kandy: Buddhist Publication Society, 1973-74.
These three small volumes contain short but useful essays on the three basic characteristics (lakkhana) of existence according to early Theravāda Buddhism--impermanence (anicca), suffering (dukkha) and nonsubstantiality (anattā).

(80) NYANATILOKA, Bhikku. Guide Through the Abhidhamma-Piṭaka, Being a Synopsis of the Philosophical Collection Belonging to the Buddhist Pali Canon, followed by an Essay on the Paṭiccasamuppāda. Colombo: Bauddha Sahitya Sabha, 1957, 179 pp.
A rather technical but important guide through the seven Abhidhamma works. A very helpful look into the contents and purpose of the works.

(81) OBERMILLER, E. "Nirvāṇa According to Tibetan Tradition." Indian Historical Quarterly 5 (1929):211-57.
Obermiller's contribution to the Western great debate on nirvāṇa. See Guy Welbon, The Buddhist Nirvāṇa and its Western Interpreters (1.1[42]).

(82) OBERMILLER, E. "A Study of the Twenty Aspects of Śūnyatā Based on Haribhadra's Abhisamayālaṁkārāloka and the Pañcaviṃśatisāhasrikā." Indian Historical Quarterly 9 (1933): 170-87.
An elucidation of the term śūnyatā, as interpreted by the Mādhyamika school, and the analysis of eight principal subjects and seventy topics in the works of Maitreya and Asanga.

(83) O'BRIEN, PAUL WILFRED, trans. "A Chapter on Reality from the Madhyāntavibhāgaśāstra." Monumenta Nipponica 9 (Apr. 1953):277-303.
Fairly good translation from the Chinese text and copious annotations on chapter 3 of Vasubandhu's work. It should be read in conjunction with Friedmann's Sthiramati: Madhyāntavibhāgatikā (14.3.2[1]) and Stcherbatsky's Madhyānta-vibhanga: A Discourse on Discrimination between Middle and Extremes (14.3.2[4]), both of which are on chapter 1. For the advanced student.

(84) OLTRAMARE, P. La formule bouddhique des douze causes: Son sens original et son interpretation théologique. Geneva: Georg, 1909, 52 pp.
A very sympathetic interpretation of the twelvefold formula of causation in early Buddhism.

(85) ORGAN, TROY WILSON. "The Silence of the Buddha." Philosophy East and West 4 (1954):125-40.
A review of the reasons for the Buddha's silence on metaphysical questions. He concludes that silence does not prevent one from metaphysicizing on Buddhist doctrines.

(86) PANDEYA, R.C. "The Mādhyamika Philosophy" (see 1.2.2.1[5]).
The author reduces the Mādhyamika (śūnyavāda) to an analytical philosophy.

(87) POTTER, KARL H. Presuppositions of India's Philosophies (see 7[23]).
A serious attempt to consider the basic conditions leading to the life of freedom (mokṣa).

(88) RAMANAN, VENKATA KRISHNIAH. Nāgārjuna's Philosophy as Presented in the Mahā-Prajñāpāramitā-Śāstra (see 7[26]).

(89) RHYS-DAVIDS, C.A.F. "Paṭiccasamuppāda." Encyclopaedia of Religion and Ethics. Vol. 9, pp. 672-74.
The article consists of a basic discussion of the problem of causation in early Buddhism.

(90) RHYS-DAVIDS, C.A.F. "Reality" (see 7[27]).

(91) RHYS-DAVIDS, C.A.F. "Relations." In Encyclopaedia of Religion and Ethics. Vol. 10, pp. 648-49.
This short article contains a critical analysis of the theory of causal correlations (paccaya) in the Theravāda Abhidhamma, especially as embodied in the Paṭṭhāna.

(92) SAIGUSA, MITSUYOSHI. Studien zum Mahāprajñāpāramitā (upadeśa) Śāstra. Tokyo: Hokuseido Verlag, 1969, 239 pp.
This is a critical dissertation in German on one of Nāgārjuna's alleged works. It discusses the author, the translations, the structure of the work, and the sources of the quotations. It also presents an exhaustive analysis of the key concepts in the work. Compare with Ramanan's work (88).

(93) SCHAYER, STANISLAV. Mahāyāna Doctrines of Salvation (see 4[28]).

(94) SCHAYER, STANISLAV. "Das Mahāyānistische Absolutum nach der Lehre der Mādhyamikas." Orientalistischer Literaturzeitung 38 (1935):401-15.
This article analyzes the Mahāyānist concept of the absolute according to Mādhyamika teaching. It is a reply to Stcherbatsky's criticism of the absolutistic interpretation of Mādhyamika.

(95) SCHAYER, STANISLAV. Review of O.O. Rosenberg's Problems of Buddhist Philosophy. Rocznik Orientalistyczny 1-2 (1916-18):292-307.
Extremely well-written critical review in English on Buddhist ontology and metaphysics. Good reading for the student at any level.

(96) SENG-CHAO. "The Immutability of Things"; "The Emptiness of the Unreal." In A Source Book in Chinese Philosophy (see 1.3[1]).
Important translations of the first two chapters of Seng-chao's Chao Lun. Compare with Liebenthal's translation of the Chao Lun (52) and Robinson's Early Mādhyamika in India and China (1.2.2.1[7]).

(97) SILVA, C.L.A. de. The Four Essential Doctrines of Buddhism (see 6[78]).

(98) SMART, NINIAN. Doctrine and Argument in Indian Philosophy (see 1.2[16]).
The work has a rather informative chapter on Buddhist metaphysics. Other chapters, for example, on causation and epistemological questions, have Buddhist doctrines interwoven.

(99) STCHERBATSKY, F. TH. The Central Conception of Buddhism and the Meaning of the Word "Dharma." London: Royal Asiatic Society, 1923.
A fundamental work on the metaphysics developed by the Abhidarma scholiasts, as for example embodied in Vasubandhu's famous compendium, the Abhidharmakośa, which represents a mixture of Sarvāstivāda and Sautrāntika ideas. Helpful table of elements is appended. Recommended for the serious student.

(100) STCHERBATSKY, TH. The Conception of Buddhist Nirvāṇa: Translation of Nāgārjuna's Mādhyamikaśastra and Candrakīrti's Prasannapadā. Leningrad: 1927. 246 pp. Reprint. The Hague: Mouton, 1965. Rev. ed. Delhi: Motilal Banarsidass, 1977.
The first part sketches the development of Buddhist philosophy in the schools of Hīnayāna and Mahāyāna. Stcherbatsky had a profound knowledge of both Western and Indian philosophy. He

attacks here the views of nirvāṇa held by de La Vallée Poussin and Keith. The second part of the book contains an English translation of chapters 1 and 25 of Candrakīrti's Prasannapadā. An important work by an important scholar.

(101) STCHERBATSKY, TH. "The 'Dharmas' of the Buddhists and the Guṇas of the Sāṅkhyas." Indian Historical Quarterly 10 (1934):737-60.
Criticism of V. Bhattacharya's view embodied in his Basic Conception of Buddhism (4) that nonsubstantiality of the individual (pudgalanairātmya) as well as of elements (dharmanairātmya) constitutes the teachings of early Buddhism. Stcherbatsky believes that the latter is upheld by the Mahāyāna schools only.

(102) STCHERBATSKY, TH. "Die Drei Richtungen in der Buddhistischen Philosophie." Rocznik Orientalistyczny 10 (1934): 1-35.
The work is directed toward Schayer's 1931 translation of chapters 5 and 12 16, of the Prasannapadā in his Ausdewahlte Kapitel. Stcherbatsky, critical of Schayer, gives his own translation of chapter 15 of the Kārikās.

(103) STCHERBATSKY, TH. The Soul Theory of the Buddhists (see 6[80]).
An authoritative analysis of the theory of nonsubstantiality as seen in the Abhidharmakośa. For the advanced student.

(104) SUZUKI, D.T. "Philosophy of the Yogācāra: The Mādhyamika and the Yogācāra." Le Muséon 5 (1904):370-86.
An important early article by Suzuki on the Mādhyamika and the Yogācāra, the two major branches of Mahāyāna Buddhist philosophy.

(105) TAKASAKI, JIKIDŌ. "Description of the Ultimate Reality." Indogaku Bukkyōgaku Kenkyū (Journal of Indian and Buddhist Studies) 9 (1961):24-33.
Takasaki, a leading authority on Tathāgata-garbha thought in Japan, discusses the description of ultimate reality in Buddhism based on his line of research.

(106) TATIA, NATHMAL. "Paṭiccasamuppāda (Causation in Pali Buddhism)." Nava-Nālandā Mahāvihāra Research Publication 1 (1957):177-239.
A rather exhaustive analysis of this important concept. Good for the beginner.

(107) TATIA, NATHMAL. "Sarvāstivāda." Nava-Nālanda Mahāvihāra Research Publication 2 (1960):75-136.
A good introduction to the Sarvāstivāda (all exist) school.

(108) THOMAS, E.J. The History of Buddhist Thought (see 1.1[39]).
Consists of two chapters dealing with the doctrines of nonsubstantiality (anattā), karma, causation, and nirvāṇa. An excellent historical introduction.

(109) TUCCI, GIUSEPPE, ed. and trans. "Śata-śāstra." In Pre-Diṅnāga Buddhist Texts on Logic from Chinese Sources. Gaekwad's Oriental Series, no. 49. Baroda: Oriental Institute, 1929.
An English translation of fifty of the one hundred verses of Āryadeva, a disciple of Nāgārjuna, who defends the Mādhyamika philosophy.

(110) TUXEN, POUL. Indledende Bemaerkningen til Buddhistik Relativisme. Copenhagen: Blunos, 1936, 102 pp.
Tuxen contributes towards a better understanding of the Mādhyamika philosophy by a study of Candrakīrti's Prasannapadā.

(111) UEDA, YOSHIFUMI. "Vasubandhu was an Ekabhaga- or Aṁsavādin." Proceedings of the 9th International Congress for the History of Religions, Tokyo (1960), pp. 201-6.
A technical essay dealing with the nature of the mind and the realms of existence according to Vasubandhu.

(112) UEDA, YOSHIFUMI. "The World and the Individual in Mahāyāna Buddhist Philosophy" (see 2[13]).

(113) VARMA, VISHWANATH PRASAD. "Early Buddhist Anātmavāda." In World Perspectives in Philosophy, Religion and Culture (Essays Presented to Prof. Dhirendra Mohan Datta). Patna: Bharati Bhawan, 1968, pp. 402-25.
A good introduction to the understanding of the non-self doctrine in early Buddhism, including a few Western interpretations of the doctrine. Very critical of Mrs. Rhys Davids's diversions from her earlier views.

(114) No entry

(115) WARDER, A.K. "Causation." Indian Buddhism (see 1.2[18]), pp. 107-56.
This chapter includes a lengthy discussion of the doctrine of causation or dependent arising (paṭiccasamuppāda) in early Buddhism.

(116) WAYMAN, ALEX. "The Yogācāra Idealism." Philosophy East and West 15 (1965):65-74.
In this review of Chatterjee's Yogācāra Idealism (6), Wayman examines the validity of the current statement, "The Yogācāra holds that consciousness is the sole reality" from the vantages of the Sāmkhya doctrines as well as other important Yogācāra doctrines.

(117) WIJESEKERA, O.H. de A. The Three Signata: Anicca, Dukkha and Anattā. Kandy: Buddhist Publication Society, 1960.
Brief, yet one of the most authoritative analyses of the early Buddhist notion of the three characteristics (tri-lakṣaṇa) of existence.

9 Philosophy of Language

(1) PANDEYA, R.C. "The Mādhyamika Philosophy: A New Approach" (see 1.2.2.1[5]).
The author reduces the Mādhyamika (Śūnyavadā) to an analytical philosophy, engaged in concepts and language.

(2) ROSEMONT, HENRY, Jr. "The Meaning is the Use: Kōan and Mondō as Linguistic Tools of the Zen Masters." Philosophy East and West 20 (1970):109-19.
Kōans and mondōs are said to be prelocutionary speech acts which have specific intent and elicit specific responses: the intent may have very little relevance to the response.

(3) ROSEMONT, HENRY, Jr. "Is Zen Buddhism a Philosophy?" Philosophy East and West 20 (1970):63-72.
Despite numerous statements supporting the nonphilosophical nature of Zen, the author analyzes the prevailing attitudes and beliefs of Zen Buddhists to conclude that Zen can indeed be referred to as a philosophy.

(4) STRENG, FREDRICK J. Emptiness (see 5[15]).
An attempt to understand Nāgārjuna's philosophy of emptiness or ultimate reality with some excursions into modern linguistic analysis.

(5) TAYLOR, RICHARD. "The Anattā Doctrine and Personal Identity" (see 6[85]).
The author takes a look at the anattā (non-self) doctrine in terms of the concept of a person, reflecting modern linguistic approaches.

(6) WIENPAHL, PAUL. "On the Meaninglessness of Philosophical Questions." Philosophy East and West 15 (1965):135-44.
Wienpahl discusses the posing of "meaningless" philosophical questions by the Rinzai sect of Zen through their use of kōans.

10 Logic

See also Buddhist Logic, 1.2.2.3

(1) CHATALIAN, GEORGE. "Jayatilleke on a Concept of Meaninglessness in Pali Nikāyas." Philosophy East and West 18 (1968):67-76.
A critique of Jayatilleke's interpretation of the concept of meaninglessness as based on a misreading of the texts.

(2) CHATTERJI, D. "Hetucakranirnāya." Indian Historical Quarterly 9 (1933):266-72.
This article presents the Tibetan text of a short tract by Dignāga on the wheel of logical reasons as well as the reconstructed Sanskrit text and an English translation. The work is viewed as an appendix to the Pramāṇasamuccaya.

(3) CHATTERJI, D. "Sources of Knowledge in Buddhist Logic" (see 7[4]).
A general accounting of the different ways of knowing in Buddhist logic.

(4) CHI, RICHARD S.Y. "A Bibliography of Indian and Buddhist Logic." Appended to his Buddhist Formal Logic. London: Royal Asiatic Society, 1969, pp. 181-222.
The bibliography is in two parts: a) Oriental texts before 1800, about 300 titles, alphabetized by title; b) Books and articles after 1800, about 400 titles, alphabetized by author. Apart from books and articles, it also includes about 100 book reviews, listed under the titles being reviewed. This bibliography contains the largest number of entries of works in this field prior to 1960.

(5) CHI, RICHARD S.Y. Buddhist Formal Logic (see 1.1[7]).
This book gives a modern interpretation of major Buddhist theories on logic: the hetucakra, the trairūpya and the list of fallacies through the application of the methodology of symbolic logic. It gives a comparison between Buddhist and Hindu systems, between Aristotelian and Indian systems, and between

Buddhist and modern systems from Gergonne to Russell. It rejects Vidyābhūsana's theory that Indian logic can be traced to ancient Greek. It also gives some possible influences upon world logic, due to the introduction of Indian logic to the West. Symbols are used extensively throughout the book. Recommended to readers who have some knowledge of symbolic logic.

(6) CHI, RICHARD S.Y. "A Comparative Study of the Categorization of Propositions in the Western and Indian Logic." Journal of Symbolic Logic 37 (1972):437-38.
This paper gives a classification of logical propositions, based on the theories of an ancient Buddhist logician and a modern mathematician, viz. Dignāga's theory of the hetucakra and E.L. Post's Theory of Elementary Propositions. It introduces a new universal language, which can express the meanings of many systems in the East and West.

(7) CHI, RICHARD S.Y. "A Semantic Study of Propositions, East and West." Philosophy East and West 26 (1976):211-23.
This is an extended version of the author's earlier paper (6). The new theory is applicable to many kinds of propositions: truth functional, quantified, classes, relations, etc. The result of this theory gives a "logical lattice" to replace the traditional "logical square." It can explain many systems in the East and the West, such as those of Aristotle, Dignāga, Uddyotakara, Gergonne, Hamilton, Hilbert, McColl, Peano, Russell, Sheffer, Wittgenstein, Lukasiewicz, and Carnap. Recommended to readers who have some knowledge of modern mathematics.

(8) CHI, RICHARD S.Y. "Topics on Being and Logical Reasoning" (see 8[7]).
Discussion on the Buddhist concepts of "being" (bhāva) and "being-in-itself" (svabhāva). Cites three different levels of reality. In a discussion of "catuṣkoṭi," this paper has rejected the views of Robinson and Jayatilleke as irrelevant. Comments briefly on the logic of Zen.

(9) DASGUPTA, S.N. "The Nature of Inference in Indian Logic." Mind 4 (1895):159-75.
A dated, but concise and coherent, exposition of the basics of Hindu logic. The author makes no distinction between Buddhist and Hindu logic.

(10) FRAUWALLNER, R. "Bemerkungen zu den Fragmenten Dignagas." Wiener Zeitschrift für die Kunde des Morganlandes 36 (1929):136-39.
The author introduces certain corrections to the book of Randle on Dignāga fragments (36) and the article by Tucci on Buddhist logic before Dignāga (50). Very technical.

(11) FRAUWALLNER, E. "Beitrage zur Apohalehre. 1. Dharmakīrti." Wiener Zeitschrift für die Kunde des Morganlandes 39 (1932): 247-85; 40 (1933):51-94.
A continuation of the author's studies on Jñānasrī's work on negation, the article contains a translation from the Tibetan of Dharmakīrti's Pramāṇavārttika. A fundamental article.

(12) FRAUWALLNER, E. "Beitrage zur Apohalehre. 2. Dharmottara (tibetischer Text, Ubersetzung und Zusammenfassung)." Wiener Zeitschrift für die Kunde des Morganlandes 44 (1937): 233-87.
Tibetan text and German translation of the Apohaprakaraṇam of Dharmottara. A continuation of the author's earlier studies on the apoha doctrine (negation) of Dharmakīrti.

(13) FRAUWALLNER, E. "Dignāga und anderes." In Festschrift Moritz Winternitz. Leipzig: Harrassowitz, 1933, pp. 237-42.
A highly technical article identifying citations of Dignāga's works in later works. Useful only for specialists on Dignāga.

(14) FRAUWALLNER, E. "Jñānaśrī." Wiener Zeitschrift für die Kunde des Morganlandes 38 (1931-32):229-34.
A synopsis of the life and works of Jñānasrī, a late Buddhist philosopher of the tenth century. Special attention is given to his work on the apoha doctrine (negation).

(15) FRAUWALLNER, E. "Zu den Fragmenten Buddhistischer Logiker im Nyāyavārttikam." Wiener Zeitschrift für die Kunde des Morganlandes 40 (1933):281-304.
The citations from Buddhist logicians in the later Hindu logical text, Nyāyavārttika by Uddyotakara Bharadvaya, are here excerpted and studied. Highly technical.

(16) GANGOPADHYAYA, M. Vinitadeva's Nyāyabindu-Ṭīkā. Calcutta: Firma L.L. Mukhopadhyaya, 245 pp.
A good introduction to the elements of Buddhist logic as seen in this classic work. The translator provides much up-to-date information on the scholarship in Buddhist logic.

(17) HATANI, RYŌTAI. "Dialectics of the Mādhyamika Philosophy (see 7[10]).
One of the few English articles by Hatani, who devoted decades to the field of Mādhyamika studies.

(18) HATTORI, MASAAKI. Dignāga: On Perception (see 7[11]).

(19) IYENGAR, H.R. RANGASWAMY. Pramāṇa Samuccaya. Tibetan Text (Romanized), Edited and Restored into Sanskrit with Vṛitti, Tīkā, and Notes. Mysore: Mysore University Publication, 1930, 110 pp.
An edition of the Tibetan text of chapter 1 with the commentaries and a reconstruction of the Sanskrit text. A valuable preface contains the essential information on Dignāga as well as summaries of the research by Tucci, Randle, and Tubianshi. The preface thus constitutes a useful introduction to Dignāga for undergraduates.

(20) JAYATILLEKE, K.N. Early Buddhist Theory of Knowledge (see 7[14]), pp. 333-68.
Logic has been discussed throughout the book, but it is particularly stressed in the chapter, "Logic and Truth," treating the important topics of truth, verification, consistency, fact, and utility. The catuṣkoṭi (four alternatives) are discussed; many illustrative cases are provided. Robinson's view on this subject is rejected here. Recommended as a useful source of information.

(21) JAYATILLEKE, K.N. "The Logic of Four Alternatives." Philosophy East and West 17 (1967):69-83.
This paper mainly refutes the view of Richard Robinson on catuṣkoṭi in the article, "Some Logical Aspects of Nāgārjuna's System" (41). Very much like Robinson, he also applied the wrong kind of logic: the quantified. As a result, the lengthy symbolic formulae occupying twenty pages are incorrect. Perhaps this controversy may provide a pseudo-case of catuṣkoṭi; two parties hold opposite views, yet neither is correct (having applied the wrong kind of symbolic logic).

(22) KAJIYAMA, YUICHI. "Bhāvaviveka and the Prāsaṅgika School" (see 8[34]).

(23) KAJIYAMA, YUICHI. "Buddhist Solipsism, a Free Translation of Ratnakīrti's Saṃtānantaradūṣaṇa." Indogaku Bukkyōgaku Kenkyū (Journal of Indian and Buddhist Studies) 13 (1965): 9-24.
Ratnakīrti, who proved in one work the existence of another mind from the standpoint of the relative truth, wrote a refutation of the existence of other people's minds (saṃtānāntaradūṣaṇa) from the standpoint of the higher truth. This is an excellent running translation of a work which "unreservedly declares solipsism as the final destination of idealism."

(24) KAJIYAMA, YUICHI. "Three Kinds of Affirmation and Two Kinds of Negation in Buddhist Philosophy." Wiener Zeitschrift für die Kunde Sudasiens 17 (1973):161-75.

A rather technical analysis of the theory of three kinds of exclusion (vyavaccheda) for the affirmation relationship between two terms, and the theory of two kinds of negation (pratiṣedha). The focus is on the particle (eva) in order to analyze the different ways in which the negation and affirmation are to be interpreted and established in the given statements. It treats statements from the writings of Nāgārjuna, Bhāvaviveka, Dignāga, and Ratnakīrti.

(25) KAJIYAMA, YUICHI. "Trikapañcakacinta: Development of the Buddhist Theory on the Determination of Causality" (see 8[35]).

(26) KEITH, A.B. Buddhist Philosophy in India and Ceylon (see 1.2[8]).
Pages 303-19 contain a synopsis of Buddhist logic with the emphasis on Dignāga and Dharmakīrti. Although now dated, the work shows keen critical insight and has more than historical interest. Perhaps useful for those who desire a brief but solid overview of Buddhist logic.

(27) KITAGAWA, HIDENORI. "A Note on the Methodology in the Study of Indian Logic." Indogaku Bukkyōgaku Kenkyū (Journal of Indian and Buddhist Studies) 8 (1960):19-29.
Uses the Dignāga system to show the inapplicability of Aristotelian logic to Indian logic.

(28) KITAGAWA, HIDENORI. A Study of Indian Classical Logic: Dignāga's System. Tokyo: Suzuki Research Foundation, 1965, 584 pp.
In Japanese. Appendix A, nos. 1 and 2, of this volume covers materials written in English. The first is "A Refutation of Solipsism," which discusses Dharmakīrti's defense of the Yogācāra system without falling into solipsism. It is largely an English translation of the Saṃtānāntarasiddhi. The second is "A Study of a Short Philosophical Treatise Ascribed to Dignāga," much of which is an abridged translation of the Chinese work, Ch'u-yin-chia-she-lun. Although in Japanese, this work is still worthy of citation and of note.

(29) MATILAL, BIMAL K. Epistemology: Logic and Grammar in Indian Philosophical Analysis. London: Mouton, 1971.
This book offers a rigorous treatment of Indian logic and epistemology. The interaction and debate of two opposing schools, viz. Buddhism and Nyāya-Vaiśeṣkika, constitute the central theme of the book. Many major topics are discussed: existence, non-being, negation, universals, quantifiers, the "inseparation relation," law of contradiction, and the status

of "examples." An indispensable work, highly recommended to serious readers at all levels.

(30) MATILAL, BIMAL K. "Reference and Existence in Nyāya and Buddhist Logic." Journal of Indian Philosophy 1 (1970): 83-110.
A rather technical comparative essay on the subject of reference and existence, either real or fictional, in the two systems of logic. That is, the analysis revolves around Udayana's (Nyāya logician) contention against Jñānasrīmitra's (tenth-eleventh century A.D. Buddhist logician) position on the matter of reference. Liberal references are made to Western logicians, such as Russell, Carnap, and Quine. For the advanced student.

(31) McDERMOTT, A.C. SENAPE. An Eleventh-Century Buddhist Logic of 'Exists.' Dordrecht: D. Reidel Publishing Co., 1970, 88 pp.
A fine translation and study of Ratnakīrti's logic, which proves universal momentariness by establishing the contraposition of an assertion of concomitance. For the advanced reader and student.

(32) MOOKERJEE, SATKARI. "The Absolutist's Standpoint in Logic." Nava-Nālandā-Mahāvihāra Research Publication 1 (1957):1-175.
This is a pioneering work that takes up the Mādhyamika's logical standpoint. It works through the ideas of Nāgārjuna, Candrakīrti, and Śrīharsa and ends by comparing their thought with the Vedantic absolutist position. Especially for the student of logic.

(33) NAKAMURA, HAJIME. "Buddhist Logic Expounded by Means of Symbolic Logic." Journal of Indian and Buddhist Studies 7 (1958):3-21.
A novel attempt at understanding the function of Buddhist logic. For the beginner. Compare similar attempt by R. Robinson (41).

(34) NISHIDA, KITARŌ, and DAVID A. DILWORTH, trans. "Religious Consciousness and the Logic of the Prajñāpāramitā Sūtra." Monumenta Nipponica 25 (1970):203-16.
Nishida, one of the most creative Japanese philosophers and practitioners of Zen, states his final religious and metaphysical position, a synthesis of some variables of Christian, Pure Land, and Zen tradition. A stimulating article.

(35) POTTER, KARL M. "Dignāga and the Development of Indian Logic." In Buddhist Formal Logic (see 1.1[7]), pp. 43-48.
This paper discusses explicitly Dignāga's trairūpya or threefold mark. Since the formulation of trairūpya is not unambiguous, it is treated here in three different stages. Comments on the role of concrete examples are also included. A stimulating article.

(36) RANDLE, H.N. Fragments from Diṅnāga. London: Royal Asiatic Society, 1926, xii + 2 + 93 pp.
Seventeen fragments on logic by Dinnāga constitute the main body of the book. They are extracted from works of Diṅnāga's opponents: Uddyotakara's Nyāya-vārttika and Vācaspati Miśra's Ṭīkā. They are exceedingly short, but vitally important documents. In order to give the reader background information of the theories of these fragments, the author appended two papers to summarize Buddhist and Hindu logical doctrines. Strongly recommended.

(37) RANDLE, H.N. Indian Logic in the Early Schools (see 1.2.2.3[5]).
A comprehensive exposition of Indian logic from its beginning, with particular stress on the Buddhist-Nyāya-Vaiśeṣika controversy. Critical insight on logic itself and not merely on history. An indispensable reference book, highly recommended to readers at the intermediate level.

(38) RHYS-DAVIDS, C.A.F. "Logic (Buddhist)." In Encyclopedia of Religion and Ethics. Vol. 8, pp. 132-33.
A short but useful summary of Buddhist logic.

(39) ROBINSON, RICHARD H. Feature Book Review of K.N. Jayatilleke's Early Buddhist Theory of Knowledge. Philosophy East and West 19 (1969):69-81.
Half of this review is actually a rejoinder of Jayatilleke's criticism of Robinson's article on catuṣkoṭi. It is interesting to read the continued arguments on the most puzzling topic of Buddhism.

(40) ROBINSON, RICHARD H. "Mysticism and Logic in Seng-chao's Thought" (see 4[27]).

(41) ROBINSON, RICHARD H. "Some Logical Aspects of Nāgārjuna's System." Philosophy East and West 6 (1957):291-308.
This is the first article that treated the puzzling topic of catuṣkoṭi (four alternatives) by means of symbolic logic. Catuṣkoṭi has several different types; some are quantified, and some are unquantified. The puzzling point lies in the unquantified cases (truth functional logic), while the quantified cases are not puzzling at all and there is no need of treatment. His symbolism is quantified, therefore the real problem has not been solved.

(42) SANGHVI, SUKHLALJI. Advanced Studies in Indian Logic and Metaphysics. Calcutta: Firma K.L. Mukhopadhyaya, 1961, 122 pp.

Though the main focus is on Jaina logic, this work can be recommended to aspiring students of logic because of its wide and involved references to other Indian logical systems. Buddhist logical concepts are liberally treated. The entire work makes a fine introduction to a comparative logical study.

(43) SHAH, NAGIN J. Akalaṅka's Criticism of Dharmakīrti's Philosophy. Ahmedabad: L.D. Institute of Indology, 1967, 316 pp.

A worthy study on a Jaina logician's critique of a Buddhist logician's philosophy. Good for the advanced student.

(44) SHARMA, DHIRENDRA. "Buddhist Theory of Meaning (Apoha) and Negative Statements." Philosophy East and West 18 (1968): 3-10.

Discussion of the theory of meaning according to the Dignāga school. It is designed to solve the problems of the universal (samanya) and the particular error (bhedagraha), the relation between substance and attributes (dharmi-dharma), and the word and its meaning (śabdārthasambandha).

(45) SHARMA, DHIRENDRA. The Negative Dialectics of India: A Study of the Negative Dialecticism in Indian Philosophy. The Netherlands: n.p., 1970, 155 pp.

Contains some contributions made by later Buddhist logicians on the subject of negation and negative epistemology. For the student of logic.

(46) SHASTRI, DHARMENDRA NATH. Critique of Indian Realism: A Study of the Conflict between the Nyāya-Vaiśeṣika and the Buddhist Dignāga School (see 7[33]).

(47) SIERKSMA, F. "Rtsod pa, the Monarchal Disputations in Tibet." Indo-Iranian Journal 8 (1964):130-52.

This article describes the institution of the Tibetan monarchal debates as it was remembered by a Geluga "incarnation" from Khams who went to Lhasa and became a Dge-bses ("Ph.D."). An interesting and informative work.

(48) STCHERBATSKY, T. Buddhist Logic. 2 volumes. Osnabruck: Biblio Verlag, 1970. (Orig. pub. Leningrad: 1930. Reprint. New York: Dover, 1962.)

Stcherbatsky's two volumes have become the best-known and most useful works on Buddhist logic. Volume 1 contains not only a scholarly synopsis of Buddhist logic, but also a survey of the entire realm of Buddhist philosophy. Volume 2 is mainly a translation from the Tibetan of the Nyāyabindu of Dharmakīrti along with the commentary by Dharmottara. Both volumes can be difficult going for novices in the field of either Buddhism or logic; however, with the aid of a good teacher, there is nothing in them that should be incomprehensible to the dedicated student.

(49) STEINKELLNER, ERNST, ed. and trans. Dharmakīrti's Hetubindhu. 2 vols. Osterreichische Akademie der Wissenschaften. Philosophisch-historische Klasse. Sitzungberichte, 252.Bd.1-2 Abh. Veroffentlichungen der Kommission für Sprachen und Kulturen Sud- und Ost-asiens, no. 4-5. Wien: Hermann Bohlaus Nachf., 1967. 337 pp.
An invaluable translated work on Dharmakīrti's text on logical reasoning (Hetubindhu). For the advanced student.

(50) TUCCI, GIUSEPPE. "Buddhist Logic before Diṅnāga (Asaṅga, Vasubandhu, Tarka-śāstras)" (see 1.2.2.3[7]).
A general summary of the author's research on early Buddhist logic. Rather technical, but good for advanced students.

(51) TUCCI, GIUSEPPE. The Nyāyamukha of Diṅnāga: The Oldest Buddhist Text on Logic. Heidelberg: Harrassowitz, 1930, 72 pp. Reprint. San Francisco: Chinese Materials Center, Inc., 1976.
The text is an important early paper by Dignāga, a prelude to his masterpiece, Pramāṇasamuccaya. It is retranslated from the Chinese translation of Hsuan-tsang. Wherever there is a correspondence between this book and the Pramāṇasamuccaya, the translator has put the Tibetan text in the footnotes. The Chinese version is almost incomprehensible to most Chinese native speakers. This English translation can help Chinese scholars to understand Chinese. An indispensable reference book.

(52) TUCCI, GIUSEPPE. "Is the Nyāyapraveśa by Diṅnāga?" Journal of the Royal Asiatic Society (Jan. 1928):7-13.
A technical article, bibliographic in nature, proposing that the Nyāyapraveśa is not by Dignāga, but by his pupil, Śaṅkarasvāmin.

(53) TUCCI, GIUSEPPE. Pre-Diṅnāga Buddhist Texts on Logic from Chinese Sources. Gaekwad's Oriental Series, 49. Baroda: Oriental Institute, (1929), 338 pp. Reprint. San Francisco: Chinese Materials Center, 1976.
Four texts, including Nāgārjuna's Vigraha-vyāvarttanī, which refutes the anticipated objections to the negativism of śūnyatā, and Ārya Deva's Śataśāstra, which refutes the dogmatic speculations of some Buddhists and non-Buddhists. They apply the method of dialectic, which is the prelude to the establishment of formal logic by Dignāga.

(54) VIDYĀBHŪṢAṆA, SATIS CHANDRA. A History of Indian Logic, Ancient, Medieval and Modern. Calcutta: Calcutta University Press, 1921, 648 pp.
This encyclopaedic volume covers the entire history of Indian logic from 640 B.C. to 1900. It has traced the origin of Hindu logic to ancient Greece. Its content concerns more history than logic itself. A great deal of names, titles, dates, and quotations, but very little logical theory. Recommended as a useful historical handbook.

(55) WAYMAN, ALEX. "The Rules of Debate According to Asaṅga." Journal of the American Oriental Society 78 (1958):29-40.
Provides a portion of the Śrāvakabhūmi that deals with correct reasonings and fallacies regarding doctrinal debates. An interesting article for all.

(56) WAYMAN, ALEX. "Who Understands the Four Alternatives of the Buddhist Texts?" Philosophy East and West 27 (1977):3-21.
This is the latest paper on the puzzling topic of catuṣkoṭi (four alternatives). Cites many previous papers on this subject, having critically studied their views. It concludes: ". . . no one understands the four alternatives, but perchance one does understand the four alternatives in a disjunctive system. . . ."

(57) YAMAGUCHI, SUSUMU. "Traité de Nāgārjuna. Pour écarter les vaines discussions (Vigraha-vyāvartanī), traduit et annoté." Journal asiatique 215 (July-Sept. 1929), pp. 1-86.
An annotated French translation of one of the five classical treatises of the Prāsaṅgika branch of the Mādhyamika. An English translation of this work is contained in Tucci's Pre-Dignāga Buddhist Texts on Logic from Chinese Sources. For advanced students interested in Nāgārjuna.

11 Social and Political Philosophy

(1) ANESAKI, MASAHARU. "The Foundation of Buddhist Culture in Japan." Monumenta Nipponica 6 (1943):1-12.

Dealing with the events of the late sixth and early seventh centuries, so decisive for the later development of Japan, Anesaki shows how Shōtoku Taishi (Prince Shōtoku) reformed all the various phases of life in Japan on the basis of Buddhism then recently introduced to the country. An admirable account of Shōtoku Taishi's views on political philosophy.

(2) BENZ, ERNST. Buddhism or Communism: Which Holds the Future of Asia? Translated by Richard and Clara Winston. New York: Doubleday & Co., 1965, 234 pp.

Focused on twentieth-century Buddhist movements, especially since the emergence of many new Asiatic nations after 1945, Benz goes through a rapid panoramic survey of the contemporary political and social conditions in these countries. He does this to exhibit the ferment of a Buddhist revival in Asia proper, including China and the Soviet Union. Of interest is the final chapter on the Buddhist critique of Communism.

(3) BHAGVAT, DURGA N. Early Buddhist Jurisprudence: Theravāda Vinaya-Laws (see 3[2]).

(4) CH'EN, KENNETH K.S. The Chinese Transformation of Buddhism (see 1.3[4]).

Deals with the interplay of Chinese indigenous thought with Buddhism.

(5) HORNER, I.B. Women under Primitive Buddhism. Delhi: Motilal Banarsidass, 1975, 391 pp. (Orig. pub. London: Routledge & Kegan Paul, 1930.)

A much-needed work on the roles and aspirations of laywomen and almswomen in early Buddhism, based on the Buddha's tolerant attitude towards women's entrance into the saṅgha.

(6) NAKAMURA, HAJIME. "The Indian and Buddhist Concept of Law" (see 3[17]).

(7) PARDUE, PETER A. Buddhism: A Historical Introduction to Buddhist Values and the Social and Political Forms They Have Assumed in Asia (see 1.1[25]).

(8) RAHULA, WALPOLA. History of Buddhism in Ceylon: The Anuradhapura Period, 3rd Century B.C.-10th Century A.D. (see 1.2.1[14]).
Rahula presents an exhaustive analysis of the establishment of Buddhism in Ceylon and the social, religious, and political developments in both monastic and lay lives. A solid work that can be recommended to all.

(9) RHYS-DAVIDS, T.W. Buddhist India (see 1.2[13]).

(10) SPIRO, MELFORD E. Buddhism and Society (see 3[21]).

(11) VARMA, VISHWANATH PRASAD. "The Philosophical and Sociological Foundations of Early Buddhist Religion." Journal of the Bihar Research Society (Patna) 1 [Buddha Jayanti Special Issue] (1956):193-208.
A good introduction to the understanding of the philosophical and sociological basis for the nontheistic nature of Buddhism.

(12) WAGLE, NARENDRA. Society at the Time of the Buddha (see 1.2.1[16]).

(13) WARDER, A.K. Indian Buddhism (see 1.2[18]).

(14) WIJESEKARA, O.H. de A. Buddhism and Society (see 3[27]).

12 Philosophy of History

(1) BROWN, DELMAR. "Buddhism and Historical Thought in Japan before 1221." Philosophy East and West 24 (1974):215-25.
A view of the Buddhist historical concept in early Japan.

(2) HORI, ICHIRŌ. "The Phenomenological Development of the Pure Land School in Japan." Religious Studies in Japan (see 1.2.2[10]), pp. 143-51.
Phenomenological analysis of one of the important segments of Japanese Buddhism, i.e., the Pure Land school. Hori points out that the Pure Land school had deep roots among farmers and fishermen as well as among the "out-caste" peoples.

13 Aesthetics

(1) CHAUDHARY, RADHAKRISHNA. "Some Aspects of Buddhism as Gleaned Through Indian Art." Journal of the Bihar Research Society (Patna) [Buddha Jayanti Special Issue] (1956):47-65.
A very helpful survey of the evolution of Buddhist art from the concept of arhat to that of Buddhahood, together with representations of the various deities. Good analysis of the various forms found in the Buddhist centers, such as Bharhut, Sāñchi, Bodhgāya, Gandhāra, Mathurā and Ajantā.

(2) HERRIGEL, E. Zen in the Art of Archery (see 16.2[7]).

(3) HISAMATSU, SHIN'ICHI. Zen and the Fine Arts (see 6[33]).
This is a liberal but faithful English translation from the Japanese done by Gishin Tokiwa. One of the finest systematic accounts of Zen aesthetics by a "Zennist" who lays bare his understanding of seven elements of Zen in the arts. Recommended for both beginners and scholars.

(4) HISAMATSU, SHIN'ICHI. "Zen: Its Meaning for Modern Civilization" (see 2[4]).
Includes a discussion of formless beauty.

(5) SUZUKI, D.T. Essays in Zen Buddhism. Third Series. (See 4[31]).
Chapter 7 is on Buddhist, especially Zen, contributions to Japanese culture. Suzuki asserts his own seven elements of Zen as manifested in the arts.

(6) SUZUKI, D.T. Sengai: The Zen Master. Greenwich: New York Graphic Society, 1971, 191 pp.
The best work on Sengai. Has a very good introduction to Sengai and an abundance of highly philosophical running commentaries on his drawings and calligraphic works. For the beginner.

(7) SUZUKI, D.T. *Zen and Japanese Culture*. New York: Pantheon Books, 1959, 478 pp. Paperback reprint. Princeton: Princeton University Press, 1970.

This is by far the most charming and delightful of Suzuki's many books on Zen. He beautifully brings into focus the essentials of Zen in the various cultural forms, such as swordsmanship, haiku, and tea ceremony. An important contribution to Japanese aesthetics. Can be used profitably by both the general reader and the scholar.

(8) WALEY, ARTHUR. *Zen Buddhism and Its Relation to Art*. London: Luzac & Co., [1922] 1959, 32 pp.

An early general treatment of the subject.

14 Authoritative Texts

14.1 Theravāda Texts

14.1.1 Abhidhamma Piṭaka

14.1.1.1 Dhamma-saṅgaṇī

(1) RHYS-DAVIDS, C.A.F., trans. A Buddhist Manual of Psychological Ethics. Pali Text Society Translation Series, no. 41. London: Pali Text Society, 1900 (reprint 1974).
This is the first book in the Abhidhamma Piṭaka. It is a compendium of mental states or processes. Highly technical.

(2) TIN, MAUNG, and C.A.F. RHYS-DAVIDS, trans. The Expositor (Aṭṭasālinī). 2 vols. Pali Text Society Translation Series, no. 8. London: Pali Text Society, 1920. Reprint. 1958.
This is an important commentary work by Buddhaghoṣa on the first book of the Abhidhamma Piṭaka, the Dhamma-saṅgaṇī (A Buddhist Manual of Psychological Ethics, [1]). Buddhaghoṣa is quite meticulous in analyzing the many technical terms of the mental states and processes.

14.1.1.2 Vibhaṅga

(1) THITTILA, U., trans. The Book of Analysis. Pali Text Society Translation Series, no. 39. London: Pali Text Society, 1969.
This is the second book of the Abhidhamma Piṭaka. It continues the discussion of the mental states or processes and further analyzes the nature of man's organic makeup in the hope of achieving the ultimate goal of enlightenment.

14.1.1.3 Dhātu-kathā

(1) NARADA, U., trans. Discourse on Elements. Pali Text Society Translation Series, no. 34. London: Pali Text Society, 1962.

This is the third book in the Abhidhamma Piṭaka. A further discussion of the mental states or processes but focussed on the elements (dhātu) as they relate to other states.

14.1.1.4 Puggala-paññatti

(1) LAW, B.C., trans. Designation of Human Types. Pali Text Society Translation Series, no. 12. London: Pali Text Society, 1922.

This is the fourth book in the Abhidhamma Piṭaka. Discusses the different ways in which human types can be designated in the stages toward enlightenment.

14.1.1.5 Kathā-vatthu

(1) AUNG, S.Z., and C.A.F. RHYS-DAVIDS, trans. Points of Controversy or Subjects of Discourse. Pali Text Society Translation Series, no. 5. London: Pali Text Society, 1915. Reprint. 1960.

This is the fifth book in the Abhidhamma Piṭaka. Discusses and refutes the heretical views, covering the principal doctrines of Buddhism. Some have referred to the text as a logical work.

14.1.1.6 Yamaka

The sixth book in the Abhidhamma Piṭaka, the Yamaka (Book of pairs), is untranslated.

14.1.1.7 Paṭṭhāna

(1) NARADA, U., trans. Conditional Relations. Pali Text Society Translation Series, no. 37. London: Pali Text Society, 1969.

This is the seventh book in the Abhidhamma Piṭaka. Discusses the very difficult subject of twenty-four conditions (paccaya) in the rise of momentary existence.

14.1.2 Abhidhammatthasangaha

(1) AUNG, S.Z., and C.A.F. RHYS-DAVIDS, trans. Anuruddha: Compendium of Philosophy. London: Pali Text Society, 1910.
Contains a summary of the major doctrines of Theravāda Abhidhamma. A critical introduction by Aung attempts to explain some of the obscure concepts, like life-principle (bhavaṅga).

14.1.3 Abhidharmakośa

(1) La VALLÉE POUSSIN, L. de., trans. Vasubandhu, L'Abhidharmakośa de Vasubandhu. 6 vols. Abhidharmakośa. Paris: Paul Geuthner, 1923-25.
A translation of Hsuan Tsang's version of Vasubandhu's Abhidharmakośa. Contains a compendium of the doctrines of the Sarvāstivada and Sautrāntika schools. One of the most important works of Sanskrit Abhidharma.

14.1.4 Aṅguttara-nikāya

(1) WOODWARD, F.L., and E.M. HARE, trans. The Book of the Gradual Sayings. Pali Text Society Translation Series, nos. 22, 24-27. London: Pali Text Society, 1932-1936.
The fourth major collection of the early discourses attributed to the Buddha.

14.1.5 Dīgha-nikāya

(1) RHYS-DAVIDS, T.W., and C.A.F. RHYS-DAVIDS, trans. Dialogues of the Buddha. 3 vols. Sacred Books of the Buddhists, nos. 2-4. London: Pali Text Society, 1899-1921.
The first of the major collections of the early discourses of the Buddha, containing thirty-four lengthy discourses treating various philosophical and religious topics.

14.1.6 Majjhima-nikāya

(1) HORNER, I.B., trans. Middle Length Sayings. 3 vols. London: Pali Text Society, 1954-1959.
The second major collection of the early discourses of the Buddha, containing 152 discourses of medium length dealing with a variety of topics. Philosophically the most important collection. See also 14.1.5(1).

14.1.7 Saṃyutta-nikāya

(1) RHYS-DAVIDS, C.A.F., and F.L. WOODWARD, trans. The Book of the Kindred Sayings. 5 vols. Pali Text Society Translation Series, nos. 7, 10, 13, 14, 16. London: Pali Text Society, 1917-30.

The third major collection of discourses attributed to the Buddha containing shorter pieces topically arranged. See also 14.1.5 and 14.1.6.

14.1.8 Milindapañha

(1) HORNER, I.B., trans. Milinda's Questions. 2 vols. Sacred Books of the Buddhists, nos. 22, 23. London: Luzac & Co., 1963, 1964.

Though the author is unknown, this is one of the most important works in early general Buddhism. It crystallizes the principal doctrines, such as non-self and impermanence, by way of dialogues between a monk and a king.

(2) RHYS-DAVIDS, T.W., trans. Questions of Milinda. 2 vols. Sacred Books of the East, nos. 35, 36. Oxford: Oxford University Press, 1980, 1984.

This is an earlier, but reliable, translation of the Milindapañha. See also Horner (1).

14.1.9 Sutta-nipāta

(1) CHALMERS, ROBERT, trans. Buddha's Teachings. Harvard Oriental Series, no. 37. Cambridge: Harvard University Press, 1932.

One of the earliest and most authoritative texts of the Buddhist canon.

14.1.10 Vinaya Piṭaka

(1) HORNER, I.B., trans. The Book of the Discipline. 5 vols. Sacred Books of the Buddhists, nos. 10, 11, 13, 14, 20, 25. London: Oxford University Press, 1938, 1940, 1942, 1951, 1952.

This unique work on monastic discipline is a source of Buddhist social, ethical, political, and devotional life. It analyzes the 227 rules that are binding, including those for women or nuns.

(2) RHYS-DAVIDS, T.W., and H. OLDENBERG, trans. The Vinaya Texts. Sacred Books of the East, nos. 13, 17, 20. Oxford: Oxford University Press, 1881, 1882, 1885.
This is an earlier but incomplete translation of the Vinaya Piṭaka, leaving out the final section on Parivara-patha, which contains summaries and classifications of the rules.

14.1.11 Visuddhimagga

(1) ÑĀṆAMOLI, Bhikkhu, trans. Buddhaghoṣa: The Path of Purification. Colombo: R. Semage, 1956.
See (2) for annotation.

(2) TIN, P. MAUNG, trans. Buddhaghoṣa: The Path to Purity. 3 vols. Pali Text Society Translation Series, nos. 11, 17, 21. London: Pali Text Society, 1922-1931.
The most sacred and authoritative text of the Theravāda school of Buddhism, containing an anlysis of the teachings of the school in terms of three major fields of discipline--morality (sīla), concentration (samādhi), and insight or knowledge (paññā).

14.2 Mahāyāna Texts

(1) Buddhist Mahāyāna Texts. 2 vols. in 1. Sacred Books of the East, no. 49. Delhi: Motilal Banarsidass, 1965. The Larger Sukhāvatī-vyūha. Translated by F. Max Müller (2: 1-85); The Smaller Sukhāvatī-vyūha, translated by F. Max Müller (2:87-107); The Amitayur-dhyāna-sūtra, translated by Junjirō Takakusu (2:159-204). (Orig. pub. Oxford: Oxford University Press, 1874.) Reprint. New York: Dover, 1968.
Although the worship of Amitābha Buddha (Buddha of infinite light) is mentioned in various sutras, these three are the major sutras of the Pure Land school of Buddhism, the most widely read and revered sutras in China and Japan.

(2) BURNOUF, EUGENE, ed. and trans. Le lotus de la bonne loi. 2 vols. Paris: Maisonneuve, 1925, 897 pp.
This is the first scholarly work in Europe on any Buddhist sutra, first published in 1852. The second volume of the two provides detailed research on the major terms and concepts that appear in the lotus sutra. Burnouf's translation is based on a Sanskrit manuscript from Kathmandhu, Nepal, sent by Brian Houghton Hodgson (1800-1894) in 1837. Hodgson sent eighty-eight Sanskrit manuscripts to the Société asiatique, which became the center of scholarly activities in Europe.

(3) EMMERICK, R.E., trans. The Sūtra of Golden Light: Being a Translation of the Suvarṇabhāsottamasūtra. Sacred Books of the Buddhists, no. 27. London: Luzac, 1970, 108 pp.
The importance of this Tantric sutra lies in the fact that the chanting and related rituals of this sutra were used for the security and prosperity of a country.

(4) FOUCAUX, PHILIPPE EDOUARD, trans. Le Lalita Vistara: Développement des jeux, contenant l'histoire du Bouddha Çākya-Mouni. 2 vols. Paris: E. Leroux, 1884-92. 406, 240 pp.
The sutra calls itself vaipulya (a great work), a name for Mahāyāna scripture. It relates the story of Śākyamuni Buddha.

(5) KATŌ, BUNNŌ, YOSHIRŌ TAMURA, and KOJIRŌ MIYASAKA, trans. The Threefold Lotus Sūtra. New York: Weatherhill, 1975, 383 pp.
After almost half a century, a new English translation of the Lotus Sutra, the most important scripture in East Asian Buddhism, has appeared. This is largely the work of Bunno Katō, who translated the text into English from the Chinese version. William Soothill had assisted and had published an abridged edition (Oxford: Clarendon Press, 1930, 275 pp.), which was further revised by Wilhelm Schiffer with the assistance of Yoshirō Tamura.

(6) KERN, HENDRIK, trans. Saddharma-Puṇḍarīka: Or The Lotus of the True Law. Sacred Books of the East, no. 21. New York: Dover, 1963. xlii + 454 pp. (Orig. pub. Oxford: Clarendon Press, 1884.)
This is one of the most widely read and revered religious books in the world. At the heart of the sutra are three major concepts of Mahāyāna Buddhism: 1) all sentient beings can attain Perfect Enlightenment; 2) the Buddha is eternal, and 3) there are various types of Buddhism, suited to different types of people, but all lead to the same goal. This is an outdated pioneer translation from the Sanskrit, whereas the other new translations are all from the Chinese.

(7) LAMOTTE, ÉTIENNE, trans. La concentration de la marche héroïque (Śūraṅgamasamādhisūtra). Mélanges chinois et bouddhiques, no. 13. Bruxelles: Institute belge des hautes études chinoises, 1965, 308 pp.
This sutra is one of the so-called "meditation sutras," and it deals with the nature of "Hero-Going Meditation." This is another masterly and scholarly treatment of a Mahāyāna sutra by Lamotte.

(8) LAMOTTE, ÉTIENNE, ed. and trans. L'enseignement de Vimalakīrti (Vimalakīrtinirdeśa). Bibliothèque du Muséon, no. 51. Louvain: Publications universitaires, Institut orientaliste, 1962, 488 pp.
An important and a delightful sutra in which a "banker" Vimalakīrti out-argues a group of "professional" monks. This is philologically the most adequate treatment of a major Mahāyāna sutra to appear in a modern language. The translation is based on the Tibetan canonical version, and where the Chinese version differs it too is translated. The meanings of many technical terms are discussed. Lamotte's introduction, however, is not as unblemished as his translation.

(8a) LUK, CHARLES, trans. The Śūraṅgama Sūtra (Leng Yen Ching). London: Rider & Co., 1966, 262 pp.
Another translation of a sāmadhi (meditation) sutra from Chinese sources, concentrating on the ālaya-vijñāna (storehouse consciousness), in order to wipe away all forms of defilement lodged in it. The translation is based on the explanation and commentary by Ch'an Master Han Shan of the Ming Dynasty. Compare with Lamotte's French translation (8).

(9) LUK, CHARLES, ed. and trans. The Vimalakīrti Nirdeśa Sūtra. Berkeley: Shambala Books, 1972, 157 pp.
Contains Vimalakīrti's dialogues with the Bodhisattva Mañjuśrī and others. It is a sutra of a fine dramatic composition, through which the essence of the Mahāyāna philosophy is beautifully expounded.

(10) MUKHERJEE, S.K. "The Vajrasūcī of Aśvaghoṣa." Visva-Bharati Annals 2 (1949):125-84.
Aśvaghoṣa is said to have lived perhaps in the second century B.C. In this work, he ridicules the caste systems of the Brahmaṇas, while exalting the truth of the Six Perfections. An interesting point.

(11) MURANO, SENCHŪ. The Sūtra of the Lotus Flower of the Wonderful Law. Tokyo: Nichiren Shū Headquarters, 1974, 371 pp.
Translated from Kumārajīva's version of the Saddharmapuṇḍarīka-sūtra. Compared with Katō's English translation of the same sutra (5), Murano's version is smooth and idiomatic, a generally faithful rendering of the Chinese text. The work, however, lacks critical footnotes and explanations.

(12) REGAMEY, CONSTANTIN, ed. and trans. The Bhadramāyākāravyākaraṇa. Introduction, Tibetan Text, Translation, and Notes. Publications of the Oriental Commission, no. 3. Warsaw: Warsaw Society of Sciences and Letters, 1938, 135 pp.
A relatively obscure but delightful sutra, in which the Buddha says to the juggler Bhadra, "The enjoyments of all beings and their possessions are conjured up by the Māyā of their deeds; this Order of monks by the Māyā of the Dharma; I myself by the Māyā of wisdom; and everything in general by the Māyā of the complexity of conditions."

(13) REGAMEY, CONSTANTIN, ed. and trans. Three Chapters from the Samādhirājasūtra. Publications of the Oriental Commission, no. 1. Warsaw: Warsaw Society of Sciences and Letters, 1938.
This sutra entitled "King of Meditations" contains a dialogue between Chandragupta, the main speaker, and the Buddha. It shows how a bodhisattva can attain the highest knowledge by means of various types of meditations.

(14) SCHULEMANN, GUNTHER, trans. Die Botschaft des Buddha vom Lotus des Guten Gesetzes. Freiburg im Breisgau: Herder, 1937, 196 pp.
A German translation of the entire Lotus sutra.

(15) STAEL-HOLSTEIN, ALEXANDER von. A Commentary to the Kāśyapaparivarta. Peking: National Library of Peiping; National Tsinghua University, 1933, 340 pp.
See (16) for description of the work. It belongs to the literature that glorifies Mahāyāna thought.

(16) STAEL-HOLSTEIN, ALEXANDER von. Kāśyapaparivarta: A Mahāyānasūtra of the Ratnakūṭa Class. Shanghai: Commercial Press, 1926, 234 pp.
This important Mahāyāna sutra has two parts: ethical and philosophical. Holstein states, "Among the philosophical sections of the Kāśyapaparivarta it is the exposition of the 'middle path,' the true way of viewing things (Text, 52-63), which specifically attracts our attention. We find much there which reminds us of the writings of Nāgārjuna and of Āryadeva. Some passages ascribed to these doctors of the Mādhyamika school are indeed as if they were based on the Kāśyapaparivarta."

(17) SUZUKI, DAISETZ TEITARŌ. "The Avataṃsaka Sūtra, epitomized by Japanese scholars and translated into English." Eastern Buddhist 1 (1921):1-12, 147-55, 237-42, 282-90.
The Buddhāvatamsaka-sūtra has been one of the most important scriptures in the East. No complete translation into any modern

language is available, due to the voluminous nature of the sutra. It deals with the profoundly metaphysical nature of reality, the interpenetrative nature of being.

(18) WELLER, FRIEDRICH. Index to the Indian Text of the Kāśyaparivarta. Harvard Sino-Indian Series, vol. 2, pt. 1. Cambridge: Harvard Yenching Institute, 1935, 61 pp.
A useful index of references to Buddhist technical terms as they appear in the literature.

(19) WELLER, FRIEDRICH. Index to the Tibetan Translation of the Kāśyapaparivarta. Harvard Sino-Indian Series, vol. 1. Cambridge: Harvard-Yenching Institute, 1933, 252 pp.
These indexes cite references to Buddhist technical terms as they appear in the literature.

(20) WELLER, FRIEDRICH. Zum Kāśyapaparivarta. Vol. 1, Mongoloscher Text. Abhandlungen der Sachsischen Akademie der Wissenschaften zu Leipzig. Philologisch-Historische Klasse, vol. 54, no. 2. Berlin: Akademie Verlag, 1962, 122 pp.
A Mongolian text of the sutra.

(21) WELLER, FRIEDRICH. Zum Kāśyapaparivarta. Vol. 2, Verdeutschung des sanskrit-tibetischen Textes. Abhandlungen der Sachsische Akademie der Wissenschaften zu Leipzig. Philologisch-Historische Klasse, vol. 57, no. 3. Berlin: Akademie Verlag, 1965, 163 pp.
A German translation of the sutra from Sanskrit and Tibetan sources.

(22) YAMADA, ISSHI, ed. Karuṇāpuṇḍarīka. 2 vols. London: School of Oriental and African Studies, University of London, 1968.
Although containing little material that would add to our knowledge of other Mahāyāna texts, the work, as the title suggests, describes the unlimited compassion of Śākyamuni for sentient beings. It is an excellent edition of the text from Sanskrit manuscripts. It also contains a summary of the contents in English. A model editorial work on a Mahāyāna sutra.

(23) YAMAMOTO, KŌSHŌ, trans. The Mahāyāna Mahāparinirvāṇa-sūtra: A Complete Translation from the Classical Chinese Language in 3 Volumes. Karin Buddhological Series, no. 5. Ube: Karinbunko, 1973-75.
The author says that this is the first and complete translation into English of the Daihatsunehangyō, i.e., the Mahāyāna Mahāparinirvāṇa-sūtra, translated from Sanskrit into classical

Chinese by Dharmaraksha (385-433) in the years 416-23, the complete text of which now remains only in the Chinese version, except for a few fragmentary pages in Sanskrit.

(24) YOSHIMURA, SHYUKI. "The Thirty-Two Instructions in the Kāśyapaparivarta." In Indogaku-Bukkyōgaku Ronshū (Kanakura Festschrift). Kyoto: Heirakuji Shoten, 1966, pp. 55-71.
An important article on the thirty-two positive virtues that are the prerequisites for a bodhisattva.

14.2.1 Prajñāpāramitā-sūtras

(1) BEAUTRIX, PIERRE. Bibliographie de la littérature Prajñāpāramitā. Série bibliographiques, no. 3. Bruxelles: Institut belge des hautes études bouddhiques, 1971, 58 pp.
This work is a valuable recent addition to Conze's Prajñāpāramitā Literature (see 1.2.2[2]), a standard work on the subject.

(2) CONZE, EDWARD, trans. Aṣṭasāhasrikā Prajñāpāramitā (see 4[5]).

(3) CONZE, EDWARD, ed. and trans. The Gilgit Manuscript of the Aṣṭadaśasāhasrikāprajñāpāramitā. Pt. 1, Chapter 55 to 70, Corresponding to the 5th Abhisamaya. Pt. 2, Chapter 70 to 82, the 6th to 8th Abhisamaya. Serie orientale Roma, nos. 26, 46. Rome: Istituto italiano per il medio ed Estremo Oriente, 1962, 1974.
A monumental edition of the Gilgit manuscript in Sanskrit, with the translation. Another good source for the understanding of the bodhisattva nature and the quest for wisdom (prajñā).

(4) CONZE, EDWARD. The Large Sūtra on Perfect Wisdom, with the Divisions of the Abhisamayālaṅkara. 2 vols. London: Luzac, 1961-64. Pts. 2 and 3, 1964, 663 pp. Reprint. Berkeley: University of California Press, 1975, 679 pp.
Another monumental translation by Conze on the wisdom (prajñā) literature.

(5) CONZE, EDWARD. Materials for a Dictionary of the Prajñāpāramitā Literature. Tokyo: Suzuki Research Foundation, 1967, 447 pp.
An indispensable tool for the study of the Prajñāpāramitā literature. The dictionary is complete for the Aṣṭasāhasrikā, the Ratnaguṇasamcayagāthā, the bhūmi chapter of the Large Prajñāpāramitā and chapters 55-70 of the Aṣṭadaśasāhasrikā.

(6) CONZE, EDWARD, trans. The Perfection of Wisdom in Eight Thousand Lines and its Verse Summary (see 4[5]).

(7) CONZE, EDWARD. The Short Prajñāpāramitā Texts. London: Luzac, 1974, 217 pp.
The book contains English translations of "The Questions of Suvikrāntavikrāmin," "The Perfection of Wisdom in 700 Lines and 500 Lines," "The Diamond Sūtra," "The Heart of Perfect Wisdom," "The Perfection of Wisdom in a Few Words," "The Holy and Blessed Perfection of Wisdom in 50 Lines," "The Perfection of Wisdom for Kausika," "The Questions of Nāgāsrī," and "The Sūtra on Perfect Wisdom, Which Explains How Benevolent Kings May Protect Their Countries." The Tantric texts are "The Perfection of Wisdom in 150 Lines," "The 108 Names of the Holy Perfection of Wisdom," "The 25 Doors to Perfect Wisdom," and "The Blessed Perfection of Wisdom, the Mother of all the Tathāgatas, in One Letter."

(8) CONZE, EDWARD, ed. and trans. Vajracchedikā Prajñāpāramitā-sūtra (see 8[13]).

(9) HIKATA, RYŪSHŌ, ed. Suvikrāntavikrāmi-paripṛcchā-sūtra (see 1.2.2[7]).
In addition to the edited text, the book contains a long essay on the Prajñāpāramitā literature, a bibliography of the Prajñāpāramitā-sutras, and tables comparing the different versions of the sutras. They will be of great help to everybody.

(10) KONOW, STEN, ed. The First Two Chapters of the Daśasāhasrikā Prajñāpāramitā: Restoration of the Sanskrit Text, Analysis, and Index (see 8[44]).

(11) THOMAS, EDWARD JOSEPH, ed. and trans. The Perfection of Wisdom: The Career of the Predestined Buddhas. The Wisdom of the East Series. London: Murray, 1952, 90 pp.
Extracts from the Prajñāpāramitā-sutras.

(12) TUCCI, GIUSEPPE, ed. and trans. The Triśatikāyāh Prajñāpāramitāyāh Kārikāsaptatiḥ by Asaṅga. In Minor Buddhist Texts. 3 vols. Serie orientale Roma, nos. 9, 43. Rome: Istituto italiano per il medio ed Estremo Oriente, 1956-71. Vol. 1, sec. 1, pp. 1-192.
This includes Tucci's commentary on the Vajracchedikā, including chapter 2, "Analysis of the Vajracchedikā according to Vasubandhu," and Appendix II, "The Gilgit Text of the Vajracchedikā," by N.P. Chakravarti. The commentary is important in that it discusses Asaṅga's comments on the Diamond Sutra from the Yogācāra point of view.

14.2.2 Abhisamayālaṅkāra and Related Works

(1) CONZE, EDWARD, trans. Abhisamayālaṅkāra. Serie Orientale Roma, no. 6. Rome: Istituto italiano per il medio ed Estremo Oriente, 1954, 223 pp.
A very scholarly translation into English from the original Sanskrit. There is no introduction, annotation, or other explanatory material; therefore this work can be used only by those already possessing some knowledge of Buddhist philosophy. The Sanskrit-Tibetan indexes are useful for advanced students.

(2) JAINI, PADMANABH S. "The Āloka of Haribhadra and the Sāratama of Ratnākaraśānti: A Comparative Study of the Two Commentaries of the Aṣṭasāhasrika." Bulletin of the School of Oriental and African Studies 35 (1972):271-84.
This is a comparative study of the Abhisamayālaṁkārāloka of Haribhadra and the Sāratama of Ratnākaraśānti that summarizes the contents of the Prajñāpāramitā-sutra in 8,000 Lines.

(3) OBERMILLER, E. Analysis of the Abhisamayālaṁkāra. 2 vols. London: Luzac, 1933-36, 275 pp. Fasc. 1, 106 pp.
A pioneering work on the significance of the Abhisamayālaṁkāra, including a very helpful introduction to this genre (i.e., wisdom, prajñā) of treatises. Sanskrit, Tibetan and the English translation of the first fascicle. The Abhisamayālaṁkāra is a brief summary of the larger version of the Prajñāpāramitā-sutra.

(4) OBERMILLER, E. "The Doctrine of Prajñāpāramitā as Expounded in the Abhisamayālaṁkāra of Maitreya" (see 4[25]).
An important article by Obermiller who initiated the studies on the Abhisamayālaṁkāra in the West.

(5) PENSA, CORRADO, ed. L'Abhisamayālaṁkāravritti di Āryavimuktisena: Primo abhisamaya. Serie Orientale Roma, no. 37. Rome: Istituto italiano per il medio ed Estremo Oriente, 1967, 135 pp.
This is a Sanskrit edition of Āryavimuktisena's commentary on the Abhisamayālaṁkāra, published nearly forty years after the discovery of the manuscripts by Tucci.

(6) STCHERBATSKY, THEODORE, and E. OBERMILLER, eds. and trans. Abhisamayālaṁkāra-Prajñāpāramitā-Upadeśa-Śāstra, the Work of Bodhisattva Maitreya. Fasciculus I: Introduction, Sanskrit Text and Tibetan Translation. Bibliotheca Buddhica, no. 23. Osnabruck: Biblio Verlag, 1970, 40 + 72 pp. (Orig. pub. Leningrad, 1929.)
As an epitomized account of the vast Prajñāpāramitā literature, the Abhisamayālaṁkāra is an invaluable aid to its comprehension.

This text was first edited by the illustrious Russian scholars. Stcherbatsky was a pupil of Minaev, Buher, and Jacobi. Obermiller in turn, was a student of Stcherbatsky. Having been devoted to the study of this difficult text, they gave a detailed synopsis of the text in English in this book.

(7) TUCCI, GUISEPPE, ed. The Commentaries on the Prajñāpāramitās. Vol. 1, The Abhisamayālaṁkārāloka of Haribhadra, being a commentary on the Abhisamayālaṁkāra of Maitreyanatha and Aṣṭasāhasrikā-prajñāpāramitā. Gaekwad's Oriental Series, no. 62. Baroda: Oriental Institute, 1932, 589 pp.
The Abhisamayālaṁkāra is a very important but difficult text to understand. Haribhadra, however, interpreted the Prajñāpāramitā-sutras according to the system seen in this text.

(8) TUCCI, GUISEPPE, ed. "Minor Sanskrit Text on the Prajñāpāramitā. I. The Prajñāpāramitā-piṇḍārtha of Diṅnāga." Journal of the Royal Asiatic Society, 1947, pp. 53-75.
This text is unique, for Dignāga summarizes (hence, piṇḍārtha) the Prajñāpāramitā-sutra from the point of view of the doctrine of the three self-natures of the Yogācāra.

(9) WOGIHARA, UNRAI, ed. Abhisamayālaṁkārāloka Prajñāpāramitā-vyākhyā (Commentary on Aṣṭasāhasrikāprajñāpāramitā), by Haribhadra, Together with the Text Commented on. 2 vols. in 7. Toyo Bunko publications, series D, vol. 2. Tokyo: Toyo Bunko, 1932-35.
Having improved on Rajendralal Mitra's edition of the Aṣṭasāhasrikā Prajñāpāramitāvyākhyā, Wogihara incorporated these amendments into his own edited text.

14.2.3 Mādhyamika-śāstra

(1) CANDRAKĪRTI, ACHARYA. Cinq chapitres de la Prasannapadā. Translated by J.W. de Jong. Buddhica, 1st ser.: Mémoires, vol. 9. Paris: P. Geuthner, 1949, 167 pp.
This is a translation by an oustanding scholar of chapters 18-22 of the Prasannapadā.

(2) CONZE, EDWARD, ed. and trans. The Gilgit Manuscript of the Aṣṭadaśasāhasrikāprajñāpāramitā (see 14.2.1[3]).

(3) DATAR, INDUMATI. "A Study of the First Chapter of Buddhapālita's Mūlamadhyamakavrtti." Journal of the Asiatic Society of Bombay 26 (1951):129-39.
Includes a translation from Tibetan to Sanskrit of the introduction and chapter 1. Buddhapālita's line was called Prāsaṅgika,

and Bhāvaviveka's line Svātantrika. "Prāsaṅga" means a kind of reductio ad absurdum, while "svātantra" means the point of view that advocates one's own antithesis by means of syllogisms. In the line of Buddhapālita was Candrakīrti (author of the Prasannapadā, whose ideas later became prevalent in Tibet. For this reason, this is an important text in the study of the Mādhyamika system.

(4) GOKHALE, VASUDEV. "Der Sanskrit-Text von Nāgārjuna's Pratītyasamutpādahṛdayakārikā." In Studia Indologica: Festschrift für Willibald Kirfel zur Bollendung seines 70. Lebensjahres. Bonner orientalistische Studien, vol. 3. Bonn: 1955, pp. 101-106.

An excellent treatment of the important verses of Nāgārjuna who declared, "Whatever has origination in dependence we call voidness. That is the designation when there is depending. Precisely that is the Middle Path."

(5) INADA, KENNETH K., trans. Nāgārjuna: A Translation of his Mūlamadhyamakakārikā. Tokyo: Hokuseido Press, 1970, 204 pp.

The work contains an introductory essay in which Inada places the thought of the Kārikā in the context of Buddhist philosophical analysis and critically discusses various philosophical ideas and interprets them to Western audiences. The Sanskrit verses are transliterated before a verse-by-verse translation of the Middle Stanzas. A beneficial work for students who wish to tackle this important but difficult text.

(6) KAJIYAMA, YUICHI. "Bhāvaviveka's Prajñāpradīpaḥ (1 Kapitel)." Wiener Zeitschrift für die Kunde sud- und Ost-asiens und Archiv für Indische Philosophie 7 (1963):37-62; 8 (1964): 100-130.

In about the sixth century A.D., Buddhapālita and Bhāvaviveka each wrote a commentary on the Madhyamaka-kārikā, and the school split into two streams thereafter. This is a German translation of Bhāvaviveka's commentary from the Tibetan text (Tōhoku no. 3853) by an outstanding Japanese scholar. This translation, however, covers chapter 1 only. There is a Chinese version (Taishō 30, no. 1565), but it is less reliable than the Tibetan version.

(7) LAMOTTE, ÉTIENNE. "Le traité de l'acte de Vasubandhu: Karmasiddhiprakarana." Mélanges chinois et bouddhiques 4 (1935-36):151-82.

The French translation of chapter 17 of the Prasannapadā appears in the appendix of this book.

(8) La VALLÉE POUSSIN, LOUIS de, ed. Mūlamadhyamakakārikās (Mādhyamikasūtras) de Nāgārjuna avec la Prasannapadā Commentaire de Candrakīrti. Bibliotheca buddhica, no. 4. St. Petersburg: Imprimerie de l'Académie Imperiale des Sciences, 1913, 658 pp.

This edited work, which includes the Kārikā of Nāgārjuna, reveals the significance of the eight negations and the middle path. Among the commentaries that evolved from the Kārikā, only Candrakīrti's Prasannapadā is extant in Sanskrit. This edition from St. Petersburg by de La Vallée Poussin is a masterpiece of exegesis, since he consulted a wide range of related literature.

(9) MIYAMOTO, SHŌSON. "The Study of Nāgārjuna." Ph.D. dissertation, Oxford University, 1928, 166 pp. plus translation, 151 pp.

Among the eight great commentaries on the Madhyamaka-kārikā within the Tibetan tradition those of Devaśarman, Guṇamati, and Guṇasrī are no longer extant. Piṅgala's commentary, however, has been preserved in the Chinese version as translated by Kumārajīva, and is known as the Middle treatise (Chung Lun; Taishō 30, no. 1564). Miyamoto translated the work into English. A copy of his unpublished dissertation is available at the Library of the Institute for Advanced Studies of World Religions (5001 Melville Library, State University of New York, Stony Brook, New York 11794).

(10) SCHAYER, STANISLAV, trans. "Feuer und Brennstoff. Ein Kapital (10) aus dem Mādhyamika-Śāstra des Nāgārjuna mit der Vṛtti des Candrakīrti." Rocznik Orientalistyczny 7 (1929-30):26-52. Also in Ausgewahlte Kapital aus der Prasannapadā. Einleitung, Ubersetzung und Anmerkungen (Krakow: Polska Akademja Umiejetnosci, 1931).

Schayer, a Polish Indologist, furthered Mādhyamika studies by translating chapters 5, 10, 12, 13, 14, and 16 of the Prasannapadā into German.

(11) Streng, FREDERICK J., trans. "Fundamentals of the Middle Way." In Emptiness (see 5[15]), pp. 181-220.

This is a complete translation of Nāgārjuna's famous work, Mūlamadhyamakakārikā. For the advanced student.

(12) WALLESER, MAX, ed. Buddhapālita: Mūlamadhyamakavṛtti. Tibetische Ubersetzung. Bibliotheca Buddhica, no. 16. Osnabruck: Biblio Verlag, [1913-14] 1970, 192 pp.

This is an edited Tibetan text of Buddhapālita's (ca. 470-540) commentary on the Madhyamaka-kārikā of Nāgārjuna. This commentary was severely criticized by Bhāvaviveka but defended by

Candrakīrti. This prompted the subdivisions within the Mādhyamika school, i.e., the Prāsaṅgika-mādhyamika and the Svātantrika-mādhyamika.

(13) WALLESER, MAX, trans. Die Buddhistische Philosophie und ihre geschichtliche Entwicklung. 4 vols. Heidelberg: C. Winter, 1904-27. Vol. 2, Die Mittlere Lehre des Nāgājuna: Nach der tibetischen Version ubertragen, 1911, 188 pp.
This is a German translation of the Akutobhayā, a commentary on the Madhyamaka-kārikā.

(14) WALLESER, MAX, trans. Die Buddhistische Philosophie und ihre geschichtliche Entwicklung (see [13]). Vol. 3, Die mittlere Lehre des Nāgārjuna: Nach der chinesischen Version ubertragen, 1912, 191 pp.
This is a German translation of Piṅgala's commentary on the Madhyamaka-kārikā translated by Kumārajīva, and known as the Middle treatise (Chung Lun).

(15) WALLESER, MAX, ed. Ga-lashjigs-med: Die tibetische Version von Nāgārjuna's Kommentar Akutobhayā zur Madhyamaka-kārikā. Nach der Pekinger Ausgabe des Tanjur. Materialien zur Kunde des Buddhismus, no. 2. Heidelberg: 1923, 114 pp.
This is an edited Tibetan text of the Akutobhayā, which is a short commentary ascribed to Nāgārjuna, according to Tibetan tradition. Recent studies by S. Yamaguchi, however, have proved that this commentary was falsely ascribed to Nāgārjuna.

(16) WAYMAN, ALEX. "Contributions to the Mādhyamika School of Buddhism." Journal of the American Oriental Society 89 (1969):141-52.
This review reexamines the celebrated verses of Nāgārjuna's Madhyamaka-kārikā XXIV, 18-19 and concludes, "Specialists in the Mādhyamika have uniformly mistranslated the verse XXIV, 18, and accordingly have failed to put Nāgārjuna's 'middle path' in proper focus."

14.2.4 Vigrahavyāvartanī

(1) JAYASWAL, K.P., and RĀHULA SĀNKṚTYĀYANA, eds. "Vigrahavyāvartanī by Nāgārjuna with the Author's Own Commentary." Journal of the Bihar and Orissa Research Society 23 (1937): Appendix, i-x, 1-31.
In this work, Nāgārjuna attacks the heresies and praises the truth of śūnyatā. In 1936, Sānkṛtyāyana discovered a Sanskrit manuscript of the Vigrahavyāvartanī, written in Tibetan ume script, in the Salu Monastery.

(2) JOHNSTON, EDWARD HAMILTON, and ARNOLD KUNST, eds. "The Vigrahavyāvartanī of Nāgārjuna." Mélanges chinois et bouddhiques 9 (1948-51):99-152.
This is the definitive Sanskrit edition of the text.

(3) MOOKERJEE, SATKARI, ed. "The Mādhyamika's Logical Position in the Vigrahavyāvartanī." Nava-Nālanda-Mahāvihāra Research Publication 1 (1957):7-41.
A liberal but forceful rendition of Nāgārjuna's refutation of opposing views on the Mādhyamika. See also translations by G. Tucci (5) and F. Streng (4).

(4) STRENG, FREDERICK J., trans. "Vigrahavyāvartanī: Averting the Arguments." In Emptiness (see 5[15]), pp. 221-27.
A faithful rendition from the Sanskrit of Nāgārjuna's important work. See also translations by G. Tucci (5) and S. Mookerjee (3).

(5) TUCCI, GIUSEPPE, ed. and trans. "Vigrahavyāvartanī by Nāgārjuna." In Pre-Diṅnāga Buddhist Texts on Logic. Gaekwad's Oriental Series, no. 49. Baroda: Oriental Institute, 1929, 373 pp.
This is a short but important treatise by Nāgārjuna, who defends the Mādhyamika system by refuting objections. Tucci's translation is from the Chinese and Tibetan sources. See also translations by F. Streng (4) and S. Mookerjee (3).

(6) YAMAGUCHI, SUSUMU, trans. "Traité de Nāgārjuna: Pour écarter les discussions (Vigraha-vyāvartanī)" (see 10[57]).
The Hui-cheng Lun, which was also translated into Tibetan, is ascribed to Nāgārjuna. Yamaguchi was the first to publish a French translation and study of it, based primarily on the Tibetan version.

14.2.5 Mahāyānaviṃśaka

(1) BHATTACHARYA, VIDHUSHEKHARA, ed. and trans. Mahāyānaviṃśaka of Nāgārjuna: Reconstructed Sanskrit Text, Tibetan and Chinese Versions with English Translation. Visvabharati Studies, no. 1. Calcutta: Visvabharati Book-Shop, 1931, 44 pp.
This is another English translation of the text, with the reconstructed Sanskrit text as well as the Tibetan recension (Tōhoku no. 3833).

(2) TUCCI, GIUSEPPE, ed. and trans. "Mahāyānaviṃśika of Nāgārjuna." In Minor Buddhist Texts (see 14.2.1[12]), vol. 1, sec. 2, pp. 193-207.

After the publication of Bhattacharya's reconstruction of the Sanskrit text, Tucci discovered, in the Nor Monastery, a manuscript in the Saradā script thought to date from the eighth or ninth century. This colophon records: "Mahāyānaviṃśaka of Ārya Nāgārjuna," but it is impossible to determine which Nāgārjuna has been cited.

(3) YAMAGUCHI SUSUMU, trans. "Nāgārjuna's Mahāyāna-Viṃśaka." Eastern Buddhist 4 (1926-27):56-72, 169-76. Reprinted in A Source Book in Indian Philosophy. Edited by S. Radhakrishnan and Charles A. Moore. Princeton: Princeton University Press, 1957, pp. 338-39.

The Mahāyānaviṃśaka (Ta ch'eng erh shih sung lun: Taisho 30, no. 1576, translated during the Sung dynasty by Shih-hu), extant in both Sanskrit and Tibetan, is also attributed to Nāgārjuna. Yamaguchi Susumu first published it in Eastern Buddhist in an English translation along with the Sanskrit and Tibetan texts. This is a compact presentation of Nāgārjuna's thought. In this work, however, rather idealistic strains are set forth, as Yamaguchi comments.

14.2.6 Dharmasaṃgraha

(1) MÜLLER, F. MAX, and H. WENZEL, eds. The Dharmasaṃgraha, an Ancient Collection of Buddhist Technical Terms. Prepared for publication by Kenjiu Kasawara. Anecdota Oxoniensia, Aryan Series, 1, pt. 5. Oxford: Clarendon Press, 1885, 89 pp.

Shih-fu's Fo shuo fa chi ming shu ching (Taishō 17, no. 764), which is a collection of Buddhist technical terms, must be highly regarded, although various Sanskrit texts of the Dharmasaṃgraha (i.e., Saptābhidhānottara) have also been transmitted and are generally accepted as Nāgārjuna's work.

(2) WELLER, FRIEDRICH, trans. Der chinesische Dharmasaṃgraha, mit einem Anhang uber das Lakkhanasuttanta des Dīghanikāya. Leipzig: H. Haessel, 1923, 198 pp.

This is a German translation of the Chinese text (Fa chi ming shu ching) or Dharmasaṃgraha.

14.2.7 Suhṛllekha

(1) BEAL, SAMUEL, trans. Suh-ki-li-lih-kiu: The Suhrllekha or 'Friendly Letter', written by Lung-shu (Nāgārjuna) and addressed to King Sadvaha. Translated from the Chinese edition of I-Tsing, with the Chinese text. London: Luzac, 1892, 51 pp.
This is a good translation of the text from the Chinese translation of the original.

(2) WENZEL, HEINRICH, trans. "'Nāgārjuna's Friendly Epistle,' tr. from the Tibetan." Journal of the Pali Text Society, 1886, pp. 1-32.
This is an English translation of a Tibetan text of the Friendly Epistle allegedly by Nāgārjuna.

(3) WENZEL, HEINRICH, ed. and trans. Suhṛllekha: Brief des Nāgārjuna an König Udayana, Ubersetzung aus dem Tibetischen. Leipzig: Boss, 1886, 27 pp.
This is a German translation of a Tibetan text of the Friendly Epistle (Tōhoku no. 4496 Suhṛllekha) allegedly by Nāgārjuna. I-Ching's translation of one fascicle of the Lung shu p'u sa chuan chieh wang Chuan (Taishō 32, no. 1674), which is a similar type of literature, and two other similar Chinese translations Taishō 32, nos. 1672-73). Therefore, this is an important and rare text in which the social and political philosophy of Mahāyāna Buddhism are expressed.

14.2.8 Ratnāvalī and Catuḥstava

(1) La VALLÉE POUSSIN, LOUIS de. "Les quatres odes de Nāgārjuna." Le Muséon 32 (1913):1-18.
In the Tibetan tradition, the Catuḥstava (Four hymns of praise) is ascribed to Nāgārjuna, although scholarly opinion regarding its content and arrangement varies. In 1913, de La Vallée Poussin released both the Tibetan texts and his French translations of the Nirupamastava (Tōhoku no. 1119), the Lokātītastava (Tōhoku no.1120), the Cittavajrastava (Tōhoku no. 1121), and the Paramārthastava (Tōhoku no. 1122).

(2) PATEL, PRABHUBHAI. "Catuḥstava." Indian Historical Quarterly 8 (1932):316-31, 689-705; 10 (1934):82-89.
Patel reproduced the Tibetan texts of the Nirupamastava and the Lokātītastava, as well as the Acintyastava (Tōhoku no. 1128), and the Stutyātītastava (Tōhoku no. 1129), this time including his own reconstruction of the Sanskrit texts.

(3) TUCCI, GIUSEPPE, ed. "Catuḥstavasamāsārtha of Amṛtākara." In Minor Buddhist Texts (see 14.2.1[12]), vol. 1, sec. 4, pp. 233-46.
In the Ṅor Monastery, Tucci discovered a Sanskrit text of the Catuḥstavasamasārtha commentary on the Catuḥstava, which he published in 1956. This commentary was written by Amṛtākara. Although part of the commentary on the Lokātītastava is lost, those on the Niraupamyastava, Acintyastava, and the Paramārthastava have been recovered.

(4) TUCCI, GIUSEPPE, ed. and trans. "The Ratnāvalī of Nāgārjuna." Journal of the Royal Asiatic Society, 1934, pp. 307-25; 1936, pp. 237-52, 423-35.
Tucci discovered a Sanskrit manuscript of the Ratnāvalī in Nepal, which he published along with an English translation. Although the manuscript was incomplete, since it was missing chapter 3, it is highly valued as a political instruction given by Nāgārjuna to a Śātavāhana king. Hideo Wada, on the basis of the Sanskrit text, made a study of it as a Buddhist treatise on political administration, while Hajime Nakamura, after extensive and diverse research in Buddhist literature, argued that it dealt in fact with Buddhist political thought, and determined that the Ratnāvalī was indeed a work of Nāgārjuna.

(5) TUCCI, GIUSEPPE, ed. and trans. "Two Hymns of the Catuḥstava of Nāgārjuna." Journal of the Royal Asiatic Society, 1932, pp. 309-25.
Tucci published Sanskrit versions of the Niraupamyastava and the Paramārthastava, which were based on manuscripts he had purchased in Nepal; included are an English translation and a Tibetan text.

14.2.9 Vaidalyasūtra and Prakaraṇa

(1) KAJIYAMA, YŪICHI, ed. "The Vaidalyaprakaraṇa of Nāgārjuna." Miscellanea Indologica Kiōtiensia 6 (1965):129-55.
The Vaidalya-prakaraṇa is a commentary on the Vaidalya-sūtra. The sutra consists of seventy-two short sutras. This is an edited Tibetan text of the Vaidalya-prakaraṇa; the Sanskrit original is not extant.

14.2.10 Mahāprajñāpāramitopadeśa and Related Works

(1) AIYASWAMI SASTRI, N., ed. and trans. "Bhavasamkrāntisūtra." Journal of Oriental Research, Madras 5 (1931).
Many works attributed to Nāgārjuna can be found in Tibetan and Chinese, yet the corresponding Sanskrit texts are as yet

unrecovered. However, efforts have been made to reconstruct the Sanskrit texts based on Tibetan and Chinese texts. This is an example of such a work which is a reconstruction of the Sanskrit text based on the Ta ch'eng p'o yu lun (Taishō no. 1574), and on the Tibetan (Tōhoku nos. 3840, 4162, 4558).

(2) LAMOTTE, ÉTIENNE, trans. Le traité de la grande vertu de Sagesse de Nāgārjuna. 3 vols. Louvain: Institut Orientaliste, 1944, 1949, 1970.
This is Lamotte's translation of the Mahāprajñāpāramitāśāstra or Prajñāpāramitopadeśa. The author of this work treats so many topics that it requires a scholar of great learning to do full justice to its richness. Nobody could have been more qualified than Lamotte. Reviews: P. Demiéville, Journal asiatique (1950): 375-95; J.W. de Jong, Asia Major 17 (1971):105-12.

(3) RAMANAN, VENKATA KRISHNIAH, ed. Nāgārjuna's Philosophy as Presented in the Mahā-prajñāpāramitā-śāstra (see 7[26]).
This work is extant only in Chinese and is entitled the Ta chih tu lun, being the commentary to the Pañcavimśatisāhasrikā-prajñāpāramitā-sūtra. Here we can find a natural continuation and development of the ideas found in the Madhyamaka-kārikā. The wide range of topics and materials found in this work make it in a real sense an encyclopedia of Buddhist doctrine. The authorship cannot be solely attributed to Nāgārjuna, as Hikata and Saigusa have shown clearly. Undoubtedly an important work.

(4) SAIGUSA, MITSUYOSHI. Studien zum Mahāprajñāpāramitā (upadeśa) śāstra (see 8[92]).
This is a thorough analytical study of the Mahāprajñāpāramitā (upadeśa) śāstra in German by a Japanese scholar.

14.2.11 Rāhula's Works

The works ascribed to Āryadeva's disciple Rāhulabhadra include the Fa hua ching ch'i tsan erh shih sung (Twenty verses in praise of the Lotus Sutra) and the Tan pan so ch'i tsan erh shih sung (Twenty verses in praise of Prajñāpāramitā). Haraprasād Śāstri has proven that the first chapter (in twenty-one verses) of the Aṣṭasāhasrikā Prajñāpāramitā Sūtra (which is included in a publication edited by Rajendralala Mitra, Aṣṭasāhasrika: A Collection of Discourses on the Metaphysics of the Mahāyāna School of the Buddhists. Calcutta: Asiatic Society, 1888, 530 pp.) was added later and identifies it as Rāhulabhadra's Verses in praise of Prajñāpāramitā (Tan pan so ch'i).

14.2.12 Āryadeva's Works

(1) BHATTACHARYA, VIDUSHEKHARA, ed. and trans. 'The Catuḥśataka of Āryadeva,' Sanskrit and Tibetan Texts with Copious Extracts from the Commentary of Candrakīrti, Reconstructed and Edited. Viśva-Bharati Studies, no. 2. Santiniketan: Viśva-Bharati, 1931, pt. 2, 308 pp.
In this work, Bhattacharya added the Tibetan version and an English translation to his previously published Sanskrit edition (2).

(2) BHATTACHARYA, VIDHUSHEKHARA. "The Catuḥśataka of Āryadeva, with Extracts from the Commentary of Candrakīrti, Reconstructed from the Tibetan Version with an English Translation." Proceedings and Transactions of the Fourth Oriental Conference, Allahabad 2 (1926):831-71.
This is a revision of Vaidya's edition (6), containing a Sanskrit version of chapter 7 as well as chapters 8-16.

(3) GOKHALE, VASUDEV, trans. Akṣara-satakam: The Hundred Letters: A Mādhyamaka Text by Āryadeva, after Chinese and Tibetan Materials. Materialien zur Kunde des Buddhismus no. 14. Heidelberg: Institut für Buddhismus, 1930, 24 pp.
One of the three important works of Āryadeva, the other two being the Śata-śāstra and the Catuḥśataka.

(4) ŚAŚTRI, HARAPRASĀD. "Catuḥśatika by Ārya Deva." Memoirs of the Asiatic Society of Bengal 3 (1914):449-514.
This is a work of Āryadeva, a direct disciple of Nāgārjuna, who demolished the views of the Hīnayāna and the non-Buddhist schools from the standpoint of Mādhyamika. Fragments of the Catuḥśataka were discovered in the Calcutta manuscripts; Haraprasād Śāstri published them along with Candrakīrti's commentary.

(5) THOMAS, FREDERICK WILLIAM, and HAKUJU UI, trans. "The Hand Treatise, a Work of Āryadeva." Journal of the Royal Asiatic Society, 1918, 267-310.
This is an English translation of the reconstructed Sanskrit version of the Hastavālaprakaraṇavṛtti based on the Tibetan recension. The book contains the Tibetan text (Tōhoku nos. 3844-48) and commentaries (nos. 3845-3849) as well as Chinese texts.

(6) VAIDYA, P.L., ed. and trans. Études sur Āryadeva et son Catuḥśataka. Paris: P. Guethner, 1923, 175 pp.
P.L. Vaidya rearranged the Sanskrit fragments discovered in the Calcutta manuscripts, and, using the Tibetan version, reconstructed the latter half of the text, from chapter 8 to chapter 16 of the Catuḥśataka, which had been lost. He then published this work along with a French translation.

14.2.13 Bhāvaviveka (Bhāvya)'s Works

(1) AIYASWAMI ŚĀSTRI, N. "Karatalaratna." Viśva-Bharati Annals 2 (1949):33-99.

This translation and that of de La Vallée Poussin (8) deal with Bhāvaviveka's Chang-chung-lun (Jewel in the palm of the hand), one of his short but important works. De la Vallée Poussin's work is the French translation of the extant Chinese text. Śāstri's work is a Sanskrit restoration on the basis of the same Chinese text, with an introduction.

(2) AIYASWAMI ŚĀSTRI, N. "Madhyamārthasamgraha of Bhāvaviveka." Journal of Oriental Research 5 (1931):41-49.

Although the authenticity of the authorship is still in dispute, in this small work with thirteen verses, the doctrine of the two truths is forcefully presented.

(3) GOKHALE, VASUDEV. "Masters of Buddhism Adore the Brahman Through Non-adoration." Indo-Iranian Journal 5 (1962): 271-75.

See (5) for annotation.

(4) GOKHALE, VASUDEV. "The Second Chapter of Bhāvya's Madhyamakahṛdaya." Indo-Iranian Journal 14 (1971):40-45.

See (5) for annotation.

(5) GOKHALE, VASUDEV. "The Vedānta Philosophy Described by Bhāvya in his Madhyamakahṛdaya." Indo-Iranian Journal 2 (1958):165-80.

In these three works, Gokhale presents a partial English translation of Bhāvya's major work entitled the Madhyamakahṛdaya (Heart of the Mādhyamika) and the autocommentary called the Tarkajvālā (Flame of reasoning).

(6) IIDA, SHŌTARŌ. "The Nature of Saṃvṛtti and the Relationship of Paramārtha to It in Svātantrika-Mādhyamika." In The Problem of Two Truths in Buddhism and Vedanta. Edited by Mervyn Sprung. Dordrecht and Boston: Reidel, 1973, pp. 64-77.

This is a study based on a newly edited Sanskrit manuscript of chapter 3 of the Madhyamakahṛdaya of Bhāvya or Bhāvaviveka and the autocommentary, the Tarkajvālā, the extant Tibetan text.

(7) KAJIYAMA, YŪICHI. "Bhāvaviveka's Prajñāpradīpah (1 Kapitel)" (see 14.2.3[6]).

This is a German translation of chapter 1 of the Prajñapradīpa, a commentary on the Madhyamakakārikā of Ñāgārjuna.

(8) La VALLÉE POUSSIN, LOUIS de. "Le joyau dans la main." Mélanges chinois et bouddhiques 2 (1932-33):68-138.
See (1) for annotation.

(9) NAKAMURA, HAJIME. "Upaniṣadic Tradition and the Early School of Vedānta as Noticed in Buddhist Scripture." Harvard Journal of Asiatic Studies 18 (1955):74-104.
See (11) for annotation.

(10) NAKAMURA, HAJIME. "The Vedānta as Presented by Bhāvya." Journal of the Oriental Institute, Baroda 14 (1965):287-96.
See (11) for annotation.

(11) NAKAMURA, HAJIME. "The Vedānta Thought as Referred to in the Texts of Bhāvya." In Professor Hiriyanna Birth Centenary Commemoration Volume. Mysore: University of Mysore, 1972, pp. 174-76.
Based on the extant Tibetan texts of Bhāvaviveka's or Bhāvya's works, Nakamura sheds light on the pre-Śaṅkara Vedānta school. Very important articles.

14.2.14 Candrakīrti's Works

(1) AIYASWAMI ŚĀSTRI, N., ed. "The Madhyamakāvatāra of Candrakīrti, Chapter 6, With the Author's Bhāṣya. Reconstructed from the Tibetan Version." Supplement to Journal of Oriental Research, Madras 4 (1930); 5:(1931):17-32; 6:(1932): 41-48.
Provides a reconstructed Sanskrit version of chapter 6 of the Madhyamakāvatāra, the most important chapter of the book, which explores the sixth stage of bodhisattva practice.

(2) JONG, J.W. de, ed. "La Madhyamakaśāstrastuti de Candrakīrti." Oriens Extremus 9 (1962):48-56.
This short but important article contains the edited Sanskrit and Tibetan texts with the French translation of the stuti (commendation) of the Mādhyamikaśāstra by Candrakīrti.

(3) La VALLÉE POUSSIN, LOUIS DE, ed. Madhyamakāvatāra par Candrakīrti. Biblioteca Buddhica no. 9. Osnabrück: Biblio Verlag, 1970, 427 pp. (Orig. pub. St. Petersburg, 1907-12.)
Tibetan edition of (4).

(4) La VALLÉE POUSSIN, LOUIS de, trans. Madhyamakāvatāra, traduit d'après la version tibétaine." Le Muséon 8 (1907): 249-317; 11 (1910):272-358; 12 (1911):235-328.

The text is not extant in Sanskrit, but it is an important work in the Mādhyamika school. Its importance lies in the fact that Candrakīrti herein develops his thought systematically, whereas in contrast, his Prasannapadā is a commentary on the Madhyamakakārikā of Nāgārjuna. The French translation is incomplete.

14.2.15 Śāntideva's Works

(1) BARNETT, LIONEL DAVID, trans. The Path of Light. Rendered for the First Time into English from the Bodhicharyāvatāra of Śānti-deva, a Manual of Mahāyāna Buddhism. The Wisdom of the East Series. London: J. Murray, 1909, 111 pp.

Śāntideva, a poet-philosopher, describes how to set one's mind on enlightenment and how to make "emptiness" and the Six Perfections (pāramitās) the basis of an enlightened life. This is the first English translation of this important popular text.

(2) BENDALL, CECIL, ed. Cikṣāsamuccaya, a Compendium of Buddhistic Teaching, Compiled by Çāntideva Chiefly from Earlier Mahāyāna-sūtras. Bibliotheca Buddhica, no. 1. Indo-Iranian Reprints, vol. 47. Osnabrück: Biblio Verlag, 1970, 419 pp. (Orig. pub. St. Petersburg, 1897-1902.)

The Śiksāsamuccaya is a sort of spiritual guide book leading towards the enlightenment. It quotes from various sutras; therefore it is a source book containing even sutras nonextant in the original Sanskrit. This excellent edition is prepared from Nepalese manuscripts.

(3) BENDALL, CECIL, and W.H.D. Rouse, trans. Śikshāsamuccaya: A Compendium of Buddhist Doctrine, Compiled by Śāntideva, Chiefly from Earlier Mahāyāna Sūtras. Indian Texts Series. Delhi: Motilal Barnarsidass, 1971, 328 pp. (Orig. pub. London: J. Murray, 1922.)

The English translation was commenced by Bendall and posthumously completed and published by Rouse.

(4) FILLIOZAT, JEAN. "Śiksāsamuccaya et Sūtra-samuccaya." Journal asiatique 252 (1964):473-78.

These two works of Śāntideva contain the fragments of texts nonextant in Sanskrit.

(5) FINOT, LOUIS, trans. La Marche à la Lumière: Bodhicaryāvatāra, Poème Sanscrit de Çāntideva. Les Classiques de l'Orient, no. 2. Paris: Bossard, 1920, 166 pp.
This is another French translation of the text for public consumption.

(6) La VALLÉE POUSSIN, LOUIS de, ed. Bodhicaryāvatārapañjikā, Prajñākāramati's Commentary to the Bodhicaryāvatāra of Çantideva. Biblioteca Indica, nos. 983, 1031, 1090, 1126, 1139, 1305, 1399. Calcutta: Asiatic Society, 1904-14. 7 vols.
Every important Indian text has at least one commentary. This is an edited Sanskrit text of Prajñākāramati's commentary, the complete edition with copious notes.

(7) La VALLÉE POUSSIN, LOUIS de. "Bouddhisme, études et matériaux." In Ādikarmapradīpa, Bodhicaryāvatāraṭikā. London: Luzac, 1898, pp. 253-338.
This is a Sanskrit edition of chapter nine (only) of Prajñākāramati's commentary to the Bodhicaryāvatāra.

(8) LIEBENTHAL, WALTER, trans. Satkārya in der Darstellung seiner buddhistischen Gegner: Die Prakṛti-parīkṣā im Tattvasamgraha des Śāntirakṣita zusammen mit der Pañjikā des Kamalaśīla. Beitrage zur indischen Sprachwissenschaft und Religionsgeschichte, no. 9. Stuttgart-Berlin: W. Kohlhammer, 1934, 152 pp.
This is a German translation of a section of Prakṛti-parīkṣā with Kamalaśīla's commentary.

(9) MATICS, MARTON L., trans. Entering the Path of Enlightenment: The Bodhicaryāvatāra of the Buddhist Poet Śāntideva (see 3[15]).

(10) MINAYEV, IVAN PAVLOVITCH, ed. "Çāntideva: Bodhicaryāvatāra. Spasenie po uceniju pozdnejsih buddhistov." Zapiski Imperatorskoi Rossiiskoi Akademii Nauk [Annals of the Imperial Russian Academy of Science] 4 (1889):153-228.
Śāntideva, who appeared around 700 A.D., produced such works as the Bodhicaryāvatāra (The path to enlightenment). His philosophical foundation is the Mādhyamika standpoint. Minayev's Sanskrit edition is filled with the fragrant religio-philosophical verses that exhibit the process of "emptiness at work."

(11) ŚĀSTRI, HARAPRASĀD, ed. "Bodhicaryāvatāram." Journal of the Buddhist Text Society of India 2 (1894):1-32.
The availability in several places of Sanskrit manuscripts of this text indicates the popularity of these verses.

(12) SCHMIDT, RICHARD, trans. Der Eintritt in den Wandel in Erleuchtung, Bodhicaryāvatāra, von Śāntideva: Ein buddhistisches Lehrgedicht des 7 Jahrhunderts n. Chr. Dokumente der Religion, no. 5. Paderborn: F. Schöningh, 1923, 144 pp.
A German translation of Śāntideva's Entering the Path of Enlightenment. See (9).

(13) STÖNNER, H. "Sentralasiatische Sanskrittexte in Brāhmīschift aus Idikustšari, Chinesisch-Turkistān 1-2." Sitzungsberichte der Akademie der Wissenschaften, 1904, 1310-13.
The fragments of the Śikṣāsamuccaya discovered in Idikustsari in Central Asia testify to the wide dissemination of the text.

(14) VLADIMIRTSOV, B. IA., ed. Bodhicaryāvatāra, Çāntideva: Mongol'skii perevod Chos-kyi hod-Zer'a. Biblioteca Buddhica, no. 28. Osnabrück: Biblio Verlag, 1970, 184 pp. (Orig. pub. Leningrad, 1929.)
The Mongolian version. Introduction in Russian.

(15) WELLER, FRIEDRICH. Tibetisch-Sanskritischer Index zum Bodhicaryāvatāra. 2 vols. Abhandlungen der Sachsischen Akademie der Wissenschaften zu Leipzig. Philologisch-Historische Klasse, 46, no. 2; 47, no. 3. Berlin: Akademie-Verlag, 1952-55.
Index of Sanskrit-Tibetan vocabularies.

14.2.16 Śāntarakṣita's Works

(1) ICHIGO, MASAMICHI. "A Synopsis of the Madhyamakālamkāra of Śāntarakṣita, 1." Journal of Indian and Buddhist Studies 20 (1972):36-42.
This synopsis, based on the extant Tibetan text, covers 97 verses of the Madhyamakālamkāra and Śāntirakṣita's autocommentary (vṛtti) and Kamalaśīla's subcommentary (Pañjikā). The subject matter is the extermination of the external objects and "internal" consciousness from the point of view of logic (yukti) and the authoritative scriptures (āgama).

(2) JHA, GANGANATHA, trans. The Tattvasaṅgraha of Śāntarakṣita, with the Commentary of Kamalaśīla (see 1.2.2.2[6]).
Jha's English translation is the key to this voluminous and difficult text.

(3) KRISHNAMĀCHARYA, EMBAR, ed. Tattvasaṅgraha of Śāntarakṣita, with the Commentary of Kamalaśīla. 2 vols. Gaekwad's Oriental Series, nos. 30, 31. Baroda: Oriental Institute, 1926.
Śāntirakṣita, as a Nirākāravādi-Yogācāra, wrote the voluminous compendium entitled Tattvasaṃgraha, to which his disciple Kamalaśīla appended a commentary. This work is literally a treasure house, containing the major tenets of the philosophical schools of that time. The discovery of the text in a Jain archive and the obtaining of permission for the editorial work involved a Mahārāja and several scholars. Krishnamācharya's edition is preceded by a long introduction by B. Bhattacharya.

(4) KUNST, ARNOLD. Probleme der Buddhistischen Logik in der Darstellung des Tattvasaṅgraha. Mémoires de la commission orientaliste, no. 33. Cracow: Académie polonaise des sciences et des lettres, 1939, 145 pp.
Kunst's German translation of the 18th chapter of the Tattvasaṃgraha, Anumāna-parīksa (Examination of inference), together with Kamalaśīla's pañjikā (commentary).

14.2.17 Miscellaneous Mahāyāna Texts

(1) RUEGG, DAVID SEYFORT, trans. The Life of Bu Ston Rin po che: With the Tibetan Text of the Bu ston rNam thar. Serie Orientale Roma, no. 34. Rome: Istituto italiano per il medio ed Estremo Oriente, 1966, 192 pp.
This excellent scholarly work presents the life of the illustrious Tibetan Master of the Law, the great Bu ston Rin chen grub, according to an account of his life composed by one of his chief disciples, sGra tsad pa Rin chem rnam rgyal. Recommended to all.

(2) THAKUR, ANANTALAL, ed. Jñānaśrīmitranibandhāvali: Buddhist Philosophical Works of Jñānaśrīmitra. Patna: K.J. Jayaswal Research Institute, 1959, 644 pp.
An editorial work should not be set aside by the beginner by reason of the inaccessibility of the original language, for it is normally preceded by an introduction and a synopsis of the text. Thakur's work is a case in point. It has a substantial introduction that literally maps not only later Indian Buddhist philosophical schools, but those of the non-Buddhists as well.

14.3 Yogācāra Texts

(1) CUTILLO, BRIAN A., and GESHE JAMPEL THARDO. The Saṃdhinirmocana-Sūtra. Planned as a book, it will be an English translation of the Tibetan text.
According to Buddhist Text Information, edited by Richard A. Gard and Nora A. Larke, number 2, page 6, this important work is in preparation. This is the first of an English translation series of Asanga's works from the Buddhist Studies Institute.

(2) LAMOTTE, ÉTIENNE, ed. and trans. Saṃdhinirmocana Sūtra: l'Explication des mystères. Université de Louvain, Recueil de travaux publiés par les membres des Conférences d'histoire et de philologie, 2, fasc. 34. Louvain: Bureaux du Recueil, Bibliothèque de l'Université; Paris: Maisonneuve, 1935, 278 pp.
Tibetan text edited in Roman letters. Just as Nāgārjuna's notion of śūnyatā was foreshadowed in the Prajñā-pāramitā-sūtras, so prior expressions of Vijñānavāda philosophy can be found in this sutra. The originality of this sutra can be seen in its tripartite division of reality. The only available translation of this important sutra.

(3) LAMOTTE, ÉTIENNE. "Les trois caractères et les trois absences de nature-propre dans le Saṃdhinirmocana, ch. 6." Bulletin de la classe des lettres et des sciences morales et politiques, Académie royale de Belgique, 1935, pp. 289-303.
The work deals with the doctrine of the three self-natures and the absence of the three self-natures taught in chapter 6 of the Saṃdhinirmocana-sūtra.

(4) The Mahāyāna-abhidharma-sūtra
Although no single work is available on this sutra, as it has been lost, the title should be mentioned. This sutra also followed the thought of "consciousness only," but gave to the ālayavijñāna a dependent nature, not absolute. This sutra was quoted several times in the Mahāyāna-saṃgraha-śāstra, an important text of the Yogācāra-vijñānavāda.

(5) SUZUKI, DAISETZ TEITARŌ. The Laṅkāvatāra Sūtra: A Mahāyāna Text. London: G. Routledge, 1932, 300 pp.
A good translation of one of the most important works of Mahāyāna Buddhism. The work is important in that it contains elements of yogācāra, tathāgata-garbha theory, and Zen. The translation is reliable, readable, but is best used in conjunction with the author's Studies in the Laṅkāvatāra Sūtra (6).

(6) SUZUKI, DAISETZ TEITARŌ. Studies in the Laṅkāvatāra Sūtra. London: G. Routledge, 1930, 464 pp.
This is the companion volume to Suzuki's 1932 translation of the Laṅkāvatāra Sūtra (5). It may also serve as an introduction to Mahāyāna Buddhism in general. The book is actually a series of essays on important topics treated in the sutra. Since these topics often occur at random throughout the sutra, Suzuki's essays provide extremely valuable continuity and help for anyone reading the sutra itself. One of the best general books for undergraduates.

14.3.1 Mahāyānasūtralamkāra

(1) LÉVI, SYLVAIN, ed. and trans. Asaṅga: Mahāyāna-Sūtrālamkāra. Exposé de la doctrine du grand vehicule selon le système Yogācāra. 2 vols. Bibliothèque de l'École des hautes études, sciences philologiques et historiques nos. 159, 160. Paris: H. Champion, 1907-11.
This first publication of a text of the Yogācāra school in the West systematically expounds the doctrine of the school. Volume 2 contains the French translation as well as a useful, if somewhat dated introduction. The first half of the work deals with the bodhisattva path and the second with specific problems treated from the Yogācāra point of view. There is unfortunately no English translation of this important work, which all serious students must attempt to understand. However, Lévi's translation can only be used by very advanced students.

(2) UI, HAKUJU. "Maitreya as an Historical Personage." In Indian Studies in Honor of Charles Rockwell Lanman (see 1.2.2.2[10]).
The existence of Maitreyanātha is shrouded in mythological tradition. While Lamotte has maintained that his existence was legendary, Ui maintains the contrary, which is adopted by Tucci (cf. his Minor Buddhist Texts [Rome: Istituto Italiano per il Medio ed Estremo Oriente, 1956, 8 ff.]). The following Chinese and Tibetan works have been transmitted and translated as his works: the Mahāyāna-sūtrālamkāra, the Madhyāntavibhāga, the Dharmadharmatā-vibhaṅga, the Abhisamayālaṁkāra, the Uttara-tantra, the Yogācārabhūmi and the Vajracchedika-prajñāpāramitā-śāstra.

14.3.2 Madhyāntavibhāga

(1) FRIEDMANN, DAVID LASAR. "Sthiramati, Madhyāntavibhāgatīka: Analysis of the Middle Path and the Extremes." Ph.D. dissertation, Rijksuniversiteit te Leiden, 1937, 143 pp.
A translation of the first chapter (on lakṣaṇa) of Sthiramati's commentary on this important Yogācāra work. Copious notes and references to other scholarship in the field. Not for beginning students.

(2) NAGAO, GADJIN MASATO, ed. Madhyāntavibhāga-bhāsya: A Buddhist Philosophical Treatise Edited for the First Time from a Sanskrit Manuscript. Tokyo: Suzuki Research Foundation, 1964, 231 pp.
This is a careful edition of a Sanskrit manuscript of the Kārikā and the Bhāsya together with an extensive index of Sanskrit, Tibetan, and Chinese texts. This text posits seven fundamental principles and explains how erroneous discrimination unfolds into subject and object bifurcation and that the true nature of things is actually emptiness.

(3) PANDEYA, RAM CHANDRA, ed. Madhyāntavibhāgaśāstra: Containing the Kārikās of Maitreya, Bhāsya of Vasubandhu and Ṭīkā of Sthiramati. Delhi: Motilal Banarsidass, 1970, 250 pp.
Pandeya has published a critical edition in Devanāgarī script.

(4) STCHERBATSKY, TH., trans. Madhyānta-vibhaṅga: Discourse on Discrimination between Middle and Extremes, Ascribed to Maitreya and Commented on by Vasubandhu and Sthiramati. Bibliotheca Buddhica, no. 30. Osnabrück: Biblio Verlag, 1970, 106 + 58 pp. (Orig. pub. Moscow, 1936.)
An English translation of this important Yogācāra text and two commentaries. For advanced students only.

(5) YAMAGUCHI, SUSUMU, ed. Madhyāntavibhāga-ṭīkā de Sthiramati: Exposition Systématique du Yogācāravijñāptivāda. 3 vols. Suzuki Research Foundation reprint series, nos. 7-9. Tokyo: Suzuki Research Foundation, 1966. (Orig. pub. Nagoya: Hajinkaku, 1934-37.)
Sylvain Lévi discovered this important manuscript in Nepal and one of his pupils, Yamaguchi, edited the text. The partial editions of the texts by V. Bhattācharya and G. Tucci are available. The Madhyānta-vibhāga literature consists of the original verses by Maitreya or Asaṅga, divided into five chapters, plus a commentary by Vasubandhu in the bhāṣya style as well as ṭīkā-type commentary by Sthiramati.

14.3.3 Dharmadharmatāvibhaṅga

(1) YAMAGUCHI, SUSUMU, and JŌSHŌ NOZAWA, eds. "The Dharmadharmatāvibhaṅga and the Dharmadharmatāvibhaṅga-vṛtti." In Studies in Indology and Buddhology, Presented in Honour of Pr. Susumu Yamaguchi. Kyoto: Hōzokan, 1955, pp. 9-50.
Tibetan texts, edited and collated, based upon the Peking and Derge editions. The work focuses on the nature of the dharmas and the mind pure in its own self-nature, and rigorously discusses the relationship of phenomena and the Absolute from the standpoint of Yogācāra-Vijñānavāda thought. No European translation is available. Although this text is extant only in Chinese and Tibetan, the Sanskrit fragments are contained in the Appendix of S. Lévi's Mahāyāna-sūtrālamkāra (14.3.1[1]) 1:190-91. This fact was discovered by Hideo Kawai; Nozawa incorporated the Sanskrit fragments in this edition.

14.3.4 Bodhisattvabhūmi and Śrāvakabhūmi

(1) BENDALL, CECIL, and LOUIS de La VALLÉE POUSSIN, trans. "Bodhisattva-Bhūmi: A Text-book of the Yogācāra School. An English Summary with Notes and Illustrative Extracts from Other Buddhistic Works." Le Muséon 6 (1905):38-52; 7 (1906):213-30; 12 (1911):155-91.
A very useful survey of this important Yogācāra text. More useful for beginning students than Wogihara's work (8).

(2) DEMIÉVILLE, PAUL, trans. "Le châpitre de la Bodhisattvabhūmi sur la perfection du dhyāna." Mémorial Stanislaw Schayer (1899-1941). Rocznik Orjentalistyczny (Warsaw) 21 (1957):109-128.
This is a French translation of the dhyānapāramitā, which forms the thirteenth patala of the first yogasthāna of the Bodhisattvabhūmi. A fine example of Demiéville's scholarly works.

(3) DUTT, NALINAKSHA, ed. 'Bodhisattvabhūmi,' Being Section 15 of Asaṅgapāda's Yogācārabhūmi. Vol. 46. Tibetan Sanskrit Works Series no. 7. Patna: K.J. Jayaswal Research Institute, 1966, 234 pp.
This editorial work includes a preface, introduction, and an analysis of the chapters. The Sanskrit is edited from the photographic copy brought from the Sha-lu monastery in Tibet by Rāhula Sāṅkṛtyāyana in 1938 and deposited in the K.P. Jayaswal Institute.

(4) LEUMANN, ERNST, ed. "Asaṅga's Bodhisattva-bhūmi 18$^{1-4}$ nach Wogihara's Ausgabe des Werkes. Übersichtlicher neu harausgegeben." In Studia Indo-Iranica. Ehrengabe für Wilhelm Geiger zur Vollendung des 75 Lebensjahres, 1856: 21. Juli, 1931. Edited by Walter Würst. Leipzig: Harrassowitz, 1931, pp. 21-38.

This is a Romanized Sanskrit text.

(5) RAHDER, JOHANNES, ed. Introduction; "Chapitres Vihāra et Bhūmi"; Appendix. In Daśabhūmikasūtra et Bodhisattvabhūmi. Société belge d'études orientales. Paris: Paul Geuthner, 1926, xxviii, 100, 28 pp.

The text "On Ten Stages" divides the bodhisattva's progress into ten levels (daśabhūmi) from the level of joy at benefitting self and others, to the level of spreading the teaching like clouds across the sky, and describes in gradual stages the virtue and power of each level. Rahder has also prepared an index to this text.

(6) UI, HAKUJU. Bonkan Taishō Bosatsuji Sakuin (A Comparative Index to the Bodhisattvabhūmi). Tokyo: Suzuki Gakujutsu Zaidan (Suzuki Research Foundation), 1961, 592 pp.

(7) WAYMAN, ALEX. Analysis of the Śrāvakabhūmi Manuscript (see 1.2.2.2[12]).

A thorough study of the Śrāvakabhūmi of Asaṅga based on Wayman's editorial work on the Bihar Research Society's Sanskrit manuscripts brought back from Tibet (photographic reproduction) by Rāhula Sāṅkṛtyāyana. After an introduction on literal history, Wayman translates selected passages, while at the same time, keeping the continuity of the text. Asaṅga's Paramārthagāthā, which directly precedes the Abhiprayikarthagāthā in the Yogācārabhūmi, is included.

(8) WOGIHARA, UNRAI, ed. Asaṅga's Bodhisattvabhūmi: Ein dogmatischer Text der Nordbuddhisten nach dem Unikum von Cambridge im Allgemeinen und Lexikalisch Untersucht. Leipzig: G. Kreysing, 1908, 45 pp.

The text has a great value because of its analysis and explanations of the various terminology in Mahāyāna texts.

(9) WOGIHARA, UNRAI, ed. "Bemerkungen über die nordbuddhistische Terminologie im Hinblick auf die Bodhisattvabhūmi." Zeitschrift der Deutschen Morgenländischen Gesellschaft 58 (1904):451-54.

The object of the Bodhisattva-bhūmi is to delineate the career of a bodhisattva from the very beginning to the final attainment of the perfect enlightenment.

(10) WOGIHARA, UNRAI, ed. Bodhisattvabhūmi: A Statement of Whole Course of the Bodhisattva, Being Fifteenth Section of Yogācārabhūmi. Tokyo: Taisho University, 1930-36.
This is a Sanskrit edition of the fifteenth chapter of the Yogācārabhūmi of Asaṅga. The Bodhisattva-bhūmi is the only section of the work that survives in Sanskrit. The author's resumé gives us a useful overview of this important Yogācāra compendium. For advanced students.

14.3.5 Mahāyānasaṃgraha

(1) LAMOTTE, ÉTIENNE, trans. "L'Ālayavijñāna (le réceptacle) dans le Mahāyānasaṃgraha, Asaṅga et ses commentateurs." Mélanges chinois et bouddhiques 3 (1934-35):169-255.
An annotated translation of the chapter on the storehouse consciousness in this important Yogācāra text, together with two commentaries. Extremely well done. For advanced students.

(2) LAMOTTE, ÉTIENNE, ed. and trans. La somme du grand véhicule d'Asaṅga (Mahāyāna-saṃgraha). 2 vols. in 4. Vol. 1, Versions tibétaine et chinoise (Hsuan-tsang). Vol. 2, Traduction et commentaire. Bibliothèque du Muséon no. 7. Louvain: Bureau du Muséon, 1938-39. 1:fasc. 1, chaps. 1-2; fasc. 2, chaps. 3-10. 2:fasc. 1, chaps. 1-2; fasc. 2, chaps. 3-10.
A monumental work by the great Belgian scholar. Volume 1 contains the Tibetan and Chinese texts, volume 2 the richly annotated French translation of the text. The work is extremely important for the understanding of Yogācāra thought and that of Asaṅga in particular. A projected third volume will contain Sanskrit, Tibetan, and Chinese indexes, and a fourth volume will contain a study of Yogācāra literature and a detailed exposé on the doctrines of Asaṅga. To date they have not appeared. Fundamental for any student who reads French, for the text is a comprehensive synthesis of the ten features basic to Mahāyāna Buddhism.

14.3.6 Abhidharmasamuccaya and Pañcaskandha

(1) GOKHALE, V.V. "Fragments from the Abhidharmasamuccaya of Asaṅga." Journal of the Bombay Branch of the Royal Asiatic Society 23 (1947):13-38.
The thought of Maitreya, who probably lived around 300 A.D., was further developed and systematized by the brothers Asaṅga and Vasubandhu. The Tibetan and the Chinese recensions are extant, but the Sanskrit original is lost. Recently, however, fragments

of the Sanskrit texts have been found in the Ṣa-lu and Ṅor Monasteries in Tibet by Rāhulasānkrityāyana (1934). Having made a study of these manuscripts, V.V. Gokhale reported this discovery to the scholarly world. See also Gokhale's article "A Rare Manuscript . . ." (3).

(2) GOKHALE, V.V. "The Pañcaskandhaka by Vasubandhu and its Commentary by Sthiramati." Annals of the Bhandarkar Oriental Research Institute 18 (1937).
This article contains a detailed account of the text by Vasubandhu on the five constituents of being. Useful for all students.

(3) GOKHALE, V.V. "A Rare Manuscript of Asaṅga's Abhidharmasamuccaya." Harvard Journal of Asiatic Studies 11 (1948): 207-13.

(4) PRADHAN, PRALHAD, ed. Abhidharmasamuccaya of Asaṅgha. Viśva-Bharati Studies, no. 12. Śāntiniketan: Visva-Bharati, 1950, 110 pp.
This and the following works constitute further studies and a reorganization of Gokhale's edition, combined with a restoration of missing parts of the Sanskrit text on the Tibetan text (Tōhōku 4049) and its commentary (Tōhōku 4054) as well as the Chinese recension of the text (Taishō 31, no. 1586).

(5) PRADHAN, PRALHAD. "The Manuscript of Asaṅga's Abhidharmasamuccaya." Indian Historical Quarterly 24 (1948):87-93.

(6) PRADHAN, PRALHAD. "A Short Note on Abhidharmasamuccaya of Asaṅga." PAIOC 14 (1948):61-62.

(7) RAHULA, WALPOLA, ed. and trans. Le compendium de la super-doctrine: Philosophie. Abhidharmasamuccaya d'Asaṅga. Publications de l'École française d'Extrême-Orient, no. 78. Paris: École française d'Extrême-Orient, 1971, 236 pp.
This is a French translation and a thorough study of the text.

14.3.7 Viṃśatikā, Triṃśikā, Siddhi, etc.

(1) BAGCHI, SITAMSU SEKHAR, trans. "Vijñāptimātratāsiddhi." Nava-Nālandā Mahāvihāra Research Publication 1 (1957): 367-89.
This is a translation of the Viṃśatikā (Twenty verses) of Vasubandhu from the Sanskrit. For the beginner. See also Clarence H. Hamilton's translation from the Chinese source Wei shih er shih lun (2).

(2) HAMILTON, CLARENCE HERBERT, trans. Wei Shih Er Shih Lun, or The Treatise in Twenty Stanzas on Representation-only, by Vasubandhu. American Oriental Series, no. 13. New Haven: American Oriental Society, 1938, 82 pp.
A translation into English of the Viṃśatikā of Vasubandhu. Useful for beginning students who cannot read the French of Lévi.

(3) JACOBI, HERMANN GEORG, trans. Triṃśikāvijñāpti des Vasubandhu, mit Bhāsya des Acarya Sthiramati. Beitrage zur indischen Sprachwissenschaft und Religionsgeschichte, no. 7. Stuttgart: W. Kohlhammer, 1932, 64 pp.
A German translation of the Triṃśikā, translated also in French by Sylvain Lévi. The annotation is well done; there are many corrections to the Sanskrit text published by Lévi. For specialists.

(4) La VALLÉE POUSSIN, LOUIS de, trans. "Vasubandhu. Viṃśakakārikāprakaraṇa. Traité des vingt ślokas avec le commentaire de l'auteur." Le Muséon 13 (1912):53-90.
The Viṃśatikā (Treatise in twenty verses) mainly elucidates the theory of "consciousness-only-and-no-external-world." De La Vallée Poussin made his French translation from the Tibetan text, for the Sanskrit text was not available at the time.

(5) La VALLÉE POUSSIN, LOUIS de, trans. Vijñāptimātratāsiddhi: La Siddhi de Hsuan-tsang. 2 vols. and index. Buddhica: Documents et travaux pour l'étude du Bouddhisme, 1st ser., Mémoires, vols. 1, 5, 8. Paris: P. Guethner, 1928-48.
A complete, annotated translation, into French, of the great commentary of Hsuan-tsang to the Viṃśatikā of Vasubandhu. Absolutely essential for Yogācāra studies. It is much superior to the 1973 English translation by Wei Tat (9) and should be used by all serious students of the text.

(6) LÉVI, SYLVAIN, ed. Matériaux pour l'étude du système Vijñāptimātra: Traduction de la Viṃśatikā et de la Triṃśikā. Bibliothèque de l'École des hautes études, sciences historiques et philologiques, no. 260. Paris: H. Champion, 1932, 206 pp.
Lévi's works are important not only in the field of Buddhist studies, but also in other related fields. This is one of his works that has had an enduring influence.

(7) LÉVI, SYLVAIN, ed. Vijñāptimātratāsiddhi: Deux traités de Vasubandhu: Viṃśatikā (La vingtaine) accompagnée d'une explication en prose, et Triṃśikā (La trentaine) avec le commentaire de Sthiramati. Bibliothèque de l'École des hautes études, sciences historiques et philologiques, no. 245. Paris: Champion, 1925, 54 pp.

This edition opened a new avenue to the study of the Vijñāpti-mātratāvādin through the availability of the Sanskrit original as well as the system of Sthiramati. While the twenty verses criticize the view of naive realism, as it were, the thirty verses explain the transformations of the ālaya-consciousness.

(8) SĀNKṚTYĀYANA, RĀHULA, ed. "Sanskrit Restoration of Yuan Chwang's Vijñāpti-Matratāsiddhi-śāstra." Journal of the Bihar and Orissa Research Society 19, Appendix (1933):1-72; 20 (1934):73-152.
This is a partial restoration of the Sanskrit text of an important Yogācāra text extant only in Chinese.

(9) WEI TAT, trans. Ch'eng Wei-shih Lun: The Doctrine of Mere-Consciousness by Hsuan-tsang. Hong Kong: Ch'eng Wei-Shih Lun Publication Committee, 1973, 818 pp.
Not to be compared with the French translation of de La Vallée Poussin, but the only recourse for students who do not read French. One useful feature of the work is that the Chinese and English are on facing pages. Thus the book is beneficial for students who wish to read the Chinese original.

14.3.8 Svabhāva-traya and Related Works

(1) BASU, ANATHNATH. "Śīlaparikathā." Indian Historical Quarterly 7 (1931):28-33.
The Śīlaparikathā is a short tract attributed to Vasubandhu that attempts to demonstrate that moral precepts (śīla) are more effective than gift giving (dāna). This article consists of an edition of the Tibetan text, Sanskrit reconstruction, and an English translation. Of interest to students of Vasubandhu only.

(2) KAJIYAMA, YUICHI. "Controversy between the Sākāra- and Nirākāra-vādins of the Yogācāra School: Some Materials." Indogaku Bukkyōgaku Kenkyū (Journal of Indian and Buddhist Studies) 14 (1965):26-37.
This article deals with the two subschools of the Yogācāra-vijñanavāda, as described in Kajiyama's "An Introduction to Buddhist Philosophy" (3).

(3) KAJIYAMA, YUICHI, trans. "An Introduction to Buddhist Philosophy: An Annotated Translation of the Tarkabhāṣā of of Moksākāragupta" (see 1.2.2[9]).
Having reached their apex in the post-Gupta period, the Madhyāmika and the Vijñāptimātrāta schools then branched out to several subschools in compliance with the religiophilosophical tendencies of the time. As for the Vijñāptimātratā school, the two sub-

schools, i.e., the Sākāravijñanavādin and the Nirākāra-vijñana-vādin evolved, centering around the interpretations of the thirty verses. Kajiyama gives a detailed account of this state of affairs.

(4) La VALLÉE POUSSIN, LOUIS de. "Le petit traité de Vasubandhu-Nāgārjuna sur les trois natures." Mélanges chinois et bouddhiques 2 (1932-33):147-61.

The doctrine of svabhāva-traya i.e., the tripartite division of the metaphysical foundation of phenomena into the purely mentally constructed nature (parikalpita), relative nature (paratantra), and perfect reality (parinișpanna), is the cardinal doctrine of the Yogācāra-vijñanavāda. De La Vallée Poussin's work contains an edition of a Sanskrit manuscript on the subject and its French translation.

(5) MUKHOPĀDHYĀYA, SUJITKUMAR, ed. The Trisvabhāvanirdeśa of Vasubandhu. Visvabharati Series, no. 4. Calcutta: Visvabharati Book-Shop, 1939, 71 pp.

A short treatise (thirty-eight verses) on the three self-natures (trisvabhāva) of the Vijñānavāda school. Sanskrit text and Tibetan versions edited with an English translation and introduction. The appendix contains an exhaustive list (seventeen pages) of similar phrases taken not only from Buddhist literature, but also from Upanișadic sources.

14.3.9 Tathāgatagarbha Texts

(1) OBERMILLER, EUGENE. "The Sublime Science of the Great Vehicle to Salvation; a Manual of Buddhist Monism, The Work of Ārya Maitreya, with a Commentary by Āryasaṅga." Acta Orientalia 9 (1931):81-306.

This is a translation of the Ratnagotravibhāga from the Tibetan text. Obermiller's interpretation of the text is based on a commentary by Tsong-kha-pa's disciple and successor, Rgyal-tshab Darma Rinchen (1364-1432). An important work.

(2) RUEGG, DAVID SEYFORT. La théorie du Tathāgatagarbha et du gotra. Publications de l'École française d'Extrême-Orient, no. 70. Paris: École française d'Extrême-Orient, 1969, 531 pp.

A monumental work that exemplifies the illustrious tradition of Western scientific Buddhist Studies. Ruegg deals with the relatively neglected subject of the tathāgatagarbha and gotra theory of Mahāyāna Buddhism from the points of view of soteriology and "gnoséologie." An overview of this important thought is critically presented, based on extensive and exhaustive Sanskrit and Tibetan materials. A scholarly work for advanced students.

(3) RUEGG, DAVID SEYFORT, trans. Le traité du Tathāgatagarbha de Bu ston Rin Chen Grub: Traduction du De bžin gšegs pa'i sñin po gsal žin mdzes par byed pa'i rgyan. Publications de l'école française d'Extrême-Orient, no. 74. Paris: École française d'Extrême-Orient, 1973, 162 pp.

This is a sister volume to Ruegg's monumental work, Théorie du Tathāgatagarbha et du gotra (2). This excellent scholarly translation is essential for an understanding of Tathāgatagarbha thought.

(4) TAKASAKI, JIKIDŌ. A Study on the Ratnagotravibhāga (Uttaratantra): A Treatise on the Tathāgatagarbha Theory of Mahāyāna Buddhism. Serie Orientale Roma, no. 33. Rome: Istituto italiano per il medio ed Estremo Oriente, 1966, 439 pp.

This is a translation from the Sanskrit text edited by E.H. Johnston, The Ratnagotravibhāga Mahāyānottaratantraśāstra (Patna: Bihar Research Society, 1950). Several passages of the Sanskrit text have been translated by E. Conze in Buddhist Texts Through the Ages (see 1.1[9]), pp. 130-31, 181-84, 216-17. Takasaki's translation is preceded by a long and useful introduction and a synopsis. A basic tool for the study of the Tathāgatagarbha thought.

(5) WAYMAN, ALEX, and HIDEKO WAYMAN, eds. and trans. The Lion's Roar of Queen Śrīmālā: A Buddhist Scripture on the Tathāgatagarbha Theory. Columbia College Program of Translations from the Oriental Classics. New York: Columbia University Press, 1974, 142 pp.

Provides an excellent scholarly translation, and includes 1) a comprehensive exposition of the literary history and the structure of the sutra; 2) a classification of persons, i.e., the different stages of progress in Buddhist life according to the sutra; 3) the main points of the doctrine contained in the sutra. The Śrī-mālā sūtra is most important for the understanding of the Tathāgatagarbha doctrine. Extensive footnotes and two appendixes are followed by an exhaustive bibliography. Recommended to all.

14.3.10 Miscellaneous Yogācāra Texts

(1) TAJIMA, RYŪJUN. Étude sur le Mahāvairocana-sūtra (Dainichikyō), avec la traduction commentée du premier chapitre. Paris: Maisonneuve, 1936, 148 pp.

Provides an important document for the study of Tantric Buddhism; contains a useful bibliography.

(2) TUCCI, GIUSEPPE. "A Fragment from the Pratītyasamutpāda of Vasubandhu." Journal of the Royal Asiatic Society, July 1930, pp. 611-23.
This is said to be a commentary to the Pratītyasamutpāda sūtra. Even a fragment is very important in view of the scarcity of the original Sanskrit texts of Buddhist literature.

14.4 Tantric Texts

14.4.1 Kriyātantra (dhāraṇī)

(1) AGRAWALA, V.S. "The Geographical Contents of the Mahāmayūrī." Journal of the United Provinces Historical Society 15 (1942):24-52.
A catalogue of the Mahāmayūrī.

(2) BAGCHI, P.C. "The Geographical Catalogue of the Yakṣas in the Mahāmayūrī." Sino-Indian Studies, 3, pts. 1-2.
Another geographical catalogue.

(3) BLONAY, GODEFROY de, ed. Matériaux pour servir à l'histoire de la déesse bouddhique Tārā. Bibliothèque de l'École des hautes études, vol. 107. Paris: Bouillon, 1895, 64 pp.
Includes the Ārya-tāra-bhaṭṭarikayānamastottaraśataka-stotra, a Sanskrit text (pp. 48-53) and French translation (pp. 54-57) and Āryatārāsragdhara-stotra, a Sanskrit text (pp. 34-40) and a French translation (pp. 41-47).

(4) DAWA-SAMDUP, KAZI, ed. and trans. Shrīchakrasaṃbhāra Tantra, a Buddhist Tantra. Tantrik texts, vol. 7. London: Luzac, 1919, 1 vol.
Consult the introduction for the essentials of the tantra.

(5) GANAPATI SASTRI, TARUVAGRAHARAM, ed. The Āryamañjuśrīmūlakalpa. 3 vols. Trivandrum Sanskrit Series, vols. 70, 76, 84. Trivandrum: Superintendent, Government Press, 1920-25.
This is an important tantric text in which Śākyamuni gives instructions to Mañjuśrī on the magic rites with mantras, mudrās, and maṇḍalas. Thus, the contents of the sutra fall within Mantrayāna, although the sutra declares itself to be an Avataṃsaka-sūtra.

(6) HODGSON, BRIAN HOUGHTON. Essays on the Languages, Literature and Religion of Nepal and Tibet. London: Trubner, 1874, 145 pp.
Hodgson reports on the popularity of the Pañcarakṣa, i.e., 1) mahā pratisāra, 2) mahāsāhasrapramardinī, 3) mahāmayūrī,

4) mahā-sitavati and 5) mahārakṣa-mantrānusārinī. The pañcarakṣa is also used for path-taking in the court.

(7) HOERNLE, AUGUSTUS FREDERIC RUDOLF. "The Unknown Languages of Eastern Turkestan." Journal of the Royal Asiatic Society, 1910, pp. 834, 1283-1300; 1911, 447-77, 201-3.
This is a partial edition of the Sanskrit text of the Mahāpratyaṅgirādhāraṇī discovered in Central Asia.

(8) IWAMOTO, YUTAKA. "Kleinere Dhāraṇī Texte." Beitrage zur Indologie (Kyoto) 2 (1937):10-12.
This is a Sanskrit edition of the Vajra-vidārinī, or Vajra-vidāraṇa-nama-dhāraṇīhṛdayopahṛdaya.

(9) KARPELES, SUZANNE. "Lokeṣvaraśatakam, ou cent strophes en honneur du seigneur du monde, par Vajradatta." Journal asiatique, 1919, pp. 357-465.
The work contains a French translation of the Śataka, a commentary by Vajradatta, and a discussion of the text.

(10) KONOW, STEN, ed. "The Aparimitayuḥ Sūtra, the Old Khotanese Version and the Sanskrit Text and the Tibetan Translation." In Manuscript Remains of Buddhist Literature Found in Eastern Turkestan. Edited by A.F. Rudolf Hoernle. Oxford: Clarendon Press, 1916, pp. 289-329.
These fragments of the Sanskrit manuscripts were unearthed from the sands of Central Asia. Painstaking editorial work has been carried out from the time of the discovery in the last decades of the nineteenth century.

(11) LALOU, MARCELLE, ed. Iconographie des étoffes peintes (pata) dans le Mañjuśrīmūlakalpa. Buddhica, Documents et travaux pour l'étude du bouddhisme, 1st ser.: Mémoires, vol. 6. Paris: P. Geuthner, 1930, 116 pp.
This is a French translation of chapters 4-7 with the Tibetan text. Her other works on the text are "Mañjuśrīmūlakalpa et Tārāmūlakalpa" (12) and "Un traité de magie bouddhique," in Études d'Orientalisme publiées par Le Musée Guimet à la mémoire de Raymonde Linossier, 2 vols. (Paris: E. Leroux, 1932, 2: 303-22).

(12) LALOU, MARCELLE, trans. "Mañjuśrīmūlakalpa et Tārāmūlakalpa." Harvard Journal of Asiatic Studies 1 (1936):327-49.
The text contains the beginning portion of chapter 13 of the Āryamañjuśrīmūlakalpa and a portion of chapter 14.

(13) LALOU, MARCELLE. "A Tun-huang Prelude to the Kāraṇḍavyūha." Indian Historical Quarterly 14 (1938):198-200.
Lalou gives a description of the Sanskrit manuscripts brought back by Pelliot from Tun-huang.

(14) La VALLÉE POUSSIN, LOUIS de, ed. Bouddhisme: Études et matériaux. Académie Royale de Blegique. Mémoires couronnés et Mémoires des savants étrangers, vol. 55. London: Luzac, 1896-1898, pp. 119-150.
One of the unique features of Tantric Buddhism is the recitation of dhāraṇīs. This is a form of concentration of mind and contemplation of profound mysteries through the use of certain letters and words that symbolize these mysteries. The chapters on these dhāraṇīs occupy an important part of the Mahāyāna texts.

(15) La VALLÉE POUSSIN, LOUIS de, trans. Svayambhūpurāṇa dixième chapitre. Université de Gand. Recueil de travaux publiés par la faculté de philosophie et lettres, fasc. 9. Gand: H. Eugelcke, 1893, 19 pp.
The manuscript of the text originates from the Bir library of Kathmandhu, Nepal.

(16) La VALLÉE POUSSIN, LOUIS de, and ROBERT GAUTHIOT, eds. "Fragment final de la Nīlakaṇṭhadhāraṇī." Journal of the Royal Asiatic Society, 1912, pp. 629-45.
There is no branch of Buddhist studies that remains untouched by de La Vallée Poussin's masterful hand, including the dhāraṇīs.

(17) LEUMANN, ERNST. "Der Anfang der Aparimitayur-dhāraṇī." In Zur nordarischen Sprache und Literatur: Vorbemerkungen und vier Aufsätze mit Glossar. Schriften der Wissenschaftlichen Gesellschaft in Strassburg, no. 10 Strassburg: 1912, pp. 75-82.
This is an editorial work on the Aparimitayur-dhāraṇī.

(18) LÉVI, SYLVAIN, ed. and trans. Asaṅga: Mahāyāna-Sūtrālamkāra: Exposé de la doctrine du grand véhicule selon le système Yogācāra (see 14.3.1[1]).
Lévi stresses that the practice of dhāraṇīs was emphasized at the height of the development of the Mahāyāna philosophical schools.

(19) LÉVI, SYLVAIN. "Le catalogue géographique des Yakṣa dans la Mahāmayūrī." Journal asiatique, 1915, pp. 19-138.
The work is a detailed comparison among Sanskrit, Chinese, and Tibetan recensions of the Mahāmayūrī, with copious notes rich in geographical information.

(20) LÉVI, SYLVAIN. "Nīlakaṇṭhadhāraṇī." Journal of the Royal Asiatic Society, 1912, pp. 1063-66.
An article on the dhāraṇī of the "Blue-necked" Avalokiteśvara.

(21) MacDONALD, ARIANE, ed. and trans. Le Maṇḍala du Mañjuśrīmūlakalpa. Collection Jean Przyluski, vol. 3. Paris: A. Maisonneuve, 1962, 190 pp.
The Mañjuśrīmūlakalpa, an important work of the Kriyā-tantra class, emphasizes the external ritualistic "works" (kriyā) thereby occupying a celebrated place from the standpoint of history and practice. MacDonald's study of the text comprises an introductory study (pp. 1-95), translation of chapter 2 and 3 of the Sanskrit work (pp. 97-149) and an edited text of the Tibetan version of the same (pp. 151-174), besides an index. An important contribution to the study of maṇḍalas.

(22) MAJUMDER, PRABHAS CHANDRA. "The Kāraṇḍavyūha: Its Metrical Version." Indian Historical Quarterly 24 (1948):293-99.
This is a Sanskrit edition of the dhāraṇī section of the Kāraṇḍavyūha[-mahāyānasūtra].

(23) MEISEZAHL, R.O., ed. and trans. "The Amoghapāśahṛdaya-dhāraṇī, the Early Sanskrit Manuscript of the Reiunji." Monumenta Nipponica 17 (1962):265-328.
A translation of the dhāraṇī.

(24) MEISEZAHL, R.O. "The Amoghapāśahṛdaya Manuscript Formerly Kept in the Reiunji Temple and Its Collateral Texts in Tibetan Translation." Mikkyōgaku Mikkyōshi Ronbunshū (Studies of Esoteric Buddhism and Tantrism) (Koyasan University, Koyasan), 1965, pp. 179-216.
This is an editorial work of the Amoghapāśahṛdaya, which was employed as a charm by the people for their mental satisfaction, spiritual elevation, and protection against evil.

(25) MINAYEV, IVAN PAVLOVITCH. Buddizm, Izsledovaniya i Materialui [Materials for the study of Buddhism]. Part 2, Materialui. St. Petersburg, 1887, 159 pp. Translated into French as Recherches sur le Bouddhisme, by R.H. Assier de Pompignan. Annales du Musée Guimet. Bibliothèque d'études, vol. 4. Paris: E. Leroux, 1894. 315 pp.
Contains an edition of the Paramārtha-nāma-saṃgīti, one of the Kriyātantras (rituals).

(26) OLDENBURG, SERGEI FEDOROVICH. Mahāmayūrī. Zapiski Vostoernago Otdelenia Imp. Russk. Arkheol Obshechestva. St. Petersburg, 1897-99.
This is an editorial work on the Mahā-mayūrī, the third of the Pañcarakṣa.

(27) WADDELL, LAURENCE AUSTINE. The Buddhism of Tibet, or Lamaism. Cambridge: W. Heffer, 1958, 598 pp. (Orig. pub. 1894.)
According to an Indian classification, Buddhism has three divisions, i.e., the Śrāvaka-yāna, the Pratyeka-buddha-yāna and the Bodhisattva-yāna. The Bodhisattva-yāna in turn is divided in two, i.e. the Pāramitā-yāna and the Mantrayana, which is equivalent to Tantric Buddhism. The Mantrayāna has a further two to seven divisions. Among them, four or five divisions are generally in use. They are: 1) the Kriyā class, 2) the Caryā class, 3) the Yoga class, 4) the Mahāyoga or Uttarayoga class, and 5) Anuttarayoga or Yoginī class. The fourfold classification combines the fourth and fifth categories. A much dated early work on Lamaism.

(28) WALLESER, MAX, ed. and trans. Aparimitayur-jñāna-nāma-mahāyāna-sūtram: Nach einer nepalesischen Sanskrit-Handschrift mit der tibetischen und chinesischen Version. Sitzungsberichte der Heidelberger Akademie der Wissenschaften. Philosophisch-historische Klasse. Jahrgang 1916. 12. Abhandlung. Heidelberg: C. Winter, 1916, 41 pp.
This work on the Aparimitayur-jñāna-nāma-mahāyāna-sutras is based on the Central Asian manuscripts.

(29) WAYMAN, ALEX. "Analysis of the Tantric Section of the Kanjur Correlated to Tanjur Exegesis." In Indo-Asian Studies. Edited by Raghu Vira. 2 vols. Śatapiṭaka series. Indo-Asian literatures, vols. 31, 37. 1:118-25. New Delhi: International Academy of Indian Culture, 1963-65.
Because certain groups of texts display much that is similar, the classification of Tantras was standardized into the following four classes: Kriyā, Caryā, Yoga and Anuttarayoga-tantras, a system by which the Tibetan Tantric canon is arranged.

14.4.2 Caryātantra

(1) TAJIMA, RYŪJUN. Les deux grands maṇḍalas et la doctrine de l'ésotérisme Shingon. Bulletin de la Maison franco-japonaise, n.s., vol. 6. Tokyo: Maison Franco-Japonaise; Paris: Presses universitaires de France, 1959, 352 pp.
The formation of the Mahāvairocana-sūtra and the Vajraśekhara-sūtra marks an epoch in the history of Tantric Buddhism. The sūtras employed a systematization of maṇḍalas in an attempt to harmonize a variety of popular beliefs with Buddhist thought. Tajima's work is a critical edition of the Tibetan text.

14.4.3 Anuttaratantra/Guhyasamājatantra

(1) BAGCHI, SITAMSU SEKHAR, ed. Guhyasamāja Tantra or Tathāgataguhyaka. Buddhist Sanskrit Texts, no. 9. Darbhanga: Mithila Institute of Post-Graduate Studies and Research in Sanskrit Learning, 1965, 177 pp.

"The Guhyasamāja Tantra is one of the earliest Tantric texts and it commands a position of unique importance in the realm of the Buddhist Tantric literature." This tantra is, according to Hadano Hakuyu, presumed to have been compiled about the second half of the eighth century. Bagchi's work contains an English introduction (pp. i-viii) followed by a Hindi introduction (pp. ix-xviii) and the edited text in Devanāgarī.

(2) BHATTACHARYYA, BENOYTOSH, ed. Guhyasamāja Tantra, or Tathāgataguhyaka. 2d ed. Gaekwad's Oriental Series, no. 53. Baroda: Oriental Institute, [1931] 1967, xxxviii + 212 pp.

The Anuttarayoga-tantra is divided into three classes, i.e. the Mahāyoga (Upāya)-tantra class, the Yoginī (Prajñā)-tantra class, and the Advaya (Yuganadddha)-tantra class. As for the second, the Guhyasamāja-tantra enjoys the spotlight. The Sanskrit text has eighteen chapters, but the Tibetan translation leaves out the eighteenth chapter, which is distinguished as another work, the Uttaratantra.

(3) FREMANTLE, FRANCESCA MARY. "A Critical Study of the Guhyasamāja Tantra." Ph.D. dissertation, University of London, 1971.

A much needed study of this tantra.

(4) MATSUNAGA, YŪKEI, ed. "The Guhyasamāja-tantra: A New Critical Edition." Journal of Koyasan University (Koyasan-Daigaku-Ronso) 9 (1974):1-44.

This edition by Matsunaga, one of the leading authorities on Tantric Buddhism in Japan, contains the romanized Sanskrit text of chapters 1-12. This section is called the Mūlatantra, which in turn is divided into two parts, i.e. from the first to the twelfth and from the thirteenth to the seventeenth chapters.

(5) MIBU, TAISHUN. "On the Theory of Five Buddhas in Guhyasamāja-tantra." Indogaku Bukkyōgaku Kenkyū (Journal of Indian and Buddhist Studies) 21 (1973):10-24.

Mibu traces the structure and development of theory of the five Buddhas in the Guhyasamāja-tantra. Highly technical article.

(6) SNELLGROVE, DAVID, trans. "Supreme Enlightenment." In Buddhist Texts through the Ages (see 1.1[9]), pp. 221-24.
An English translation of chapter seven of the Guhyasamājatantra is available here.

(7) TUCCI, GIUSEPPE. "Some Glosses upon the Guhyasamāja." Mélanges chinoise et bouddhique 3 (1934-35):339-53.
This is a review of Benoytosh Bhattacharya's edition of the Sanskrit text Guhyasamāja Tantra (2). Tucci discusses the various points of the text, i.e., the number of chapters, the number of supreme Buddhas, the nature of mantra, etc. Interesting points for advanced students.

(8) WAYMAN, ALEX. Yoga of the Guhyasamājatantra: The Arcane Lore of Forty Verses. Delhi: Motilal Banarsidass, 1975.
Translation of chapters six and twelve of the Guhyasamājatantra from Wayman's reedited Sanskrit, along with Sanskrit selections from the Pradīpoddyotana MS (which is the most important commentary on that Tantra) and translation of the same selections; translation of the Akṣobhya-maṇḍala of the Guhyasamājatantra. The main part of the work is a synthetic commentary on the forty verses with copious extracts from the Tanjur (Tibetan) commentaries on the Tantra and the annotations of Tson-kha-pa.

(9) WINTERNITZ, MORITZ. "Notes on the Guhyasamāja-Tantra and the Age of the Tantras." Indian Historical Quarterly 9 (1933):1-10.
These notes are based on no. 18 of the "Descriptive Catalogue of Sanskrit Manuscripts in the Government Collection under the Care of the Asiatic Society of Bengal, vol. 1, Buddhist Manuscripts." A highly technical article.

14.4.4 Pañcakrama

(1) La VALLÉE POUSSIN, LOUIS de, ed. Études et textes tantriques. Vol. 1, Pañcakrama. Recueil de travaux publiés par la faculté de philosophie et lettres de l'Université de Gand, fasc. 16. Gand: Université de Gand, 1896, 56 pp.
This is the Sanskrit edition of the important text called the Pañcakrama. The term krama indicates a gradual realization toward enlightenment preceded by piṇḍakrama which is prescribed for the considerations regarding the body (Kāyaviveka). The five Kramas are: Vajrajapa, Sarvasuddhīvisuddhī, Svadhīṣṭhana, Paramarahāsyasukhābhisambodhi and Yuganaddha. This important work of de La Vallée Poussin contains: an introduction and the texts of the Piṇḍi-krama, the Pañca-krama, and the commentary (Tippani) by Paṇḍita Parahitaraskṣita. The introduction is the reproduction

of de La Vallée Poussin's "Note sur le Pañcakrama," Proceedings of the 10th International Congress of Orientalists, Geneva, 1894, pt. 1, pp. 137-46.

14.4.5 Advayasiddhi

(1) SHENDGE, MALATI J., ed. and trans. Advayasiddhi: A Study. The Maharashtra State University Oriental Series, no. 8. Baroda: Oriental Institute, 1964, 30 pp.

This small work, Advayasiddhi, written by Princess Lakṣimīnkaradevī, a younger sister of King Indrabhūti (ca. 687-717), is well introduced, edited and translated into English. The text is one of the "Seven classes of realization" (Śrīguhyasiddhinam or Grub pa sde bdun).

14.4.6 Kālacakra Tantras

(1) HOFFMANN, HELMUT H.R. "Kālacakra Studies I. Manichaeism, Christianity and Islam in the Kālacakra Tantra." Central Asiatic Journal 13 (1969):52-73.

This work is the first of the series in which Hoffmann presents a free and informal series of smaller or bigger treatises about the numerous aspects and problems connected with the Kālacakra-tantra and related works in Sanskrit as well as in Tibetan.

(2) HOFFMANN, HELMUT. "Das Kālacakra, die letzte Phase des Buddhismus in Indien." Saeculum 15 (1964):125-31.

The work gives general information about the Kālacakra and its related problems. In the Kālacakara, for example, the halting of the Muslim invasion through the alliance of Buddhists, Vaiṣṇavas, Saivas, etc., is stated.

(3) HOFFMANN, HELMUT. "Literarhistorische Bemerkungen zur Śekoddeśaṭīkā des Nadapada." Walther Schubring zum 70. Geburtstag dargebracht von der deutschen Indologie (Hamburg), 1950, pp. 140-147.

This study deals with the commentary entitled the Śekoddeśaṭīkā by Nadapada or Naropa. Naropa's authorship, however, is questioned by Hakuyu Hatano (cf. "Fundamental study on the formation of 'Kālacakra-tantra" Mikkyō Bunka 8 [1950]:18-37.)

(4) RAGHU, VIRA, and LOKESH CHANDRA, eds. Kālacakra-Tantra and Other Texts in Tibetan, Mongolian and Sanskrit. 2 vols. Sata-piṭaka Series. Indo-Asian literatures nos. 69, 70. New Delhi: International Academy of Indian Culture, 1966, 698 pp.

The Kālacakra (Wheel of time) was introduced about A.D. 967 from a country where Indian civilization had to struggle with others. It was compiled roughly between A.D. 1027-87, and was current from the closing years of the eleventh century to the opening years of the twelfth. The edition gives, besides the Sanskrit text, the Tibetan and Mongolian translation.

14.4.7 Hevajratantra

(1) SNELLGROVE, DAVID L., ed. and trans. The Hevajra Tantra: A Critical Study. 2 vols. London Oriental Series, vol. 6. London: Oxford University Press, 1959.
This is a complete study of the Hevajra Tantra, one of the most interesting sutras in the Anuttarayoga class. It is complete with an introduction and translation (vol. 1) and the Sanskrit and Tibetan texts in the separate volume. The practice of yogins and yoginīs, the worship of Dākinī, etc. are all contained in this esoteric text, which demands a careful and guided reading.

14.4.8 Cittaviśuddhiprakaraṇa

(1) PATEL, PRABHUBHAI BHIKHABHAI, ed. Cittaviśuddhiprakaraṇa of Āryadeva: Sanskrit and Tibetan Texts. Viśva-Bharati Studies, no. 8. Santiniketan, 1949, 108 pp.
Although about thirty works are attributed to Āryadeva according to the Tibetan tradition, the authorship of many cannot be ascertained. Among them, this work is interesting because of its esoteric contents. There is a Japanese translation, but no European translation is available. (Cf. Ryōjō Yamada, "The Cittaviśuddhiprakaraṇa Sanskrit and Tibetan Versions with Japanese Translation," Bunka 3 [1936]:1-65.) Patel's introduction originally appeared in Indian Historical Quarterly 9 (1933):705-21.

(2) SNELLGROVE, DAVID, trans. "The Cleansing of Thought." In Buddhist Texts Through the Ages (see 1.1[9], p. 221.
English translation of the Cittaviśuddhiprakaraṇa of Āryadeva.

14.4.9 Mystic Songs of Sahaja

(1) BAGCHI, PRABODH CHANDRA, ed. Caryāgītikośa of Buddhist Siddhas. In collaboration with Śānti Bhikṣu Śāstri. Shantiniketan: Viśvabharati, 1956, 215 pp.
The work was completed by Shānti Bhikṣu Shāstri after the death of Bagchi in 1956. It has an informative preface covering the discovery, progress report, and future plan of studies of the gītis and dohas of Siddhas followed by an introduction that

sketches "a number of images," such as the boat, the rat, Vīṇā, the elephant, the deer, the union, the fermentation of wine, carding the cotton, etc. The edition is carefully done, having numerous footnotes showing variants in the Tibetan text.

(2) BAGCHI, PRABODH CHANDRA. Dohakośa (Apabhraṃśa-Texts of the Sahajayāna School). Pt. 1. Texts and Commentaries. Calcutta Sanskrit Series. Calcutta: Metropolitan Publishing House, 1938, viii + 167 pp.

The following earlier works of P.C. Bagchi are also available: "A Note on the Language of the Buddhist Dohas," Calcutta Oriental Journal 1 (1934); "Some Aspects of Buddhist Doha," Calcutta Oriental Journal 1 (1934); "Dohakośa with Notes and Translations," Journal of the Department of Letters (Calcutta) 23: (1935) 180 pp.; "Sibilants in the Buddhist Dohas," Indian Linguistics 5 (1935).

(3) GUENTHER, HERBERT V., trans. The Royal Song of Saraha: A Study in the History of Buddhist Thought. Seattle: University of Washington Press, 1969, 214 pp.

Saraha was a famous yogin who lived in India sometime between A.D. 800 and 1000. Like Milarepa, Saraha gave his teachings in songs that are collectively known as the three cycles of dohas. Guenther has here translated and annotated one of the cycles, the king dohas, as well as translating their Tibetan commentaries. The translation and footnotes are clear and to the point. Difficult points are carefully explained both by Guenther and the Tibetans so that one can study Saraha's teaching without getting lost in detailed analysis. Highly recommended.

(4) SHAHIDULLAH, MUHAMMAD, ed. Les chants mystiques de Kanha et de Saraha: Les dohakośa (en apabhraṃśa avec les versions tibetaines) et les Caryā (en vieux-bengali). Textes pour l'étude du bouddhisme tardif. Paris: A. Maisonneuve, 1928, 234 pp.

The last stage of esoteric Buddhism in India is called the Sahaja-yāna, which is active even today in the Bengal region. (See Nagendra Nath Vasu, The Modern Buddhism and Its Followers in Orissa [Calcutta: Calcutta University Press, 1911], 181 pp.) Among the works of the Sahaja-yāna, the Dohakośa of Kanha, the Caryācārya-ṭīkā of Siddhācārya, the Dharma-pūjā-vidhi of Raghunandin, and the Śūnya-purāṇa of Pamaipaṇḍita, are more famous and the texts are available. These texts are written in the Apabhraṃśa dialect. Shahidullah compares the Apabhraṃśa verses with their Tibetan translations.

(5) SNELLGROVE, DAVID, trans. "Saraha's Treasury of Songs." In Buddhist Texts Through the Ages (see 1.1[9]).

This is an English translation of the 112 verses of the Dohakośa, enjoyable reading for "tired philosophers."

14.4.10 Miscellaneous Tantric Texts

(1) CHANG, GARMA CH'ENG-CHI, ed. and trans. The Hundred Thousand Songs of Milarepa. 2 vols. New Hyde Park: University Books, 1962, 730 pp.

Milarepa (1040-1123) inherits the mystical songs (doha) of the Tantric poets of Bengal, through his teacher Marpa. Chang translates this great Tibetan classic for the first time in any modern language. In this book the profound ideas of Mahāyāna-Vajrayāna Buddhism are revealed in sixty-one stories in simple language. The appendix includes an introductory article, "Its Origin, Background, Function, and Translation."

(2) CONZE, EDWARD. "The Adhyardhaśatika prajñāpāramitā." Mikkyōgaku Mikkyōshi Ronbunshū (Studies of Esoteric Buddhism and Tantrism) (Koyasan University, Koyasan), 1965, pp. 101-15.

This is an English translation of a Prajñāpāramitā-sūtra, which abounds in esoteric words. Conze's authoritative translation is based on the Sanskrit and Tibetan text of the sutra edited by Shoun Togano-o.

(3) DAS, SARAT CHANDRA, ed. and trans. "Bodhi Patha Pradīpa (Byan chub lam gyi sgron-ma) by Dīpāṅkura Śrījñāna." Journal of the Buddhist Text Society of India 1 (1893): 39-48; 3 (1893):21-26; Tibetan text pt. 1 (1893):57-64.

This English translation represents one of the most important works of the great Bengali Paṇḍit Atīśa or Dīpāṅkura Śrījñāna, who undertook a journey to Tibet to restore the purity of Buddhism there. The work contains the essence of both the sutras and tantras, the path to enlightenment. As for Atīśa's life and works, see Alaka Chattopadhyaya, Atīśa and Tibet: Life and Works of Dīpamkāra Śrījñāna in Relation to the History and Religion of Tibet, with Tibetan Sources Translated under Professor Lama Chimpa (Calcutta: Indian Studies: Past and Present, 1967), 593 pp.

(4) EVANS-WENTZ, WALTER YEELING, ed. The Tibetan Book of the Great Liberation; or The Method of Realizing Nirvāṇa Through Knowing the Mind (see 5[3]).

Along with a lot of Evans-Wentz's philosophy, this book contains a translation of Padmasambhava's biography and a yogic text entitled "The Yoga of Knowing the Mind, The Seeing of Reality, Called Self-Liberation." The meditation text is a short one attributed to Padmasambhava, dealing with the illusions of

(5) GORDON, ANTOINETTE K., ed. and trans. The Hundred Thousand Songs: Selections from Milarepa, Poet-saint of Tibet. Tokyo: E. Tuttle, 1961, 122 pp.
Another work on Milarepa's famous songs.

(6) GUENTHER, HERBERT V. Buddhist Philosophy in Theory and Practice (see 1.5[8]).
Guenther attempts "to present an account of the various systems and problems of Buddhist philosophy in a single volume" based on his translations of two short but very important Tibetan texts, the Grub-pa'i mtha'i rnam'-bzhag rinpo-ch'i phreng-ba and the Yid-bzhin-mdzod-kyi grub-mtha' bsdus-pa, or "The Jewel Garland," a dGelugs-pa text, and "The Summary of Philosophical Systems" by Lama Mi-pham, a nineteenth-century Nying-ma-pa writer. A recommended book for anyone at all interested in Buddhist philosophy, although the reader must be initiated into some of Guenther's esoteric terminology "without mystification" such as "bare haecceity" (p. 41).

(7) GUENTHER, HERBERT V. "Indian Buddhist Thought in Tibetan Perspective: Infinite Transcendence Versus Finiteness." History of Religions 3 (1963):83-105.
Provides the translation of a small text by Kun-mkheni Jigs-med gling-pa entitled "The Tantra of the Reality of Transcendent Awareness (symbolically referred to as) Kun-tu bzang-po, the Quintessence of Fulfillment and Completion." Guenther then gives a comparison with the traditional system of the Vijñānavādins.

(8) GUENTHER, HERBERT V., trans. The Life and Teaching of Naropa. UNESCO Collection of Representative Works: Tibetan Series. Oxford: Clarendon Press, 1963, 292 pp.
This is translated from the original Tibetan with a philosophical commentary on the oral transmission. Naropa was a famous Indian Buddhist scholar who became the elder teacher at Nalanda University. Fascinating and sometimes humorous, the biography is an excellent example of the "crazy wisdom" of the Tantric siddhas, showing how Tantra is taught as a practical life experience. The second part of the book is Guenther's elucidation of the biography, interpreted in light of Western philosophy and psychology.

(9) GUENTHER, HERBERT V. Yuganaddha: The Tantric View of Life. Chowkhamba Sanskrit Series, vol. 3. Varanasi: Chowkhamba Sanskrit Series Office, 1969, 218 pp.
The basic premise of Tantra (and this book) is that such polarities as masculine/feminine are merely " . . . two abstractions carved from an indivisible whole . . ." that man must see beyond if he is to realize liberation. Like all Mahāyāna Buddhists, the Tantrics feel that the best way to transcend dualities is to

accept them with openness and equanimity. Although the book is quite difficult in parts, it is still one of the best on the topic.

(10) GUENTHER, HERBERT V., and LESLIE S. KAWAMURA, trans. Mind in Buddhist Psychology. Tibetan Translation Series. Emeryville: Dharma, 1975, 133 pp.
This is a translation of "The Necklace of Clear Understanding: An Elucidation of the Working of Mind and Mental Events" by the eighteenth-century dGe-lugs-pa writer Ye-shes rgyal-mtshan. The work is a straightforward description of the various types of mental events present in everyday consciousness. The events are classified together with similar mental activities in several groupings, e.g. the six basic emotions, the twenty proximate factors of instability, etc., and are then dealt with individually. Each topic is begun with a definition taken from the Abhidharmasamuccaya and then discussed in terms of its positive, negative, and neutral aspects (if applicable) and its manifestations in the mind. Although short, the work succeeds in covering the subject matter in a clear and readily understandable way.

(11) KASCHEWSKY, RUDOLF, ed. Das Leben des Lamaistischen Heiligen Tsongkhapa Blo-bzan-grags-pa (1357-1419), dargestellt und erlautert anhand seiner Vita "Quellort allen Gluckes." 2 vols. Asiatische Forschungen, vol. 32. Wiesbaden: Harrassowitz, 1971.
This excellent scholarly study deals with the life and works of Tsong-kha-pa. It includes: "Einleitung" (pp. 1-57), "Deutsche Fassung der Vita Quellort Allen Gluckes" (pp. 61-256) and a reproduction of the text.

(12) TATTABHUSAN, H.G., ed. and trans. Kāmaratna Tantra. Shillong: Assam Government Press, 1928, 110 pp.
An edition of this interesting tantric text with an English translation and twenty pages of diagrams.

(13) WANGYAL, GESHE THUPTEN, comp. The Door of Liberation. New York: Girodias Associates, 1973, 323 pp.
The book has a prefatory note by Tenzin Gyatsho, the fourteenth Dalai Lama. Geshe Wangyal is from the famous Drepung Monastery near Lhasa and founder of the Lamaist Buddhist Monastery of America (Labsum Shedrup Ling). His first book contains a translation of several Tibetan texts concerning lineage of teachers including the Kadampa, excerpts from the Damamūrkha-sūtra and the writings of Tsong-kha-pa: "The Essence of Good Explanation, Praise of Munīndra," "The Three Principles of the Path," "The Concise Meaning of the Stages of the Path," and "The Foundation of All Excellence."

14.5 Japanese Buddhist Texts

14.5.1 Shingon

(1) HAKEDA, YOSHITO S., trans. Kūkai: Major Works. UNESCO Collection of Representative Works, Japanese Series. New York: Columbia University Press, 1972, 303 pp.

Provides an account of Kūkai's life, a summary and exegesis of the most important themes of his writing, and a translation of the principal portions of eight of Kūkai's works on religion. An important work recommended to all. For those who can use them, Hakeda's works in Japanese are of value:

"Sokushin Jōbutsugi" [the doctrine of attaining Buddhahood while living in human body]. Mikkyō Bunka 27 (1954):1-12; 28 (1954): 13-22; 29-30 (1955):23-32; 31 (1955):1-12; 32 (1956):1-10; 33 (1956):1-14; 34 (1956):1-10; 38 (1957):1-19.

"Unjigi" [The doctrine of the syllable Hūṃ]. Mikkyō Bunka 17 (1952):1-10; 18 (1952):11-20; 19 (1952):21-32; 20 (1952):33-42; 21 (1953):43-54; 22 (1953):55-62; 23 (1953):63-72; 24-25 (1953): 73-82.

"Shōji Jissōgi" [A treatise on the meaning of voice and syllable and reality]. Mikkyō Bunka 7 (1949):1-10; 8 (1950):1-10; 9-10 (1950):1-12; 11 (1950):1-12; 12 (1950):1-12; 13 (1951):1-12.

(2) TAJIMA, RYŪJUN. Les deux grands maṇḍalas et la doctrine de l'ésotérisme Shingon (s-e 14.4.2[1].

This is an important work on a pair of Maṇḍalas, the Garbha-dhātu and the Vajra-dhātu. On the basis of these Maṇḍalas, the two methods of Tantric practices are organized.

14.5.2 Nembutsu (including Pure Land)

(1) ANDREWS, ALLAN A. "The Essentials of Salvation: A Study of Genshin's Ōjōyōshū." Eastern Buddhist 4 (Oct. 1971):50-88.

Two centuries before Hōnen (1133-1212), a Tendai monk, Genshin (942-1017) provided answers to the essentials of Nembutsu. Does Nembutsu require supporting practices? Is it a form of meditation? A good basic article.

(2) ANDREWS, ALLAN A. The Teachings Essential for Rebirth: A Study of Genshin's Ōjōyōshū. A Monumenta Nipponica Monograph. Tokyo: Sophia University, 1973, 133 pp.

The first book-length study of Genshin's influential work. Recommended to all who wish to prove the Pure Land system.

(3) IMADATE, TOSUI. The Tannishō (Tracts on Deploring the Heterodoxies). Kyoto: Eastern Buddhist Society, 1928, 51 pp.
An excellent translation of this famous work.

(4) The Kyōgyōshinshō or the Teaching, Practice, Faith, and Attainment. Translated by Kōshō Yamamoto. Tokyo: Karinbunko, 1958, 518 pp.
An earlier translation by a scholar of Pure Land Buddhism.

(5) MIYAJI, KAKUE. "Salvation for the Wicked--Some Comments on Section 13 of 'Tan-ni-shō.'" Journal of the Institute of Buddhist Culture (Kyoto Joshigakuen Bukkyōbunka Kenkyūsho Kenkyūkiyō) 5 (1975):1-25.
This excellent scholarly study surveys the doctrine of akunin-shōki (salvation for the wicked), which is an important but often misunderstood teaching of Shinran.

(6) SHINRAN. The Kyōgyōshinshō: The Collection of Passages Expounding the True Teaching, Living, Faith and Realizing of the Pure Land. Translated by Daisetz Teitarō Suzuki. Kyoto: Shinshū Ōtaniha, 1973, 442 pp.
This is not only one of the most important books on the study of Pure Land Buddhism, but also on Buddhism in general. This is the main work of Shinran Shōnin and the basic scripture of the Jōdo Shin sect that he founded. The book falls into two parts: the first four chapters (True Teaching, True Living, True Faith, and True Realization) and the remaining two chapters on True Buddha and the land of the Transformation-body. An extensive glossary with 442 items (pp. 203-329), 14 charts, and a copious index (pp. 357-442) are included.

(7) SHINRAN. The Tanni-shō: Notes Lamenting Differences. Translated and annotated by Ryosetsu Fujiwara. Ryūkoku translation series, no. 2. Kyoto: Ryūkoku Translation Center, Ryūkoku University, 1962, 146 pp.
The Tanni-shō is not a systematic presentation of the doctrine of Shin Buddhism, but the abundant citations of Shinran's words makes the book one of the most influential scriptures of Japanese Buddhism. The volume contains the Japanese text, the Romanization of it, and translation. Supplementary notes and glossary are included.

(8) Shinran-shōnin's Tannishō with Buddhist Psalms. Translated and compiled by Inagaki Saizō. Nishinomiya City: Eishinsha, 1949, 220 pp.
Yet another translation of this famous work.

(9) The Shinshū Seiten: The Holy Scriptures of the Shin Sect. Honolulu: Honpa Hongwanji Mission of Hawaii, 1955, 522 pp.
A collection of basic Shin works translated into English.

(10) SUZUKI, DAISETZ TEITARŌ. Collected Writings on Shin Buddhism. Kyoto: Shinshū Ōtaniha, 1973, 262 pp.
This volume embraces a pair of publications by Shinshū Ōtaniha. Suzuki's writings on the subject of Shin Buddism cover over half a century, the period during which he taught at the Shin-affiliated Otani University. He was at the time engaged in editing Eastern Buddhist, which he founded in 1921, and in which many of his own articles appeared. Important articles on Shin Buddhism are edited and contained in this volume. They are: "The Development of the Pure Land Doctrine in Buddhism," "A Miscellany on the Shin Teaching of Buddhism," "Infinite Light," "What is Shin Buddhism?," "The Life of Shinran Shōnin and the Tannishō."

(11) TANNISHŌ KENKYŪKAI. Perfect Freedom in Buddhism: An Exposition of the Words of Shinran, Founder of the Shin Sect, the Largest Buddhist School in Japan. Translated by Shinji Takuwa. Japanese Life and Culture Series. Tokyo: Hokuseidō Press, 1968, 174 pp.
The original Japanese text is the outcome of joint study of the Tannishō Study Group. An authoritative introduction includes: "Faith of the Ignorant," "Blessed are the Wicked," "Neither Self Effort nor a Moral Goodness," etc.

(12) Tannishō: A Tract Deploring Heresies of Faith. Kyoto: Higashi Hongwanji Shamusho, 1961, 61 pp.
Another translation of this famous work. This version also includes the Japanese text.

(13) YAMAMOTO, KŌSHŌ, ed. Private Letters of Shinran Shōnin. Tokyo: Okazakiya Shōten, 1956, 115 pp.
An edited work that reveals Shinran's thoughts on many subjects.

(14) YAMAMOTO, KŌSHŌ, trans. The Words of St. Rennyo: Complete Translations of the Rennyoshōnin--Goichidaiki-Kikigaki and the Anjinketsujosho. Ube: Karinbunko, 1968, 196 pp.
According to the translator, the Shin Buddhists possess three popular but important works in the Japanese language. These are the Tannishō, the Anjinketsujosho, and the Rennyoshōnin-goichidaiki-kikigaki. The latter is a mélange, requiring further finish. Yet, people at times call this the "Analecta Confucius of the Shin Buddhists." The reason is that it contains the words of Rennyo, the greatest of the Shin "apostles," who tells us how to carry on a life of faith.

14.5.3 Zen

(1) ABE, MASAO. "Dōgen on Buddha Nature." Eastern Buddhist 4 (May 1971):28-71.
This excellent article examines the celebrated book of Shōbōgenzō on the opening of the Buddha nature: "All sentiment beings without exception have the Buddha nature: Tathāgata is permanent with no change at all."

(2) BLYTH, R.H. Zen and Zen Classics. Vol. 4, Mumonkan. Tokyo: Hokuseido Press, 1966, 340 pp.
The Mumonkan (Gateless barrier) is a basic Zen text written by Mumon (Wu-men) in 1229. It comprises forty-eight cases, each with lengthy commentaries on the subject at hand. Blyth had undertaken this admirable translation to be one of an eight-volume work. He did not, however, live to complete the work; there are only five rearranged volumes in the Zen and Zen Classics series. Other volumes can profitably be consulted since interspersed among them are translations from the original Chinese and Japanese texts; for example, volume 1 has Seng-ts'an's Hsin-hsin-ming (The believing mind). Chinese texts usually accompany the translations. A very good beginning.

(3) HOFFMANN, YOEL, trans. The Sound of the One Hand: 281 Zen Kōans with Answers. New York: Basic Books, 1975, 322 pp.
The kōans and their answers are taken from a heretofore guarded Zen text, Gendai Sōjizen Hyōron (A critique of present-day pseudo-Zen), which was first published in Japan in 1916. Its publication created quite a stir at the beginning in Japanese Zen circles, but all of that seems to have subsided. It includes a helpful introduction by Ben-Ami Scharfstein, "The Tactics of Emptiness."

(4) KING, WINSTON, JOCELYN KING, and GISHIN TOKIWA. "The Fourth Letter from Hakuin's Orategama." Eastern Buddhist 5 (May 1972):81-114.
Hakuin wrote the original text in 1750 at the age of 66. It was published the next year. He wrote it in answer to a question from the Lord of Nabeshima concerning the relative superiority of nembutsu and Kōan. An interesting letter.

(5) KOBORI, SŌHAKU, and NORMAN A. WADDELL, trans. "The Biography of Shidō Munan Zenji, compiled by Fufu-anju Enji." Eastern Buddhist 3 (June 1970):124-38.
Shidō Munan Zenji (1603-76) was an important Zen master; nearly all modern Zen masters, except those of the Sōtō school, belong to his line. Having completely broken away from the Zen tradition, he wrote nothing at all in Chinese. Rather, he expressed

his insight exclusively in Japanese colloquial language. His Sokushin-ki is a good example.

(6) KOBORI, SŌHAKU, and NORMAN A. WADDELL, trans. "Sokushin-ki Shidō Munan Zenji." Eastern Buddhist 3 (Oct. 1970):89-118; 4 (Oct. 1971):119-27.
A translation of Shidō Munan Zenji's work on attaining Buddhahood in this very mind.

(7) MASUNAGA, REIHŌ, trans. A Primer of Sōtō Zen (see 4[21]).
The Shōbōgenzō Zuimonki, a collection of various discourses and comments by Dōgen (1200-1253) recovered by his disciple Ejō (1198-1280). It reveals Dōgen's supramundane thought as well as mundane reflections. An important introduction to Sōtō Zen, a school of Zen relatively unknown in the West as compared to the Rinzai branch.

(8) MASUNAGA, REIHŌ. The Sōtō Approach to Zen. Tokyo: Layman Buddhist Society Press, 1958, 215 pp.
Provides a good introduction to the Sōtō branch of Zen and contains translations of selected chapters from the Shōbōgenzō of Dōgen.

(9) SASAKI, RUTH F., trans. The Record of Lin-chi: The Recorded Sayings of Ch'an Master Lin-chi Hui-chao of Chen Prefecture. Compiled by Hui-jan. Kyoto: Institute for Zen Studies, 1975, 88 pp. + Chinese text, 35 pp.
The translation was begun by the late Ruth F. Sasaki and completed by members of the Institute for Zen Studies, Kyoto. It is an excellent translation with copious notes. A basic text of Japanese Rinzai Zen.

(10) SHAW, R.D.M., trans. The Blue Cliff Records: The Hekigan Roku (Pi-yen-lu). Containing One Hundred Stories of Zen Masters of Ancient China. London: Michael Joseph, 1961, 299 pp.
Shaw has edited, translated and added his commentaries to this basic Zen text. A good beginning.

(11) SHAW, R.D.M., trans. The Embossed Tea Kettle: Orate Gama and Other Works of Hakuin Zenji. London: George Allen & Unwin, 1963, 197 pp.
The volume includes the Yasen Kanna (see [12]) and other works such as the Orategama (The embossed tea kettle) and eight "Sermons to His Peasant Parishioners." A good introduction to the life and thought of the great eighteenth-century Japanese Rinzai Zen reformer.

(12) SHAW, R.D.M., and WILHELM SCHIFFER, trans. "Yasen Kanna: (A Chat on a Boat in the Evening), by Hakuin Zenji." Monumenta Nipponica 13 (1957):101-27.
Translation of an important work by Hakuin (1685-1768), a great master of Rinzai Zen as well as a witty teacher.

(13) SHIBAYAMA, ZENKEI. Zen Comments on the Mumonkan. Translated by Sumiko Kudo. New York: Harper & Row, 1974, 361 pp.
Provides an authentic commentary by a Japanese Zen Rōshi on one of the most important documents in Zen Buddhism.

(14) SUZUKI, DAISETZ TEITARŌ. "On the Hekigan Roku (Blue Cliff Records) with a Translation of Case One." Eastern Buddhist 1 (Sept. 1965).
An authoritative translation of the Blue Cliff records, one of the most important documents in the study of Zen.

(15) WADDELL, NORMAN, trans. "The Zen Sermons of Bankei Yōtaku." Eastern Buddhist 6, no. 2 (Oct. 1973):129-51; 7, no. 6 (May 1974):124-41; no. 2 (Oct. 1974):83-107.
The Zen master Bankei Yōtaku (1622-93) was famous for his "Unborn Zen." Waddell translates the Bankei butchi kōsai zenji hogo [The dharma sermons of Bankei Butchi Kōsai Zenji], one of two collections of his sermons.

(16) WADDELL, NORMAN, and MASAO ABE. "Dōgen's Bendōwa." Eastern Buddhist 4 (May 1971):124-57.
Dōgen's second work (after Fukanzazengi); his first in Japanese. It has been said with truth that all the books of the Shōbōgenzō collection are in their essence contained in this, the first book. Bendōwa thus serves as an excellent basic introduction to Dōgen's work and thought as a whole.

(17) WADDELL, NORMAN, and MASAO ABE. "Dōgen's Fukanzazengi and Shōbōgenzō Zazengi." Eastern Buddhist 6 (Oct. 1973):115-28.
Dōgen's first utterance, "The Universal Premonition of the Principles of Zazen," the Sōtō sect's single most cherished writing.

(18) WADDELL, NORMAN, and MASAO ABE. "Dōgen's Shōbōgenzō Zenki 'Total Dynamic Working' and Shōji 'Birth and Death.'" Eastern Buddhist 5 (May 1972):70-80.
An English translation of one of the most important chapters from the Shōbōgenzō.

(19) WADDELL, NORMAN, and MASAO ABE. "The King of Samādhi's Samādhi: Dōgen's Shōbōgenzō Sammai O Zammai." Eastern Buddhist 7 (May 1974):118-23.
Rājasamādhi is, according to Nāgārjuna, "so called because all the various kinds of other samādhis are included in it. It is like all the rivers and myriad rivulets of the human world flowing into the great ocean. Or like the fact that all men are vassals of the King of the realm." An important chapter of the Shōbōgenzō.

(20) WADDELL, NORMAN, and MASAO ABE. "One Bright Pearl, Dōgen's Shōbōgenzō Ikka Myōju." Eastern Buddhist 4 (Oct. 1971): 108-18.
Provides a good English translation of a chapter of the Shōbōgenzō, which is not only treasured by the Sōtō sect, but also by students of Japanese thought and literature.

(21) WADDELL, NORMAN, and MASAO ABE. "Shōbōgenzō Genjōkōan." Eastern Buddhist 5 (Oct. 1972):129-40.
The eminent Sōtō master of the Meiji era, Nishiari Bokusan spoke of Genjōkōan in this fashion: "This is the most difficult. . . . It is Dōgen's skin, flesh, bones, and marrow. . . . His whole life's teaching begins and ends with this fascicle . . . the 95 fascicles of Shōbōgenzō are offshoots of this one."

(22) YAMPOLSKY, PHILIP B., trans. The Zen Master Hakuin: Selected Writings. New York: Columbia University Press, 1971, 253 pp.
The work contains a translation of the complete Orategama text, as well as of Yabukōji and Hebiichigo. An admirable attempt to present Hakuin's writings in English.

(23) YOKOI, YŪHŌ. The First Step to Dōgen's Zen--Shōbōgenzō-zuimonki. Tokyo: Sankibo Buddhist Book Store, 1972, 132 pp.
Another complete translation of the six collected chapters of Dōgen's lectures, in which he stressed the strenuous discipline of doing zazen. The translation is only fair, but gives sufficient insight into Dōgen's thought and life.

(24) YOKOI, YŪHŌ. Zen Master Dōgen: An Introduction with Selected Writings. New York and Tokyo: Weatherhill, 1976, 217 pp.
With the editorial assistance of Daizen Victoria, Yokoi has translated three independent works of Dōgen, i.e. Fukan Zazen-gi [A universal recommendation for zazen], Gakudō Yōjin-shū [Points to watch in Buddhist training], and Shushō-gi [The meaning of

practice-enlightenment]. In addition, there are twelve selected sections from the bulky Shōbōgenzō. A helpful introduction to Dōgen's life and thought is included.

14.5.4 Nichiren

(1) EHARA, RYŌZUI, trans. The Awakening to the Truth, or Kaimokushō. Tokyo: International Buddhist Society, 1941, 122 pp.

The Kaimokusho, one of the important writings of Nichiren, was written in 1272 A.D., when he was in exile at a forlorn hermitage on the island of Sado. In this work, he describes the process by which he reached the conclusion that he himself was destined to appear in the latter day as a messenger of the Buddha Śākyamuni, as prophesized in the Lotus Sūtra.

(2) RENONDEAU, GASTON, trans. La doctrine de Nichiren. Publications du Musée Guimet. Bibliothèque d'études, vol. 58. Paris: Presses Universitaires de France, 1953, 332 pp.

This excellent book provides the French translation of the six important works of Nichiren: Kaimokushō (Le traité qui ouvre les yeux), Kwanjin honzon-shō (L'introspection revèle l'objet fondamental de notre vénération), Sho-hō jissō shō (Traité sur le caractère vrai de toutes les essences), Sōmoku jōbutsu kuketsu (instruction verbale sur la bouddhisation des végétaux), Shokun no mimi ni kono hōmon wo ire yodozai wo manukaruru koto (Faire connaître cette doctrine à votre seigneur c'est le moyen d'échapper à la participation à ses fautes), and Hokke shuyō-sho (Traité sur l'essentiel du Lotus).

(3) RENONDEAU, GASTON, trans. "Traité sur l'état, de Nichiren suivi de huit lettres de 1268." T'oung Pao 40 (1950-51): 123-98.

This is another important translation of one of the most important writings by Nichiren, the influence of whom is being felt today, not only in religious circles of the world, but in the Japanese political scene as well.

15 Presuppositions and Methodology

(1) DHAMMARATANA, U. "The Methodology of Vibhaṅgapakaraṇa" (see 6[20]).

(2) INADA, KENNETH K. "Some Basic Misconceptions of Buddhism" (see 7[12]).

(3) KITAGAWA, HIDENORI. "A Note on the Methodology in the Study of Indian Logic" (see 10[27]).
Shows the inapplicability of Aristotelian logic to the Indian system of logic of Dignāga.

(4) POTTER, KARL H. Presuppositions of India's Philosophies (see 7[23]).

(5) ROBINSON, RICHARD H. "The Classical Indian Axiomatic" (see 7[28]).

(6) SAKURABE, HAJIME. "Abhidharmāvatāra by an Unidentified Author" (see 6[72]).

16 Comparisons of Buddhism

16.1 Comparisons of Buddhism with Western Thought

(1) ABE, MASAO. "God, Emptiness, and the True Self." Eastern Buddhist 2 (1969):15-30.
A comparative analysis of Christian and Zen mysticism, together with a discussion of the nature of the profound concept of emptiness (śūnyatā) as related to the true self.

(2) AMES, Van METER. "America, Existentialism and Zen." Philosophy East and West 1 (1951):35-47.
A general article that tries to draw comparisons between Zen and modern twentieth-century philosophies. In spite of the fact that Zen is basically joyous, while existentialism is morbid, the author finds similarities in their basically pragmatic approach to existence. An article of philosophical speculation of little use to students.

(3) AMES, Van METER. "Current Western Interest in Zen." Philosophy East and West 10 (1960):23-33.
This article traces modern American interest in Zen, and tries to offer some explanations for the phenomenon. It might be of some interest to students who want to know more about the "Zen boom" of the 1950s in America.

(4) AMES, Van METER. "Zen and American Philosophy." Philosophy East and West 5 (1956):305-20.
The article purports to show the similarity of Zen and such American pragmatic teachers as Dewey and James. Basically a continuation of the author's "Zen and Pragmatism," Philosophy East and West 4, no. 1 (1954):19-34. These articles by Ames have little value as instructional materials. They are mainly pro-Suzuki and aimed at making Zen better known in the West by showing its supposed affinities with Western thought.

16.1 16.1 Comparisons of Buddhism with Western Thought

(5) AMES, Van METER. Zen and American Thought. Honolulu: University of Hawaii Press, 1962, 293 pp.
A definitive comparative work on Zen and its relationship to American thought from early revolutionary America, through the transcendentalists, to the pragmatists. Recommended to all.

(6) AMES, Van METER. "Zen and West." In Bonnō no Kenkyū (A Study of Kleśa) (see 3[7]), 107-19.
An essay on the Western experience of Zen, its contributions and problems.

(7) ANDŌ, SHŌEI. Zen and American Transcendentalism. Tokyo: Hokuseido Press, 1970, 218 pp.
A good comparative work on Zen and the New England transcendentalists. The author goes into an exhaustive analysis of the nature of both Zen and American transcendentalism. Appendix 1 is a good comparison of Zen and Christianity. A very good beginning.

(8) BETTY, L. STAFFORD. "The Buddhist-Humean Parallels: Postmortem." Philosophy East and West 21 (1971):237-53.
Very objective analysis of the parallels drawn so far between the two philosophies. The author concludes that the parallels are to be "treated at the present state of our knowledge as nothing more than a cluster of coincidences, just so many curios in the emporium of human ideas."

(9) BISHOP, DONALD H. "Buddhist and Western Views of the Self." Eastern Buddhist 2 (1969):111-23.
A general account of the problem inherent to the non-self (anātman) doctrine. Some comparisons are loosely drawn.

(10) BLACKWOOD, R.T., and A.L. HERMAN. Problems in Philosophy: West and East. Englewood Cliffs: Prentice-Hall, 1975, 544 pp.
This is an ambitious work in East-West problems in the principal areas of metaphysics, epistemology, theology, and ethics. For example, in the section on metaphysics, Vasubandhu's Viṃśatikā (Twenty verses), in epistemology, Dharmakīrti's "Refutation of Solipsism" and selections from Stcherbatsky's Buddhist Logic, and in theology, a selection from the Milinda-pañha, are given. The Buddhist selections are quite arbitrary but at least the book as a whole focuses on the central problems in East-West dialogue.

(11) BLYTH, R.H. Zen in English Literature and Oriental Classics. Tokyo: Hokuseido Press, 1942.
A strange book, based on the supposition that Zen is something inherent in the minds of all men. The author finds Zen

attitudes in such authors as Homer, Shakespeare, and Wordsworth. A gold mine of quotes for the student of comparative literature, but not for the student of philosophy.

(12) BOYD, JAMES W. "The Teachings of Don Juan from a Buddhist Perspective." Christian Century, Mar. 1973, pp. 360-63.
Some insights into Don Juan's thought based on Buddhist principles. For the beginner.

(13) No entry

(14) CHANG CHUNG-YUAN. "Pre-Rational Harmony in Heidegger's Essential Thinking and Ch'an Thought." Eastern Buddhist 5 (1972):153-70.
The author sees a converging tendency in Zen (Ch'an) thought and Heidegger's essential or meditative thinking. A good beginning for those who are interested in comparing the two systems.

(15) CONZE, EDWARD. "Buddhist Philosophy and Its European Parallels." Philosophy East and West 13 (1963):9-23.
An excellent start for anyone looking for comparisons. Conze's companion essay, "Spurious Parallels to Buddhist Philosophy" (16) should also be read.

(16) CONZE, EDWARD. "Spurious Parallels to Buddhist Philosophy." Philosophy East and West 13 (1963):105-15.
Follow-up essay to "Buddhist Philosophy and Its European Parallels" (15). Good analysis of some of the easy assimilations of Buddhist thought to that of Kant, Bergson, and Hume.

(17) De SILVA, M.W. PADMASIRI. Buddhist and Freudian Psychology. Colombo: Lake House Investments, 1973, 195 pp.
The author attempts to see similarities in the two systems on such concepts as the mind, the unconscious, libido, ego, desires, and the death instinct.

(18) DRAKE, DAVID. "The Logic of the One-Mind Doctrine." Philosophy East and West 16 (1966):207-19.
The author takes up the mind-only doctrine (cittamātra) from the Laṅkāvatāra Sūtra and attempts to give a coherent and consistent logical structure of experience. He also refers to the works of Wittgenstein and Russell.

(19) ERNST, BENZ von. "Esoterisches Christentum." Mikkyōgaku Mikkyōshi Ronbunshū (Studies of Esoteric Buddhism and Tantrism (Koyasan University, Koyasan), 1965, pp. 319-45.
This is a comparative study between Christianity and Buddhism concerning their esoteric elements from a sociological and doctrinal perspective.

16.1 16.1 Comparisons of Buddhism with Western Thought

(20) FRAZIER, A.M. "A European Buddhism." Philosophy East and West 25 (1975):145-160.
Examination of Nietzsche's thought as it relates to classical Buddhist philosophy.

(21) FRIDELL, WILBUR M. "Notes on Japanese Tolerance." Monumenta Nipponica 27 (1972):253-71.
Although Fridell's analysis of Japanese tolerance and intolerance bears improvement, he has initiated an interesting and important topic of consideration and comparison.

(22) GLASENAPP, HELMUT von. Buddhism and Christianity. Buddhism and the Vital Problems of our Time. The Wheel publication, no. 16. Kandy: Buddhist Publication Society, 1959, 40 pp.
Two essays, originally written in German, comparing and contrasting the basic teachings of Buddhism and Christianity.

(23) GRIFFIN, DAVID R. "Buddhist Thought and Whitehead's Philosophy." International Philosophical Quarterly 14 (1974): 261-84.
An attempt to analyze and understand Buddhist concepts such as non-self, relational origination, and suffering, by the aid of related Whiteheadian concepts.

(24) GUENTHER, HERBERT V. "Towards an Experience of Being Through Psychological Purification." In Bonnō no Kenkyū (A Study of Kleśa) (see 3[7]).
A lucid presentation of Klong-chen rab'byams-pa's on the subject of purification. Guenther makes a number of comparisons with "traditional ethics," particularly in the West, which gives an interesting reading in comparative ethics. Guenther, as usual, gives a popularized version of highly specialized discussions.

(25) HARDWICK, C.S. "Doing Philosophy and Doing Zen." Philosophy East and West 13 (1963):227-234.
A comparison of the often illogical use of language in Zen teaching and the ideas developed later in life by Ludwig Wittgenstein. Interesting reading, but not for beginners.

(26) No entry

(27) HUDSON, H. "Wittgenstein and Zen Buddhism." Philosophy East and West 23 (1973):471-81.
Another attempt at bringing the two philosophies together.

(28) INADA, KENNETH K. "Munitz' Concept of the World: A Buddhist Response." Philosophy East and West 25 (1975): 309-17.
The author examines the points of contact between Munitz's and Buddhist views on reality as a means of furthering a dialogue.

(29) INADA, KENNETH K. "Vijñānavāda and Whiteheadian Philosophy." Journal of Indian and Buddhist Studies 8 (1959): 83-96.
An early attempt to seek out similarities in the two systems from the standpoint of a philosophy of organism.

(30) INADA, KENNETH K. "Whitehead's Actual Entity and the Buddha's Anātman." Philosophy East and West 21 (1971): 303-16.
An attempt to find some similarities in the two strains of process thought as a way of opening up future dialogue.

(31) JACOBSON, NOLAN PLINY. "Buddhism, Modernization and Science." Philosophy East and West 20 (1970):155-67.
A very sympathetic understanding of Buddhist principles in light of science and modernization.

(32) JACOBSON, NOLAN P. "Buddhist Elements in the Coming World Civilization." Eastern Buddhist 5 (1972):12-43.
The author gives a profound analysis of Buddhist doctrines relevant to the self-corrective process in man and society. A thought-provoking essay that can be recommended to all.

(33) JACOBSON, NOLAN PLINY. "The Possibility of Oriental Influence on Hume's Philosophy." Philosophy East and West 19, no. 1 (1969):17-37.
The author takes up the possibility that Buddhist thought may have played a major role in the initial formulation of Hume's Treatise. A novel idea worth considering.

(34) JACOBSON, NOLAN PLINY. "The Predicament of Man in Zen Buddhism and Kierkegaard." Philosophy East and West 2, no. 3 (1952):238-53.
A better "comparison" article than most. The author confines himself to a treatment of the so-called four affirmations of his two subjects. The article is more a study of Kierkegaard than of Zen, for which the author relies entirely on Suzuki.

(35) JAYATILLEKE, K.N., ROBERT F. SPENCER, and WU SHU. Buddhism and Science. Kandy: Buddhist Publication Society, 1958.
A collection of four short essays devoted to a comparison of the ideas of modern science with those of Buddhism.

16.1 16.1 Comparisons of Buddhism with Western Thought

(36) JOHNSTON, WILLIAM. The Still Point: Reflections on Zen and Christian Mysticism. New York: Harper & Row, 1971, 202 pp.
One of the finest works in the area of comparative mysticism.

(37) JOHNSTON, WILLIAM. Christian Zen. New York: Harper & Row, 1971, 109 pp.
Aiming at a comparative study of Zen and Christian thought from the point of view of the psychological and theological, the author inadvertently shows the difficulty with both objective and impassioned comparisons.

(37a) KIM HA TAI. "The Logic of the Illogical." Philosophy East and West 5 (1955):19-29.
The article attempts to show that the thinking of the modern Japanese philosopher Nishida Kitarō (1870-1945) is essentially a blend of Zen and Hegel. For professional philosophers, not students.

(38) KING, WINSTON L. Buddhism and Christianity. London: George Allen & Unwin, 1963, 240 pp.
A most sympathetic comparative view dealing with the principal doctrines in both religions. Good for the beginner.

(39) MASUTANI, FUMIO. A Comparative Study of Buddhism and Christianity. Tokyo: Young Eastern Association, 1957, 193 pp.
Accent on the similarities of the two religions and focusing on the nature of human beings, happiness, faith, and religious practice. Quite introductory, but at that level provides an objective and sympathetic comparison of Buddhism and Christianity.

(40) McCARTHY, HAROLD E. "Dewey, Suzuki, and the Elimination of Dichotomies." Philosophy East and West 6 (1956):35-48.
A sound comparative study approached from the naturalistic standpoint.

(41) McCARTHY, HAROLD E. "Poetry, Metaphysics, and the Spirit of Zen." Philosophy East and West 1 (1951):16-34.
This article is based on the statement by Suzuki that Zen finds its best expression in poetry rather than in philosophy. From here the author proceeds to investigate the existence of Zen concepts in Goethe's Faust, which he considers the most Zen-like of all Western writings. A sound, if somewhat etherial, article.

(42) McDERMOTT, A. CHARLENE. "Direct Sensory Awareness: A Tibetan View and a Medieval Counterpart." Philosophy East and West 23 (1973):343-60.
A sound comparative study of the concept of perception (pratyakṣa).

16 Comparisons of Buddhism

(43) MERTON, THOMAS. Zen and the Birds of Appetite. New York: New Directions, 1968, 141 pp.
A series of essays by the famous Trappist monk resulting from his studies of Zen in Japan. The approach is mainly religious and the tendency is to find common ground between Christianity and Zen. Part two contains an interesting dialogue between Merton and Suzuki. Could make interesting side reading for motivated undergraduates.

(44) MOORE, CHARLES A., ed. Essays in East-West Philosophy. Honolulu: University of Hawaii Press, 1951, 467 pp.
Comprises the results of the Second East-West Philosophers' Conference held in Honlulu (1949). Buddhist essays are presented by D.T. Suzuki, ("Reason and Intuition in Buddhist Philosophy"), G.P. Malalasekera, ("Some Aspects of Reality as Taught by Theravāda [Hīnayāna] Buddhism"), and S. Hanayana, ("Buddhism of the One Great Vehicle [Mahāyāna]"). Other comparative essays can be read with great profit.

(45) MOORE, CHARLES A., ed. Philosophy and Culture East and West. Honolulu: University of Hawaii Press, 1962, 832 pp.
This bulky volume contains the proceedings of the Third East-West Philosophers' Conference held in Honolulu (1959). There are a number of Buddhist-oriented essays including D.T. Suzuki's "Zen and Parapsychology." All the essays give practical expressions of Buddhist ideas.

(46) MOORE, CHARLES A., ed. Philosophy--East and West. Princeton: Princeton University Press, 1946, 334 pp.
No one intent on studying comparative philosophy can afford to neglect this pioneering work which is the result of the First East-West Philosophers' Conference held in Honolulu (1939). Buddhist ideas are interspersed throughout the volume, but most notable are the chapters by J. Takakusu, "Buddhism as a Philosophy of Thusness," and by D.T. Suzuki, "An Interpretation of Zen-Experience."

(47) MOORE, CHARLES A., ed. The Status of the Individual in East and West. Honolulu: University of Hawaii Press, 1968, 606 pp.
This is the final volume edited by C.A. Moore, the results of the Fourth East-West Philosophers' Conference held in Honolulu (1964). The theme, status of the individual, is approached from both the Theravāda and Mahāyāna traditions. Other Buddhist-oriented essays are also included, for example, D.T. Suzuki's "The Individual Person in Zen."

16.1 16.1 Comparisons of Buddhism with Western Thought

(48) NAKAMURA, HAJIME. "Buddhist Logic Expounded by Means of Symbolic Logic (see 10[33]).
This thought-provoking article by an outstanding international scholar represents an attempt to apply present-day symbolic logic to centuries-old Buddhist assertions such as that of śūnyatā. This highly informative and stimulating article is recommended to everybody.

(49) NAKAMURA, HAJIME. "Contribution of Eastern Thought and Buddhism to World Culture." Van Hanh Bulletin 5 (1973): 121-57.
An important article by Nakamura, the author of "The Ways of Thinking of Eastern Peoples." Good reading for all.

(50) NAKAMURA, HAJIME. "The Kinetic Existence of an Individual." Philosophy East and West, 1, no. 2 (1951):33-39.
An analysis of the non-self (nairātmya) doctrine and a comparison of it with Greek thought, especially that of Heraclitus.

(51) NAKAMURA, HAJIME. "A New Way of Approach in Buddhist Studies." Religious Studies in Japan (see 1.2.2[10]).
Nakamura, who is firmly established in the fields of Buddhist studies and comparative philosophy, first laments the "desperately unintelligible" nature of the writings on Buddhism as "the words of the inhabitants of Mars" and next, suggests a way out from this rather sad state of affairs in the light of comparative philosophy. An interesting observation and solution on a fundamental problem of Buddhist studies.

(52) ÑĀNAJĪVAKO, Bhikkhu, ed. Schopenhauer and Buddhism. The Wheel Publication, nos. 144-46. Kandy: Buddhist Publication Society, 1970, 93 pp.
A set of selections from Schopenhauer's works dealing with the problems raised in the Buddhist doctrine of the four noble truths, purporting to dispel the prejudices about the proper meaning of the term pessimism in his philosophy.

(53) PARSONS, HOWARD L. "The Value of Gautama Buddha for the Modern World." Eastern Buddhist 2 (1969):31-70.
A beautiful summation of basic Buddhist thought applicable to the contemporary world. A good beginning.

(54) PUHAKKA, KAISA. Knowledge and Reality: A Comparative Study of Quine and Some Buddhist Logicians. Delhi: Motilal Banarsidass, 1975, 109 pp.
The writer focuses on the central problems of logic and ontology; more specifically, on the problems of relating language to reality. In this, the meaning-reference distinction arises and

becomes the basis for the Kantian analytic-synthetic distinction. With Quine as the representative Western logician, the analysis introduces the logical thoughts of Dignāga, Dharmakīrti, and Ratnakīrti. For the advanced student.

(55) REICHELT, KARL LUDWIG. Meditation and Piety in the Far East: A Religious-Psychological Study. Translated from the Norwegian by Sverre Holth. New York: Harper, 1955, 171 pp.
Reichelt, a Norwegian Lutheran missionary in China, makes a comparison between the "general salvation" in the non-Christian religions and the "special revelation" in Christianity and seeks to point out contacts between the two. He describes "the heart-beat of the East-Asiatic religions," i.e. meditation, in the second and longer part of the book. An interesting field-report.

(56) ROSS, NANCY WILSON, ed. The World of Zen: An East-West Anthology. New York: Random House, 1960.
Relies on D.T. Suzuki's contributions but has interesting sections on Zen and the arts, humor in Zen, Zen in psychology and everyday life, universal zen, and Zen and the West. Excellent for the beginner.

(57) SHIBLES, WARREN. "Wittgenstein and Zen." In Wittgenstein: Language & Philosophy. Dubuque: Kendall/Hunt Publishing Co., 1969, pp. 84-100.
A comparative study of some of the major tenets of Zen and the ordinary-language philosophy of Wittgenstein. Some interesting insights on similar forms of approach in both systems. Recommended to all.

(58) SHUTE, CLARENCE. "The Comparative Phenomenology of Japanese Painting and Zen Buddhism." Philosophy East and West 18 (1968):285-98.
A Western phenomenological (Husserlian) approach to Japanese painting and its relationship to Zen.

(59) SMART, MINIAN. Buddhism and the Death of God: The Eighth Montefiore Memorial Lecture Presented at the University of Southampton. Southampton: Camelot Press, 1970, 16 pp.
Smart presents a concise Theravādin view on man's nature and his religious life and delves into certain convergences with the radical theologies.

(60) STEFFNEY, JOHN. "Symbolism and Death in Jung and Zen Buddhism." Philosophy East and West 25 (1975):175-85.
Argues against any conciliation between the two systems of thought on the dualistic structure of ego-consciousness.

16 Comparisons of Buddhism

16.1 16.1 Comparisons of Buddhism with Western Thought

(61) SUZUKI, D.T. Mysticism Christian and Buddhist. London: Allen & Unwin, 1957, 214 pp.
Suzuki's comparative study is largely Zen-Buddhist oriented; he focuses on Meister Eckhart as the paradigmatic exponent of Christian mysticism. In his usual inimical ways, though loosely organized, he presents the philosophical basis for the comparison. Good for the beginner.

(62) SUZUKI, D.T., E. FROMM, and R. De MARTINO. Zen Buddhism and Psychoanalysis. New York: Harper, 1960, 180 pp. Paperback reprint. New York: Grove Press, 1963.
Lengthy essays exploring the connections between the two fields. Good for the beginner.

(63) SUZUKI, D.T., A. WATTS et al. "Views and Reviews: Drugs and Buddhism--A Symposium." Eastern Buddhist n.s., 4 (1971):128-52.
Contains: D.T. Suzuki, "Religion and Drugs," pp. 128-133, A. Watts, "Ordinary Mind is the Way," pp. 134-137, R. Jordan, "Psychedelics and Zen: Some Reflections," pp. 138-140, Robert Aitken, "LSD and the New American Zen Student," pp. 141-144, Richard Leavitt, "Experiences Gradual and Sudden, and Getting Rid of Them," pp. 145-148, and Shizuteru Ueda, "The LSD Experiences and Zen," pp. 149-152. An interesting symposium.

(64) TEO, WESLEY K.H. "Self-Responsibility in Existentialism and Buddhism." International Journal for Philosophy of Religion 4 (1973):80-91.
A short comparative essay on a crucial issue in religious philosophy.

(65) TILLICH, PAUL, HANNAH TILLICH, and HISAMATSU SHIN'ICHI. "Dialogues, East and West." Eastern Buddhist, n.s. 1 (1971):89-107; 2 (1972):107-28; 3 (1973):87-114.
This is a slightly edited record of an interesting dialogue that took place in the autumn of 1957, when Hisamatsu was at the Harvard Divinity School as a University Professor.

(66) UEDA, DAISUKE. Zen and Science. Tokyo: Rishosha, 1963, 95 pp.
The author, a physicist, presents a searching analysis of the problem of causality and freedom, and the accommodation of scientific theories with Zen. For the general reader.

(67) UMEHARA, TAKESHI. "Heidegger and Buddhism." Philosophy East and West 20 (1970):271-81.
The author compares Heidegger and basic Buddhism on the questions of being, nothingness, and death. In so doing, he introduces Japanese thinkers from Dōgen to Suzuki and Nishida.

(68) VALERA, J. EDUAEDO PEREZ. "Toward a Transcultural Philosophy." Monumenta Nipponica 27 (1972):39-64; (1972):175-89.
This is an interesting article suggesting a way to a transcultural philosophy. His "Transcultural Categories" include: this-worldliness, acceptance of natural human dispositions, symbolic mentality, the question of what is real, tendency to stress a limited social bond, values, etc.

(69) WALDO, IVES. "Nāgārjuna and Analytic Philosophy." Philosophy East and West 25 (1975):281-90.
Reexamines the nature of the ontological/epistemological dilemma in the Mādhyamika system from the viewpoint of analytic philosophy.

(70) WATTS, ALAN W. The Spirit of Zen: A Way of Life, Work and Art in the Far East. 3d ed. London: John Murray, 1958.
This book should be sufficient to introduce the student to the works of Alan Watts. Basing himself mainly on Suzuki, the author extracts from Zen teachings those elements he thinks useful for Westerners. The book has no pretensions toward scholarship, but does give useful examples of the influence of Zen on the daily and aesthetic life of the Far East. Should be used with extreme caution.

(71) WELBON, GUY RICHARD. The Buddhist Nirvāṇa and Its Western Interpreters (see 1.1[42]).
An interesting discussion of the various interpretations of the concept of freedom (nirvāṇa) offered by Western scholars who studied or were influenced by Buddhism.

(72) WETTIMUNY, R.G. de S. Buddhism and Its Relation to Religion and Science. Columbo: M.D. Gunasena & Co., 1962, 380 pp.
This highly ambitious work deals mainly with traditional Buddhist concepts, which are conveniently related to modern scientific ideas. It is too general and one-sided to be of scholarly value.

(73) YAMAGUCHI, MINORU. The Intuition of Zen and Bergson. Tokyo: Enderle Bookstore, 1969, 235 pp.
An analytic comparison of Zen and Bergson focusing on intuition as the central concept. A good beginning for comparative studies.

16.2 Comparisons of Buddhism with Other Asian Thought

(1) BHARATI, AGEHANANDA. "Modern Hindu Exegesis of Mahāyāna Doctrine." Philosophy East and West 12 (1962):19-28.
The modern exegesis is limited to the Yogācāra (ālaya-vijñāna doctrine) and the Mādhyamika (śūnyatā doctrine) schools.

16.2 16.2 Comparisons of Buddhism with Other Asian Thought

(2) CHAN, WING-TSIT. "Wang Yang-ming's Criticism of Buddhism, in World Perspectives." In Philosophy, Religion and Culture (Essays Presented to Professor Dhirendra Mohan Datta). Patna: Bhrati Bhawan, 1968, pp. 31-47.
Despite the fact that his thoughts are close to Buddhism, Wang is shown to criticize the unpractical aspects of Buddhist doctrines, especially the Zen doctrine of no-mind.

(3) CHATTERJI, SUNITI KUMAR. "Tantra and Brahmanical Hinduism." Mikkyōgaku Mikkyōshi Ronbunshū (Studies of Esoteric Buddhism and Tantrism) (Koyasan University, Koyasan), 1965, pp. 145-66.
Chatterji points out three distinct elements of Tantric tradition and traces a harmonious development with Brahmanical Hinduism. Next, he sketches the Buddhist development of the same elements.

(4) EARHART, H. BYRON. "Shugendō, the Traditions of En no gyōja, and Mikkyō Influence." Mikkyōgaku Mikkyōshi Ronbunshū (Studies of Esoteric Buddhism and Tantrism) (Koyasan University, Koyasan), 1965, pp. 297-317.
Shugendō, a peculiar movement within Japanese religion founded by En no gyōja, Earhart proves, was heavily influenced by esoteric Buddhism.

(5) FU, CHARLES WEI-HSUN. "Morality or Beyond: The Neo-Confucian Confrontation with Mahāyāna Buddhism." Philosophy East and West 23 (1973):375-96.
Examines the neo-Confucian understanding and misunderstanding of Mahāyāna philosophy.

(6) GLASENAPP, HELMUT von. Vedānta and Buddhism. The Wheel Publication, no. 2. Kandy: Buddhist Publication Society, 1958, 12 pp.
Abridged English translation of an article containing an exposition of the doctrine of nonsubstantiality (anattā), especially as seen from the Mahāyāna perspective, compared and contrasted with Vedānta.

(7) HERRIGEL, E. Zen in the Art of Archery. New York: Pantheon Books, 1953. Reprint. New York: Vintage Books, 1971.
The author shows how Zen training is applied in learning archery in modern Japan. The object is to make the archer conceive of himself and his target as one, once the necessary technical skill has been learned. A charming book; shows how pervasive Zen ideas are in the Far East.

(8) INGALLS, DANIEL. "Śamkara's Arguments Against the Buddhists." Philosophy East and West 3, no. 4 (1954): 291-306.
Ingalls compares the commentaries of Śaṅkarācārya and Bhaskara on the Brahmasūtra, and the arguments Śamkara uses against the Buddhists in his Brahmasūtra-bhāsya with those he uses in commenting on the Bṛhadāraṇyaka Upaniṣad. The arguments are mainly against those Buddhists who maintain the existence of the external world (vijñānavādins).

(9) MONIER-WILLIAMS, M. "On Buddhism in its Relation to Brahmanism." Journal of the Royal Asiatic Society of Great Britain and Ireland 18 (1886):127-56.
A pioneering work, showing in detail the affinity between the two systems of thought.

(10) MOOKERJEE, SATKARI. "Influence of Buddhism on Indian Thought and Culture." Journal of the Bihar Research Society (Patna) 1 [Buddha Jayanti Special Issue] (1956):159-72.
A sympathetic, if not apologetic, essay on the similarities of Buddhism and Vedānta philosophy.

(11) MORI, MIKISABURŌ. "Chuang Tzu and Buddhism." Eastern Buddhist 5 (1972):44-69.
The author shows the strong influence of Chuang-tzu's thought on Zen and even on Pure Land Buddhism. A good beginning for those interested in Chinese Buddhism.

(12) NAKAMURA, HAJIME. Ways of Thinking of Eastern Peoples: India-China-Tibet-Japan. Honolulu: East-West Center Press, 1964, 712 pp.
This classical work of Nakamura shows how philosophies, language-patterns, and behavior-patterns dictate ways of thinking. He creatively utilizes much Buddhist literature in order to prove his thesis. This book is therefore a milepost for philosophical, linguistic and cultural analyses of the sacred texts of the East.

(13) PANIKKAR, RAIMUNDO. "The 'Crisis' of Mādhyamika and Indian Philosophy Today (see 1.2.2.1[6]).
The author begins with a critique of the Mādhyamika system, based on the interpretation by T.R.V. Murti, and explores the problem of Indian philosophy in general from the standpoint of the tension that exists between the ātman-view and the anātman-view. A very interesting attempt.

16.2 Comparisons of Buddhism with Other Asian Thought

(14) RAJU, P.T. Idealistic Thought of India (see 1.1[28]).
Though the work is a general survey of idealism in India, Raju touches on the salient points of Buddhist idealism in many places. Note especially his account of voidness.

(15) SHAH, NAGIN JIVANLAL. Akalaṅka's Criticism of Dharmakīrti's Philosophy (see 10[43]).

(16) SMART, NINIAN. Doctrine and Argument in Indian Philosophy (see 1.2[16]).
Though the work spans the various schools of Indian philosophy, the emphasis is on metaphysics and epistemology, and the religious considerations related to them. Buddhist metaphysics is given wide coverage and comparative analysis is sound. For the serious student.

(17) STRYK, LUCIEN, and TAKASHI IKEMOTO, ed. and trans. Zen: Poems, Prayers, Sermons, Anecdotes, Interviews. New York: Anchor Books, 1963, 160 pp.
A collection of Zen thought expressed in the various forms. Quite helpful to the beginner.

(18) UPADHYAYA, KASHI NATH. Early Buddhism and the Bhagavadgīta. Delhi: Motilal Banarsidass, 1971, 588 pp.
A systematic study of the conditions that gave rise to Buddhism. Good introductory survey of basic doctrines.

(19) UPADHYAYA, KASHI NASH. "The Impact of Early Buddhism on Hindu Thought, with Special Reference to the Bhagavadgīta." Philosophy East and West 18 (1968):163-73.
A comparative study showing similar strains of thought in Buddhism and the Gītā and discussing some of the advancements by the latter over the former.

(20) VARMA, VISHWANATH PRASAD. "Śrī Aurobindo's Interpretation of Buddhist Philosophy." Journal of the Bihar Research Society (Patna) 1 [Buddha Jayanti Special Issue] (1956): 99-112.
Though not a serious scholar or practitioner of Buddhist philosophy, Aurobindo did utilize its doctrines to mold his own system of spiritual metaphysics.

(21) VARMA, VISHWANATH PRASAD. "The Upanishads and the Origins of Buddhism." Journal of the Bihar Research Society (Patna) 2 [Buddha Jayanti Special Issue] (1956):372-94.
The essay goes into the differences between Upanishadic and early Buddhist thought, especially the ātman and anātman theories, and

the influence of the Upanishads upon Buddhism as, for example, in Yoga practice and the nature of karma.

(22) WAYMAN, ALEX. "Two Traditions of India: Truth and Silence." Philosophy East and West 24 (1974):389-403.
A comparative study of Upanishadic and Buddhistic approaches to truth and silence.

(23) YU, DAVID C. "Skillful-in-means and the Buddhism of Tao-sheng: A Study of a Chinese Reaction to Mahāyāna of the Fifth Century." Philosophy East and West 24 (1974):413-27.
The doctrines of skillful-in-means (upāya-kauśalya) and sudden enlightenment (tun-wu) are examined in historical context.

Author/Title Index

Subject Index

Three treatises. See Buddhism: Sanron
Three vehicles. See Buddhism: Triyāna
Tibet. See China: Tibet
T'ien-t'ai. See Buddhism: T'ien-t'ai
Ṭīkā, 10(36)
Time, 6(75); 8(2), (30), (36), (46), (48), (52), (69)
Tolerance, 3(11), (23); 16.1(21)
Totality, 8(5)
Traikālyavāda, 8(58)
Trairūpya, 10(5), (35)
Transcendentalism, 16.1(7)
Transmigration, 6(3). See also Rebirth; Saṃsāra
Transmission of the Lamp. See Ching-te ch'uan-teng-lu
Tri-lakṣaṇa, 8(117)
Trikāya, 1.1(37); 1.2.2(13)
Triṃśikā, 1.2.2.2(3), (7); 6(9), (19); 14.3.7
Tripiṭaka, 1.5(6)
Triśatikāyāḥ Prajñāpāramitāyāḥ Kārikāsaptatiḥ, 14.2.1(12)
Trisvabhāvanirdeśa, 14.3.8(5)
Triyāna. See Buddhism: Triyāna
Tsong-kha-pa (1357-1419), 14.3.9(1); 14.4.3(8); 14.4.10(11), (13)
Truth, 1.5(6); 3(25); 7(14), (18), (24), (27), (32), (34); 8(8), (9), (20), (90), (94); 10(7), (20), (23); 16.2(22). See also Two truths; Four noble truths; Satya
gTum, 6(11)
Tun-wu, 16.2(23). See also Enlightenment
Twenty Verse Treatise. See Viṃśatikā
Two truths, 1.2.2.1(1); 1.5(6); 7(18); 8(8), (9)

Udayana, 10(30)
Uddyotakara Bharadvaya, 10(7), (15), (36)
Unconscious, 16.1(17)
Understanding, 7(9); 8(23)
Universal flux, 1.1(19); 7(6); 8(69)
Universal salvation, 1.3(2)
Unwisdom. See Avidyā
Upāya-kauśalya, 16.2(23)
Upanishads, 1.2.2.1(8); 1.2.2.2(1); 3(24); 14.2.13(10); 14.3.8(5); 16.2(8), (21), (22)
Uttaratantra, 1.5(2); 14.3.1(2); 14.3.9(4); 14.4.3(2)

Vācaspati Mishra, 10(36)
Vaibhāṣika. See Buddhism: Vaibhāṣika
Vaidalyaprakaraṇa, 14.2.9
Vaidalyasūtra, 14.2.9
Vairocana, 8(14)
Vaiśeṣika, 1.2.2.3(4)
Vajrachedikā Prajñāpāramitā, 8(13); 14.3.1(2)
Vajradatta, 14.4.1(9)
Vajradhātumaṇḍala, 1.1(15)
Vajrajapa, 14.4.4(1)
Vajraśekhara-sūtra, 14.4.2(1)
Vajrasūcī, 14.2(10)
Vajra-vidāraṇa-nāma-dhāraṇīhṛdayopahṛdaya, 14.4.1(8)
Vajra-vidāriṇī, 14.4.1(8)
Vasubandhu, 1.1(12); 1.2(5); 1.2.2.2(3), (5), (7); 1.2.2.3(7); 1.3(9); 2(12); 6(1), (19), (47), (80); 7(18); 8(48), (83), (99), (111); 10(50); 14.1.3(1); 14.2.3(7); 14.3.2(3), (4), (5); 14.3.6(1), (2); 14.3.7(1), (2), (3), (4), (5), (7); 14.3.8(1), (5); 14.3.10(2); 16.1(10)
Vedanā, 6(74); 16.1(42)
Vedas, 3(24)
Vehicle, 4(11)
Veracity, 3(23)
Vibhaṅga, 14.1.1.2
Vibhaṅgapakaraṇa, 6(20); 15(1)
Vibhāṣa, 7(18)
Vibhāshāprabhā[v]ritti, 6(38); 8(31)